Conducting Educatio

MW00381117

BOLD VISIONS IN EDUCATIONAL RESEARCH: PIONEERS

Volume: BVER 30 / PION 01

Series Editor
Kenneth Tobin, *The Graduate Center, City University of New York, USA*

Editorial Board
Heinz Sunker, *Universität Wuppertal, Germany*
Peter McLaren, *University of California at Los Angeles, USA*
Kiwan Sung, *Woosong University, South Korea*
Angela Calabrese Barton, *Teachers College, New York, USA*
Margery Osborne, *Centre for Research on Pedagogy and Practice Nanyang Technical University, Singapore*
Wolff-Michael Roth, *University of Victoria, Canada*

Scope

Bold Visions in Educational Research was co-founded by Joe L Kincheloe and Kenneth Tobin for the purposes of publishing cutting edge research that incorporated incisive insights supported by rich theoretical frameworks. The editors stance was that scholars with bold visions would pave the way for the transformation of educational policies and practices. In conjunction with this idea of encouraging theoretically rich research, the editors planned a series of Pioneers—first readers in a given field. Pioneers are written for educators seeking entry into a field of study. Each Pioneer is a "starter"; an introduction to an area of scholarship, providing well-developed, theory-rich, jargon-free texts about current, state-of-the-art research that affords deep understandings of an area and lays the foundation for further studies in the same and related areas. The books are excellent texts for graduate studies, useful resources for professional development programs, and handy reference readers for early career researchers.

Conducting Educational Research

A Primer for Teachers and Administrators

Patricia D. Morrell
James B. Carroll

University of Portland, Oregon, USA

SENSE PUBLISHERS
ROTTERDAM/BOSTON/TAIPEI

A C.I.P. record for this book is available from the Library of Congress.

ISBN: 978-94-6091-202-3 (paperback)
ISBN: 978-94-6091-203-0 (hardback)
ISBN: 978-94-6091-204-7 (e-book)

Published by: Sense Publishers,
P.O. Box 21858,
3001 AW Rotterdam,
The Netherlands
http://www.sensepublishers.com

Printed on acid-free paper

TABLE OF CONTENTS

PREFACE

We designed this book for use by preservice and inservice teachers completing an education masters program. Most university programs require the completion of a mid-level research project. These projects are more in-depth than an undergraduate senior-level capstone, but not as intense an undertaking as required by a doctoral-level research study. Some, though not most, may be thesis-level work.

We have found that these preservice teachers have unique needs for educational research instruction. Typically, the fifth year students already possess a bachelor's degree. Some are older and dissatisfied with their current career choices. Others were uncertain of their career options as undergraduates. All have decided to enter the teaching profession. These students tend to have limited classroom experience, are not familiar with educational research, probably have not used statistics outside an introductory undergraduate class, and in all likelihood know nothing about qualitative design.

Similarly, inservice teachers and administrators also seek a master's degree in education. Students in these thesis and non-thesis option degree programs tend to be practicing teachers, with strong classroom experience. However, like the 5th year students, they are typically not familiar with educational research (relying on practitioner articles), and also are not fluent in statistical or qualitative methods.

Both groups of students are learning about educational research methods and designing and conducting their own initial research project while they are taking other coursework and have heavy responsibilities as classroom teachers, administrators or student teachers. Their comfort level with research is generally not high, which makes juggling work, school, and personal responsibilities even more difficult.

When it comes to coursework on research, preservice and inservice teachers both need the same basics: (a) an understanding of why educational research is important to them in their professional lives; (b) instruction on being critical consumers of educational research; and (c) guiding direction on designing, conducting, and reporting on their own research. We have designed this text to meet those goals. Specifically, the book provides:
- the background needed for preservice and inservice teachers and administrators to appreciate the importance of educational research in their daily professional lives (outside of degree requirements).
- instruction in all aspects of a typical five-chapter research design (introduction; literature review; methodology; results; conclusion/discussion/implications), with guidance to actually write a five chapter research report.
- the tools needed to locate and review published educational research.
- instruction on common qualitative methodologies.
- instruction on the types of quantitative methodologies masters-level candidates would be most likely to use.
- ways to engage the student in a reflection plan for the future.

The text leads preservice and inservice teachers and administrators step- by-step through the process of educational research, providing actual classroom examples and showing the relevance of the materials. We strived to include the essentials without being overwhelming. Ultimately, we hope the text will help teachers and administrators see both the value of becoming life-long critical consumers of educational research and the merits of using research in helping them to become teacher leaders and change agents in their own professional settings.

Features of this Text:

The following key features appear in each chapter of the text:
- **Concept Map:** Each chapter of the book begins with a concept map providing a visual outline of the chapter.
- **Chapter Overview:** The chapter overview provides a brief description of the content of the chapter.
- **Key Terms:** Key terminology appears in boldface on first introduction in the text. Definitions appear in the comprehensive glossary at the end of the text.
- **Figures and Tables:** Figures and tables supplement the text for clarification and elucidation of key concepts.
- **Examples:** Numerous student examples appear throughout the text and are designed to insure relevancy to a classroom professional.
- **Next Steps:** Each chapter closes with a lead-in to the next chapter.
- **Chapter Self-Check:** The self-checklist at the end of each chapter is designed to help students determine their understanding of key concepts.
- **Chapter Review Questions:** End-of-chapter questions help reinforce learning and measure students' understanding of the material presented in the chapter. These questions are available for use by the student or by the instructor as an outcomes assessment.

Supporting Materials:

The website that accompanies this text http://teaching.up.edu/ResearchPrimer provides both the students and instructors using this book with a variety of online resources, materials, and activities they can use to strengthen and enrich their understanding or presentation of the topics in the text.

ACKNOWLEDGMENTS

We have a number of people to thank for their assistance with the development of this text. First, we would like to thank *all* the students we have worked with over the years who have taught us what a master's level student needs. We are especially grateful to those students who allowed us to use their work as examples for this text: Debbie Bale, Stacey Boatright, Deborah Brandell, William Burns, Carolyn Cameron, Sharon Clark, Steve Colkitt, April Crysler, David Dempsey, Emily Ferguson, Carlos Gumataotao, Kim Huber, Tom Kuntz, Krista MacGregor, Tia Martini, Caroline Missal, Sherilyn Mooney, Sheryl Nash, Nancy Petersen, Robert Probert, Chris Stiles, and Ken Szopa. We also appreciate the other authors who allowed us to include portions of their work in our book.

Finally, we would like to thank the University of Portland for providing us with sabbatical time to work on this text and, more importantly, to our families for their encouragement, support, and for putting up with us throughout this endeavor: thanks Jeff, Barbara, Chris, Ian, Devon, and Adam.

INTRODUCTION OF EDUCATIONAL RESEARCH

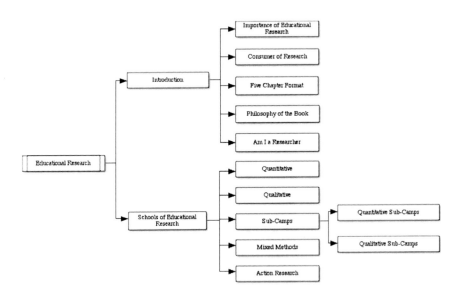

CHAPTER OVERVIEW

The first chapter sets the stage by introducing the reader to the area of educational research. It explains the importance of research, relating this to a teacher's everyday professional practice. The chapter will briefly describe the format of a typical five chapter research paper and describe the layout of the text. It will also provide a brief historical overview of educational research and describe, compare and contrast the major types of educational research methodologies.

INTRODUCTION

Let's say you want to buy a new car. What would you do? Ask some friends. Keep your eyes "open" while you drive on the freeway, looking at other vehicles. Eventually, you compare performance, price, amenities, comfort, and gas mileage. You do some test drives. You might consult the "Blue Book." You finally choose a vehicle based on your observations and findings.

Now let's say a district administrator wants your school to adopt a new reading curriculum. What questions surface? Why is the new curriculum being adopted? Is it better than the current curriculum? How does it fit into the school-wide plan?

Will it improve student understanding and achievement? What do teachers in schools who have adopted that curriculum have to say about it? What kind of inservice will be provided to you and the other teachers? Do you have a choice?

Or taking it down a notch, let's say you're taking a course at the local university and the professor is espousing a particular teaching methodology that you have not tried. Don't you think of similar questions? Is this new method really better than your current method? On what is the answer to that question based?

Or making it even more personal, let's say you do try that new method with your students and you are pleased with the results. How do you convince other colleagues in your building to try it?

THE IMPORTANCE OF EDUCATIONAL RESEARCH

So, what does buying a car have to do with buying into a new curriculum or instructional methodology? In order for us to make an informed decision about any of these, we need to have relevant data. It is more convincing to base a decision on information than on gut instinct.

That is what the processes of educational research are all about (see Figure 1-1). They provide us with information and tools that have been tested, they provide us with a way to know if the testing done was appropriate and the results can be trusted, and they provide us with a way to share our own practices and discoveries with others. We sometimes know what we are doing in our classroom is great, but we often know it because it seems to feel right or our students seem to be engaged. We don't always have convincing data that we can use to persuade someone else that what we are doing is more effective than an alternative methodology. Think of educational research as a way to provide substance to the feelings. Educational research is not just a way to come up with new ideas about teaching and learning, but most often it is a way to convince us that the ideas we already have are worth exploring—that they are worth buying into.

Educational research is important in:

- Proposing theories

- Testing theories

- Increasing our understanding

- Improving teaching and learning

Figure 1-1. The importance of educational research.

Educational research helps us by improving our understanding of how students learn and how best to teach. New articles are continually being published. Learning about the "how-tos" of educational research help us to become better consumers of what is out there. It teaches us to distinguish between legitimate claims and faulty or flawed ones.

Sometimes educational research is used to propose new theories. For example, in 1983 Gardner first proposed his theory of Multiple Intelligences. Besides accommodating different learning styles when teaching, Gardner recommended teachers should also be concerned with the strengths and weaknesses of students' intelligences. Should they? Once new theories are published, other researchers can test them. Do the ideas seem to hold true under some circumstances better than others? Do they need to be adjusted to accommodate different settings or students? In reference to multiple intelligences, thousands of studies have been completed by educational researchers to expand on Gardner's original ideas. Many of these studies were completed by classroom teachers trying to better understand how the more global theory actually works in the real world of schools and classrooms. After further research, Gardner himself added the multiple intelligence of "naturalist" (Gardner, 1999) to the list.

Perhaps most importantly, educational research is an important tool in helping us to improve our own teaching and learning. By being an informed reader, we are in a better position to make educated decisions about curriculum adoption, new teaching strategies, management ideas, and other pedagogical choices. By conducting research in our own classrooms or school, our opinions, suggestions, and ideas will be taken more seriously by teaching colleagues, administrators, parents, and school board members. Research also makes us more reflective about our own practice. All of these move us toward the ultimate goal of improved learning by our students.

BEING A CRITICAL CONSUMER OF RESEARCH

Not all research is created equal. Some studies are stronger than others: their methods are well designed and the conclusions and recommendations clearly flow from the data. Other studies are poorly designed, or the authors took great liberties in discussing the results and determining the conclusions. Findings of studies with major flaws should be suspect. Understanding how to construct a research project will help you not only with your own research but will also equip you to become a critical consumer of research. It will provide you with the tools you need to determine whether any study should be believed and its recommendations tried, or if it should be taken lightly or totally ignored. As you go through this text, the questions you will apply to your own developing project should also be applied to anything you read to help you determine the value of work written by others.

FIVE CHAPTER FORMAT

Typically, research tends to follow a general five-chapter format. It is kind of like "the" scientific method. Most of us learned a five step model to scientific problem solving (e.g., state the problem, make observations, devise a hypothesis, test the

3

hypothesis, make a conclusion). While this works well for many scientific problems, it really is not a "one size fits all" methodology—think ecological studies, as an example. The same holds true with the five-chapter design for educational research that we are about to describe. This model works for many educational studies, but not necessarily all. However, it brings an easy to understand, logical structure to your work and it is by far the most common approach to reporting on educational research.

This basic design of educational research involves the following five components:

Chapter 1 – Introduction
Chapter 2 – Review of the Literature
Chapter 3 – Study Design and Research Methods
Chapter 4 – Results
Chapter 5 – Discussion/Conclusions/Implications

Let's look at these chapters with a little more detail so you'll have a better understanding of what is ahead (see Figure 1-2). Chapter One, the Introduction, is a narrative that lets the reader know what you plan to study or examine. It sets the

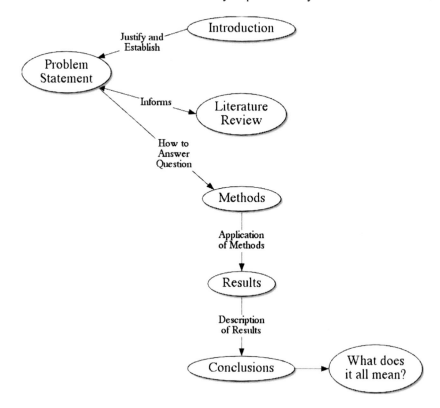

Figure 1-2. Schematic of a five chapter design.

scene for the entire study. What is the problem or purpose of the work? Why is this issue important to you, as an educator, and why is it a worthy project to pursue? Chapter One describes the significance and the need for the study. It typically provides a description of the context in which the question was raised, some history of the problem, and what theoretical constructs (ways in which the research community views the problem) have been applied to the problem. Often, also included in Chapter One are definitions of important terms. For example, "cooperative learning" has a variety of definitions. Which one pertains to the particular study? "Looping" may be a term that is not familiar to all. A definition would help the reader understand just what the study concerns. If we think of educational research as a road trip, Chapter One is stating the starting point of the proposed destination. It is the point at which you would describe why you wanted to make the trip and to state as clearly as possible where you intend to go.

Chapter Two is the Literature Review. It presents an overview of what is already known about a topic. What background is needed to understand the problem? What similar work has already been done? What has been found? What theoretical constructs are important and relevant? Going back to our road trip analogy, Chapter Two is exploring ways of getting from Point A to Point B. What are the pros and cons of driving, taking the train or bus, or flying? How long will the trip take? What roadblocks might be encountered? Chapter Two provides the background information that will help us in planning our own excursion. It is appropriate here to point to Newton's edict that "if I have seen a little further it is by standing on the shoulders of giants." All of what you read may not necessarily seem to be written by giants, but the point remains that we need to be sure that we understand what has come before in order to make good progress ourselves.

The third chapter is the methods section. In it we explain how we plan to go about gathering and analyzing data to solve the problem. Who will you be studying (e.g., your own class, all third graders, just the students in your math class)? What techniques do you plan to use to gather data (e.g., a survey, pre/post tests, observations)? How do you think you might make sense of the data you collect? Will you be running statistical tests? Coding video-tapes of lessons or categorizing classroom behaviors? This is the nuts and bolts of the road trip: what means of transportation will you take, what routes, what stops, how did you prepare for the journey. The methods section of the report on your research is important because it lets others know how you have approached your research in sufficient detail that they can make judgments about the quality of the procedures you applied to your work. You will be asking the same questions when you read other authors' work that readers of your research will be asking. Was the study conducted in such a way that I can believe the conclusions of the study?

Chapter Four is the results section. Who or what was actually studied and what did you find? Let's say you decided to drive on that road trip. Were you able to take the roads you had originally planned? Did you have any detours? Any car problems? Did everything go smoothly? What did you actually see and do while on the trip? At some point you will gather data about your research problem. In almost all cases (particularly qualitative studies) the amount of information you gather is far greater than could be comfortably listed in a research report. Your job is to condense those data into an understandable form. Depending on the type of research you are doing, there are clear conventions for how to do this. Readers of your results section will know exactly what you found after you applied your research methods to gather and analyze information around your topic. Chapter Four sets the stage for your chance to talk in the final chapter about the meaning of what you have found.

The last chapter—Conclusions— is the chapter that ties everything together and suggests plans for the future. You make sense of your data, share your insights, compare the findings to what you thought you would discover and to what you found in the literature. The research question is answered, the process and findings are discussed, and personal reflections are added. Chapter Five includes the "so what" of your findings. What does your study mean to you? Because of it, will you change your teaching style, curriculum, or some other important part of your work? Did this study lead you to think of other questions you would like to answer? If you had the opportunity to redo the study, what did you learn in hind-sight? How will your findings impact your current and future teaching? Chapter Five is the destination of your road trip. Think of it as the gathering you have with friends to show slides of your trip. Did you get to where you hoped? If you had to do it again, is there anything you would recommend be changed? Would you use the same mode of transportation and follow the same route? If so, why? If not, why not? What is likely to be your next trip? Appendix A contains an outline of the five chapter model and Appendix B is a sample student research paper. You may want to refer to these as you write your research paper.

Every piece of educational research is part of a larger puzzle and it often seems that the conclusions of your study leave more questions than answers. But, if you have followed the traditions of good research your piece of the puzzle will be a valuable contribution. It will help you and/or others plan the next "trip."

THE PHILOSOPHY OF THIS BOOK

We wrote this book to guide the first time researcher through the process of planning, conducting, and sharing the findings of an educational research project. We have been on the five-chapter journey many times ourselves and have helped numerous students take that trip. It is with our students in mind that we wrote the following chapters. Some of our students were pre-service teachers, others had been teaching for decades. Some were administrators and others were studying to be administrators. Some were young and impressionable; others were well seasoned and set in their ways. Like the Automobile Club, some of our "members" just needed a road map. Others needed possible routes pointed out to them. Many wanted everything we could give them, listing specific roads to travel, with places to visit, hotels, campgrounds, and eateries noted along the way.

Regardless of the amount of instruction you need as you embark on your first educational research journey, we want this text to provide the basic groundwork anyone needs to be successful. As noted earlier, we will use the five chapter model as our guide. We will start with some basic information about the main types of educational research methodologies, and then provide instruction in a stepwise fashion through each of the phases of conducting a study. The book is designed to be a travel guide—use the sections as you need them and spend the time with the text and supplemental materials as your needs dictate. After you have successfully completed your first "journey," we hope that you will continue to use the text as a refresher for future studies.

AM I CUT OUT TO BE A RESEARCHER?

We, the authors, have each been teaching research classes for well over a decade. Some of our students were very comfortable conducting a research study. Others were a little hesitant. Most were initially very tense. Please be aware that we plan to lead you through what would be the equivalent of a typical master's level research project. And if you have spent at least one day in a classroom working with students, you have the raw materials you need to be successful in carrying out an educational research study.

Consider: as educators, our primary goal is to optimize the learning environment and opportunities for each of our students. We do this by making continual assessments and adjusting our teaching accordingly. If for just one day you kept a tally of all the decisions you made to help you reach this goal, we guess you would: (a) get tired of making hash marks; (b) forget to make a mark each time; (c) wear down your pencil before the end of the day.

How do you make all these decisions? The questions you ask, the impressions you make, the changes you implement are based on what you learned in education classes, watching others, what you gleaned from professional development, and your own experience. While you may think your decisions are being made "instinctively," it would not take much to turn your decision-making issues into a research study. Educational research is nothing more than a systematic examination of an issue we face in our professional lives. For example, you may want to look at one of the following problems:

Why do some students have trouble with long-division problems?
What types of writing strategies are used by high achievers?
Does judicious discipline work in managing high school students?
How can I get non-volunteers to answer questions?
How could I more effectively get parents to participate in their child's learning?

Perhaps your school is thinking of moving from a middle school to a junior high, or is being restructured to be a school within a school. Is that a good change? Maybe you would like to try some new idea in your own classroom or school. Is your reading/mathematics/writing curriculum being revamped? Will it be effective?

We know you have things you would like to study in more detail (even if you can't think of what they are yet!). By following a research format you can do it in a way that provides you with the supportive data you need to defend your conclusions—to yourself and others. You can formalize what you do or think about as part of your daily professional responsibilities in ways that provide defendable information about the choices you make—you can be an educational researcher. Let's start by learning some background about educational research processes.

SCHOOLS OF RESEARCH

There are basically two main types of research paradigms: **quantitative** and **qualitative**. As the names imply, quantitative research methods have to do with quantities—numbers. Data might be pre and post test scores, ratings on a survey, amount of time spent doing homework or viewing television or playing computer and video games. They tend to answer the question "what." They generally measure characteristics of groups. Qualitative research is more interested in the "whys" and "hows" of the what, often including beliefs and opinions of individuals. Data sources might be interview transcripts, reflective writings, photographs, and observations. It is more descriptive in nature. Qualitative and quantitative camps are opposite ends of a research continuum, with a variety of mixtures of the two main ideologies in between.

Here are some additional research questions to get a better sense of these schools of research before delving more deeply into them:

1. Is the amount of time spent viewing television related to student achievement?
2. Does the new mathematics curriculum improve students' state test scores?
3. Why do students possess the attitudes they do about studying history?
4. What do teachers feel are the pros and cons of looping in the early elementary grades?
5. How do students feel about studying history?

Look at those five questions. Which of the above questions can be answered by some kind of measurement? (Do look first before continuing with the reading!!)

Did you decide questions one and two would lend themselves to gathering numbers? For the first question, we could have measurements of time and test (or other achievement) data. The second question could be answered by examining student scores taught using the old and new curricula (with some caveats). For questions three and four, however, there isn't an easy number that could be obtained. Students would probably have to be asked specifically why they felt the way they do toward studying history—was it peer influence, family influence, boring content, riveting content, the way it is taught? Likewise, to get teachers' opinions of looping, the easiest way would be to ask them to list or state what they perceive to be the pros and cons of the practice. So the first two would most likely be quantitative studies while the second two would employ qualitative methods.

What about the fifth question? The answer is—it depends. How do you want to go about collecting the data? An attitude questionnaire, with a **Likert**-type scale (strongly disagree to strongly agree) could produce a quantified idea of students' attitudes toward the subject and lead to a quantitative study. An open-ended questionnaire (where students write in responses to questions) or a conversational interview with students could produce qualitative information about the students' attitudes and lead to a qualitative study. So like most things in life, in educational research it is not always obvious how to proceed.

Which type of research is better? Some researchers (and granting agencies) believe the old adage that "numbers don't lie." They prefer hard and fast measurements. Think of "No Child Left Behind" in the United States (http://www.ed.gov/nclb/landing.jhtml) or a myriad of other government mandated assessments. Quantifiable test results are required. Others feel numbers don't tell the whole story. Take for example the TIMSS studies, the Third International Math and Science Study (http://nces.ed.gov/timss). While student scores on tests were used to compare student achievement in different countries, the teachers from various countries were videotaped. These videotapes were analyzed qualitatively to examine exactly what the teaching looked like in some countries: how were the lessons delivered, what was the nature of teacher/student interaction, what types of learning activities were included in the lesson.

Like the discussion over the appropriateness of phonics or whole language, the preferred methodology in educational research tends to swing back and forth. Originally, educational research was quantitative in nature. It adhered to a traditional five step "scientific method" approach. In the 1960s, societal changes of civil rights, diversity issues, and inclusion, encouraged the use of qualitative methods for educational research (Bogdan & Biklen, 2006). Many "how" questions were being spotlighted (how to integrate, how to accommodate different learners, how to be culturally sensitive and encourage diversity), and these questions could not be easily answered quantitatively. Qualitative research gained a stronghold. Debate over the value/rigor of qualitative studies as compared with quantitative methodologies became an issue again in the mid 1980's. Combinations of these two schools of thought became more widely used.

A struggle between qualitative and quantitative camps still exists. Qualitative studies are longer (both in the time they take to conduct and in volume of paper produced to disseminate the findings). At the 2006 National Association of Research in Science Teaching (NARST) business meeting, a lively discussion ensued about the decrease in the number of journal articles being published in the *Journal of Research in Science Teaching*, while the average number of pages in each journal had actually increased. The reason: mostly qualitative studies were being published, and compared with quantitative work, these require more pages to present their findings. Qualitative research has also been less likely to make a "contribution to theoretical knowledge" as compared with quantitative research (Zeichne, 2007, p. 43), mostly due to its limited context and generalizability. As noted by Erickson (1986), interpretative research targets "particularizability" not "generalizability." Borko, Liston, and Whitcomb (2007), in their editorial introducing a paper set on teacher education, stress the values and needs for **empirical research**; that is, research based on observation and experimentation. The pendulum still swings.

So back to the question—which type of educational research design is better? For simplicity's sake, imagine you want your students to be better readers. If you try to do this through the introduction of books into a classroom library you might want to know if the students were more excited about reading after the introduction of the books (probably a qualitative question) or you might want to know if reading scores went up (probably a quantitative question).

Which type of research is better depends on the study itself. The research approach needs to be appropriate for the specific question. While some people prefer one type of research to another, really the better method is the one that will address the problem—and sometimes both methods are needed in the same study. The question determines which type(s) of research design is required.

QUANTITATIVE RESEARCH

Let's take a more detailed look at the two schools of research. We'll start with quantitative because that is most like the typical five step process of problem solving and the design with which you are probably more familiar. In quantitative designs, you generally start with a question or a premise. Will using inquiry-based activities affect student achievement? If my students use this tutorial, will their mathematics grades improve?

Quantitative studies are linked to statistics. Most statistical studies phrase their question in the form of a hypothesis. A hypothesis is just a way of formalizing your question in the form of a statement. The hypothesis may be stated in an if/then format; for example, if I use more inquiry-based activities in my classes, then student grades will increase; if I use this tutorial with my students, their scores on the state mathematics test will increase.

Some of you may recall the "null hypothesis" from a statistics class. If you remember that phrase, you can state your hypothesis as a null hypothesis. This means you are saying the independent variable (the factor being changed) has no effect on the dependent variable (the variable being measured); for example, teaching students using an inquiry approach will not result in any change in achievement gains. (In this example, the independent variable is the type of instruction while the dependent variable is achievement gains.) Using this tutorial with my students (independent variable) will not affect their scores (dependent variable) on the state mathematics test. Quantitative researchers do this because it would be very hard to say that we have proved something will always be true when we are studying people. There are usually exceptions in any situation. So, we ask questions about how likely it is that the lack of what we thought we would see is a good explanation for what we are studying. If the lack isn't a good explanation then that tells us that what we thought we were going to see in the first place is a better explanation.

You will become more comfortable with thinking like this as you apply these ideas to your specific research. We will go over writing a quantitative problem statement in detail later. And, for most cases, the quantitative problem statement for educational research does not need to look or sound like something out of a statistics primer! The important thing is to be able to clearly state what it is you are planning to investigate.

To answer quantitative questions, you typically follow some kind of experimental design. You usually have some baseline data, try an intervention, collect more data and see if the intervention made a difference. Or you have two sets of data that you are trying to compare. For instance, to see if teaching with inquiry methods affects student learning more positively than teaching using direct instruction, you might test the students before and after using one method and then do the before and after tests using the other instructional method. After making some assumptions (like the two units are comparable in difficulty and student interest), you can compare the scores the students have on the tests of the two units. You would use statistical methods to determine if one teaching methodology did, indeed, yield greater improvements in scores than the other. As an additional example, perhaps you want to see if the age at which children started walking is related to when they started reading. Here you are not doing any intervention, but you are comparing two sets of information to see if a relationship exists between them.

Quantitative research, then, is a structured process in which you gather and analyze quantitative data. Ideally, it requires large, random samples. That is, you would use your whole class rather than a just a handful of selected students. Quantitative research follows a deductive model—you go from the general to the specific. You have an idea or theory, you apply it to your sample (class, school, etc.), and see if it holds true. The findings tend to be generalizable to other people who are similar to those who were in your study. If teaching with a more inquiry-like approach works for your students, it will probably work for all similar groups of students. If direct instruction worked better for your students, it would probably work better for other students in your school. Finally, quantitative research is concerned with outcomes—it looks at a product.

QUALITATIVE RESEARCH

Qualitative research designs are quite different from quantitative methodologies. Instead of starting with a hypothesis, you end up with one. You start with something you want to learn more about, but have no hypothesis to test. For example, rather than trying to measure student attitudes toward school, you want to find out what is it they like or dislike about school. What affects their attitudes? Rather than using an experimental set up, you study the students in an actual setting. You don't manipulate how the teacher teaches or what students are in the class, but rather look at the situation in context. You will collect descriptive rather than numerical data. You might do classroom observations, you might interview students, you might have students journal about their thoughts. You would NOT give them a list of items and ask them which statements were true about their attitudes toward school. You would have the students generate the list. In qualitative designs, we typically select small, non-random samples to study. Rather than study all students enrolled in a history class, we might study a handful that we think possess (or have been suggested to us as possessing) positive attitudes and some that have negative attitudes. Because the numbers are small and the sample is non-representative, the findings will not be generalizable. They hold true only for that specific group of students.

In qualitative research, you don't come up with an outcome or a product. Rather than a "what," you usually come up with "hows and/or whys." The data are specu-lative, based on the perceptions of those involved. You actually "conclude" with

11

a hypothesis. This may provide an excellent statement to be tested in another setting or with other research designs. After talking with and observing a select group of students, you may come up with some notion of what it is that affects students' attitudes toward school. Students might like it when they feel they have more of a say in what happens and more freedom of choice in their schools. From that you might hypothesize that students in schools with an active and strong student government would have more positive attitudes toward school; however, you could not conclude that—you are just guessing based on what you discovered with this select group—that assertion is something that would need testing (probably using a quantitative design). Qualitative research tends to be inductive. You look at specific instances and try to come up with a generalization.

So, quantitative and qualitative studies differ in important ways (See Figure 1-3).

1. *Purpose of the study*—are you looking to test something specifically or determine an outcome *or* are you interested in coming up with possible explanations or descriptions?
2. *Kinds of data collected*—are you looking at quantitative outcomes (test scores, scales, etc.) *or* observational/descriptive data (you are the primary collection tool)?
3. *Methods of data collection*—are you using an experimental set up *or* a more naturalistic approach; is the process more objective *or* subjective?
4. *Analysis of the data*—are you applying statistical procedures *or* using inductive reasoning?

Quantitative	**Qualitative**
numerical data	descriptive data
deductive model	inductive model
large, random sample	small, purposeful sample
generalizable	not generalizable
outcome oriented	process oriented

Figure 1-3. Comparison of quantitative and qualitative design.

SUBCAMPS OF QUANTITATIVE AND QUALITATIVE RESEARCH

While specific types of quantitative and qualitative research methodologies will be discussed in more detail later, it is useful to provide an overview of the types of studies that fit into these paradigms now. We think this will help solidify the similarities and differences between the two major research models.

Quantitative categories. Common quantitative designs include **experimental**, **causal-comparative**, **correlational**, and **survey** or **descriptive designs** (see Figure 1-4). An experimental design is used when you want to test a particular variable. Using our previous examples, if you want to see whether inquiry-type learning produces different achievement results than direct instruction, you would use an experimental design. The variable being tested is the type of instructional methodology (independent variable) and the outcome being measured (dependent variable) is achievement. Experimental designs allow for manipulation of independent variables and make cause/effect conclusions possible by examining data that comes from dependent variables. In actuality, in most educational research studies that we will do, we will be using a quasi-experimental design rather than a true experimental design. This is because we cannot randomly select our students. We generally work with the sample we have the easiest access to, and this is not usually randomly assigned.

- **Experimental design** – testing a particular variable

- **Causal-Comparative (Ex post facto)** – testing a variable but researcher cannot control the independent variable

- **Correlational study** – determining relationships between variables

- **Descriptive quantitative study** – gathering information to clarify characteristics of a group

- **Survey research** – relying on answers to questions

Figure 1-4. Selected types of quantitative research designs.

When you cannot control or manipulate variables but want to see the effect a variable may have, you typically are doing causal-comparative research, also known as **ex post facto research**. For example, you want to determine if reading daily to preschoolers (independent variable) affects their reading readiness in kindergarten (dependent variable). You cannot (and should not) determine which preschoolers get read to, so you compare two *intact* kindergarten groups—those that had been read to with those that had not. It is similar to an experimental design in that groups are being compared to determine an outcome (the differences in the dependent variable); but dissimilar in that the experimenter does not control the independent variable (the factor being changed).

A correlational study is used when you want to determine if a relationship exists between two or more variables. Is there a relationship between socio-economic status and performance on open-ended mathematics tasks? Is there a relationship between homework completion rate and chapter test scores? These are not cause/effect studies, but help to determine the degree of a relationship that exists between/among variables. It may be enough for your study's purposes to understand that two variables behave in the same (as one increases, the other increases) or opposite ways (one increases while one decreases) but often the results of correlational studies help in the design of further experimental studies.

Descriptive quantitative studies gather information about a group so that it is easier to understand the nature of the group. The purpose of the study is not to compare groups or to understand the impact of an intervention, but simply to have a clearer picture of the characteristics of a group. As an example, you might want to track changes in your school district's yearly expenditures over time to understand changing funding sources. In this case you are asking a descriptive question about the group being studied and not comparing groups.

A form of descriptive research is **survey research**. As the name suggests, survey research relies on answers to questions. Unlike qualitative descriptions, the data collected in this type of design are quantitative. Those in the sample respond to provided statements such as "choose from the following" or "rate on a scale from one to five." Typical data collection instruments include tests and questionnaires; pencil and paper forms that the respondents can complete on their own (or via telemarketers).

Qualitative categories. Qualitative research can be categorized in a myriad of ways, but the main types typically are **grounded theory, ethnography, case study, phenomenology**, and **historical research**. (See Figure 1-5) In a grounded theory approach, the purpose is to collect and analyze data with the intent of coming up with a theory that explains the research situation. It is considered "grounded" because it develops out of—or is grounded in—collected data. You would use this approach when existing theories do not apply to your situation or context and when studying new phenomena. You are basically trying to understand a research situation; that is, what is happening and how those involved feel about it. As an example, you may be interested in understanding why conflict exists between parents of children in special education programs and school officials or how to best integrate the use of interactive white boards in a classroom. For grounded theory, the data collection and analysis process is an iterative cycle of collecting information, identifying commonalities in the data, and verifying those commonalities, narrowing the key components as you repeat the cycle. The outcome is a potential theory that explains the relationship.

- **Grounded theory** – generating a theory to understand a problem/situation
- **Ethnography** – examines the "culture" of a group
- **Case study** – detailed account of an individual or group
- **Phenomenology** – looking at something through the eyes of those being observed
- **Historical Research** – understand events that have already occurred

Figure 1-5. Selected types of qualitative research designs.

Another common qualitative approach is an ethnography. In an ethnography, you are interested in studying the "culture" of a group. You might examine how a group is formed, how the members interact, and what type of interactions occur.

You might be interested in looking at "skateboarding culture" or behaviors of teachers in a teachers' lounge. One of our colleagues studied a group of graffiti artists to get a deeper understanding and insight into that subculture (Christen, 2003).

A case study is considered by some to be a subset of ethnography. Others consider it a separate type of qualitative design. As its name implies, a case study is an in-depth examination of one or more special "cases." A case can be a specific person or a small group. It is similar to an ethnography, but has a more defined/limited focus. One of our students was doing her practicum in a grade school that was gradually implementing a new mathematics curriculum. Teachers were given the option of when and how they wanted to start using the newly adopted, student-centered program as long as everyone had it fully adopted by the end of three years. Our student chose a small group of teachers to study, which included early adopters, resisters, and some fence straddlers. She examined how they felt about the change, about mathematics in general, and about student learning. She hoped to understand why there was such a difference in attitude and behavior concerning the implementation of this new type of curriculum.

Phenomenology is looking at something (the phenomenon) through the eyes of a subject group. That something might be an event or an interaction; the focus is on understanding the perspectives of those you are studying. You attempt to find the "commonalities of their perceptions" (Slavin, 2006, p. 147). Phenomenology applies a social constructivist viewpoint to the research process. You might be interested in studying student teacher/mentor teacher interactions or how students deal with the loss of a classroom pet.

Historical research is used to help us understand events that have already occurred. We worked with a teacher who had started the school year in a new district. The physical design of her school building was very different from any she had worked in or seen. Her research question was why the school was designed as it was. She undertook a historical research project, examining school board minutes, looking at architectural plans, speaking with members on the school building/planning committee, to gain an understanding of the reasons for the physical configuration of the building.

As with anything, these subcategories of quantitative and qualitative research are not exhaustive. There are other distinctions and subcategories within subcategories. These are just the more common approaches you're likely to encounter or pursue yourself.

MIXED METHODS

As mentioned earlier, sometimes a research study uses a combination of qualitative and quantitative methods. You may not be interested in just what teachers' attitudes are toward state-mandated curricula (which can be measured using a scaled instrument) but also why they feel that way (answered by having them answer some open-ended or interview questions). You might want to know what methods neighboring districts use to identify talented and gifted students *and* how teachers feel about those methods. You may want to examine if and how student achievement scores are affected by switching to PowerPoint presentations *and* what students think about your use of that type of medium. Using a mixture of qualitative and quantitative methods in one study is perfectly acceptable, and in some cases, necessary. Your question dictates the methodology *or* methodolog*ies* you should use! (You've heard that before.)

In a study that uses **mixed methods**, the methods can be used sequentially or simultaneously (see Figure 1-6). For example, you might initially administer a quantitative questionnaire to gain information on students' attitudes toward a specific content area. You would then use those results to help identify a sample of students with a range of attitudes from positive to negative to interview for a deeper insight into the whys of these attitudes. This is referred to as an **explanatory design**: the quantitative portion precedes the qualitative data collection. Conversely, you might follow an **exploratory design**, carrying out qualitative methods prior to quantitative methods. You might interview a sample of students first to determine their attitudes toward a subject and the factors that affect that attitude. After analyzing the data to determine pertinent themes and patterns, you would use those findings to design a quantitative questionnaire that could be administered to a larger group of students.

At times your question might require that you collect both types of data simultaneously or concurrently. You might be integrating technology into your instruction and you want to determine if (a) this change in methodology will impact quantitative student achievement and (b) whether students' behaviors in class are affected by the implementation of technology. You would use a quantitative design for the former and a qualitative design for the latter and be conducting both at the same time. This is referred to as a **triangulated design.**

In these types of mixed-methods studies, you actually have a two-pronged or compound research question. One part of the question would be answered using quantitative methods and the other using qualitative means. You could design the study as if you are doing two studies, using both types of methods and data analysis, but base your conclusions on the two sets of findings.

Explanatory

Quantitative precedes *Qualitative*

Exploratory

Qualitative precedes *Quantitative*

Triangulated

Quantitative occurs along with *Qualitative*

Figure 1-6. Models of mixed methods.

ACTION RESEARCH

There is one other main "body of research." It is **action research**. Action research can be qualitative or quantitative or use mixed methods. It follows the same planning and guidelines as other types of research. What sets it apart, is that action research is generally undertaken by individuals for their own, personal purpose—as opposed to educational researchers in college, universities or think tanks. Teachers and school administrators look at a problem in their own classroom/school/district to be able to gather information and make an informed "action plan." The purpose is generally to improve one's teaching or address a specific, local concern. Is the new tardy policy working? Is implementing judicious discipline in my history class helping students learn more deeply about democratic principles? Is using the student response system a more effective way of formative assessment than using non-technological means? Action research is not undertaken to have the findings apply to any situation except the one that is studied.

Mills (2007) categorizes action research into two main types: **practical action research** and **participatory action research**. Practical action research is research that addresses specific questions in a classroom, school, or district. The purpose is to improve teaching and learning or provide necessary information to help in decision making. Participatory action research differs from practical action research in that it involves a group of people focusing on the same problem (e.g., teachers, administrators, board members). This group of stakeholders collectively formulates the research problem, which leads to this type of action research also being dubbed **collaborative action research**. Additionally, participation action research attempts to "improve social practice by changing it" (McTaggart, 1989, Tenet 1). It is an iterative process of planning, implementing, observing the effects of the implementation, reflecting on the effects, and revising the action plan.

While there are entire books written just on action research (e.g., Mills, 2007), the basic research guidelines needed in conducting such a project parallel those outlined in this text. Depending on your question, you would follow the guidelines for conducting a qualitative, quantitative or mixed methods study. Once you are done with your data analysis, action research requires that you take one additional step. The implications section would be your action plan. Now that you have studied the issue, what do you propose be done in response to the problem?

A main drawback to conducting action research is that the researcher is an inherent part of the process, making it harder to maintain objectivity. The major advantage is action research focuses on self-reflection; and, because you are studying something that is relevant to your immediate professional practice, it is easy to keep focused on and enthused about the research question. You will be taking a systematic and critical look at an issue that will ultimately improve your effectiveness as a professional. Those of you who will be examining your own teaching practices or classroom policies may be conducting a study very similar to action research.

NEXT STEPS

Now that you are armed with a basic understanding of why you should know how research is conducted, why you should learn about designing and conducting your own research project, and the basic schools of research methodologies, the next logical step is to begin thinking about your own research project. It's time to start drawing on the empowerment that you will get from becoming an educational researcher.

CHAPTER SELF-CHECK

Having completed this chapter, you should be comfortable discussing the following:
- the importance of educational research
- what it takes to be an educational researcher
- the typical format of an educational research paper
- a comparison of qualitative and quantitative paradigms
- the description of the following quantitative methodologies: experimental design, causal-comparative, correlational, survey, descriptive
- the description of the following qualitative methodologies: grounded theory, ethnography, case study, phenomenology, historical research
- mixed methods research
- what constitutes action research

CHAPTER REVIEW QUESTIONS

1. What is the purpose of educational research?
2. Why is it important that you understand the basics of conducting educational research?
3. How is a typical research paper organized? What is included in each chapter?
4. What are the major differences between qualitative and quantitative research?
5. The text describes five main types of quantitative research. What are these? Provide a brief description of each.
6. The text also describes five main types of qualitative research. What are these? Provide a brief description of each.
7. Is it possible to mix qualitative and quantitative methodologies in the same research study? Why or why not?
8. Compare and contrast action research with qualitative and quantitative schools of research.

REFERENCES

Bodgan, R. C., & Biklen, S. K. (2006). *Qualitative research for education: An introduction to theory and methods* (5th ed.). Boston: Allyn and Bacon.

Borko, H., Liston, D., & Whitcomb, J. A. (2007). Genres of empirical research in teacher education. *Journal of Teacher Education, 58*(1), 3–11.

Christen, R. S. (2003). Hip hop learning: Graffiti as an educator of urban teenagers. *Educational Foundations, 17*(4), 57–82.

Erickson, F. (1986). Qualitative methods in research on teaching. In M. C. Wittrock (Ed.), *Handbook of research on teaching* (3rd ed., pp. 119–161). New York: Macmillan.

Gardner, H. (1983). *Frames of mind: The theory of multiple intelligences.* New York: Basic.

Gardner, H. (1999). *Intelligence reframed. Multiple intelligences for the 21st century.* New York: Basic Books.

McTaggart, R., (1989). *16 tenets of participatory action research.* A paper presented at the Third World Encounter on Participatory Research, Managua, Nicaragua. Retrieved from http://www.caledonia.org. uk/par.htm

Mills, G. E. (2007). *Action research: A guide for the teacher researcher* (3rd ed.). Upper Saddle River, NJ: Merrill.

Slavin, R. E. (2006). *Educational research in an age of accountability*. Boston: Pearson.

Zeichner, K. (2007). Accumulating knowledge across self-studies in teacher education. *Journal of Teacher Education, 58*(1), 36–46.

CHAPTER 2

WRITING A RESEARCH QUESTION

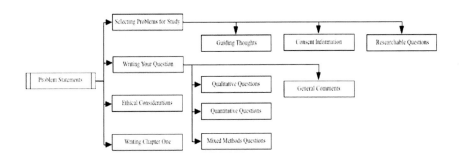

CHAPTER OVERVIEW

Chapter Two guides the reader through the process of writing a research question. It provides considerations and tips for coming up with a good and manageable question, including a discussion of ethical considerations, informed consent, and getting institutional approval. It discusses the differences in framing a qualitative, quantitative, and mixed-design problem statement, and also discusses the practicalities of doing each type of research as a classroom teacher. The chapter concludes with instruction on how to write an introductory chapter to a research proposal and study.

INTRODUCTION

When planning a trip, you need to decide on a destination or at least a route. The same is true for our research journey. We need to start with a problem statement. What questions or problems exist in your daily professional life that you would like to answer? What concern or issue do you have that you would like to explore in depth?

Writing a problem statement may be the hardest part of the whole research process. You might know you want to vacation in a tropical paradise. Once you know where you want to go, making transportation arrangements, hotel accommodations, and packing begin to fall neatly into place. But, deciding on that one destination is not as easy. It is the same with selecting a problem statement. Once you know what you will be studying, the rest of the process follows; but choosing that starting point can be difficult. So, let's work on coming up with a good problem statement.

SELECTING A PROBLEM TO STUDY

Sometimes seeing what others have done makes it easier to decide on a question for ourselves. Here are some problem statements that our students have examined:

Do students in a self-contained seventh grade classroom score higher on standardized language arts tests than seventh grade students in other instructional settings?

What were the effects of the Read Well Program on kindergartners who had Read Well instruction versus kindergartners who did not receive Read Well instruction?

Do fifth grade students think it is important to pass the state benchmarks assessments?

Are current school start times in alignment with our students' sleep/wake habits?

How do teachers who have looped grade levels with their students feel about the process?

The purpose of this study is to analyze how eighth grade mathematics students view themselves as mathematicians.

The purpose of this study is to determine if a student's reading fluency score can be correlated with their reading comprehension test scores.

The purpose of this study is to investigate the work-related stress experienced by my teaching colleagues.

This research proposes to investigate transition programs for grade six students in XX School District by comparing the characteristics of these programs with the characteristics of effective transition programs as described in the current literature.

GUIDING THOUGHTS

Have any of these spurred you on to your own question? Here are some things to consider in developing your own problem statement. These are adapted from Bogdan and Biklen (2006).

1. Be realistic. You will probably do this research project while attending other classes and/or teaching/working full time. Then there are those pesky personal responsibilities (shopping, cooking, cleaning, taking care of yourself and perhaps a family), and of course trying to find some down time to relax and keep yourself emotionally and physically healthy. Realize that you will have time constraints. Keep your study simple to start. Come up with a manageable question that can be answered in the time you have available.
2. Choose a sample that is convenient to study. While there are problems inherent in choosing your own students or colleagues, we feel your own classroom, school or district would be an optimal place to look. The main reasons we suggest this is that you have easy access to the students/staff/administration and you are a "known quantity." A major drawback is that the responses you get

may be tainted for those same reasons. Your sample may act or respond in a way that they feel you want to see rather than more naturally and truthfully. There may also be ethical considerations. We will explore these more fully later in this chapter.

3. Consider ease of access. Regardless of whether you choose to study your own teaching site or another, consider when you will be able to have access to your sample. For example, if you are going to compare teaching strategies of other teachers in your own building, are you able to do that? Do they teach during your planning period or other times you might have available? Are you just interviewing them? Can you do that before and/or after school? If you will be administering a survey to the staff, can that be done during a faculty meeting? If you are going to study a curriculum used by teachers in a neighboring district, when will you be able to meet with those teachers and see the curriculum being delivered? Can you do that during a prep period or is there a way that you can get release time to do that? Is their teaching schedule different from your own? What kind of paperwork will you need to file in order to gain access to teachers in another district? Don't set yourself up for failure by choosing to study an issue that will cause obvious concerns with data collection.

4. Do not be too abstract with your question. Rather than being interested in multiculturalism in schools, think about what really concerns you in that area. Are you interested, for example, in policy, instruction, teacher/student or student/ student relationships? Is it how teachers handle English Language Learners (ELL) in their classes or how relationships develop between ELL and the native students in the class? Are you really concerned with what services different school districts offer for ELL or teaching strategies that might be successful in working with ELL? Maybe you're interested in examining how the ELL in your classroom cope with language difficulties. While you don't want to be too narrow at the onset, you also don't want to be so broad as to have no sense of where you want to go with the question. Doing background research will help you in focusing your question, but it really helps to have some basic ideas before doing much exploring.

5. Be flexible. You have to be willing to adjust and refine your question as you progress. You may find after doing a literature review that your question should have a slightly different focus or that you really would rather go a totally different direction than you had thought. That's ok! There is a point in quantitative research where your problem statement will need to become permanently fixed but you do not need to do that initially.

6. Does your study have any importance? What would be gained by doing this study? Will it help you or others do your jobs better (practical importance)? Will it add to our knowledge about education in some important way (theoretical importance)? Will your study replicate what someone has already done to see if it works in your context? Conversely, if the question has already been rather thoroughly studied, perhaps just reading on the topic would provide you with what you need to know. In that case, it would not make a good problem statement.

7. Probably most importantly, you must be interested in your topic. If you plan to study something that you are not so excited about, it will be a chore to get the project done. Working on a topic you don't really have a vested interest in will not make or keep you motivated to collect and analyze your data, and your findings may be irrelevant for yourself. Research takes time and (as already discussed) provides much in terms of personal and professional development. Invest this time wisely. Given all the other demands on your time, it is important that you feel what you devote to your research project is a good use of this limited resource.

IDENTIFYING A PROBLEM AREA

If you are having problems coming up with a problem, here are some prompts that may be helpful:

- Is there an educational phenomenon you wish to describe (e.g., a move from a middle school to a junior high school; a historical overview of a change in curriculum; effects of block scheduling)?
- Is there something you have observed and would like to try and explain (e.g., why some students have trouble with long-division problems; what writing strategies are used by higher achievers; what thought processes do good problem solvers use)?
- Do you have a problem you want to try and develop a solution for (e.g., how can I make my students more self-directed learners; how can I get non-volunteers to answer questions; how can I better help my ADHD students to learn)?
- Is there a study you have read that you would like to replicate (e.g., check the validity of research findings with your population)?
- Have you heard a problem or concern raised at faculty meetings, committee groups, etc. that you would be interested in addressing?
- Look at the *Review of Educational Research* for ideas.
- Read the literature and see what the implication sections have to offer.
- Look at "hot topics" in current education to see if there is something that really piques your interest (e.g., whole language v. phonics; engineering design; alternative assessments).

If you are still stumped, for a few days or a week, journal at the end of each day on what happened in your classes or school. Read your journal. What recurrent issues arise? Can one of these act as the basis for your problem statement?

WHAT MAKES A RESEARCHABLE QUESTION?

The purpose of your research project is to answer your research question. So, in order to be researchable, you have to be able to answer your question, supported by the data you collected. Questions based on opinion, personal philosophies or beliefs are generally not researchable. For example, you cannot research the question "Should school uniforms be mandated?" This is a debatable question, but not one that is researchable as stated.

If your district is considering having all students wear a mandated school uniform and you would like to research that topic, you need to reframe the problem. You may want to see if the number of student behavioral referrals decrease if such a dress code is mandated. You may want to see if students have higher standardized test scores in schools with a mandated uniform as compared to schools with a less stringent dress code. Perhaps you are interested in how teachers/students/parents feel about having a mandated uniform for school attendance. All of these can be answered. While the last item (how people feel) is based on opinion, if your question is phrased to determine how a specific type of constituent in schools with a mandated uniform policy feel or how those constituents in a school that is considering such a dress code policy feel about it, that is a question that can be asked, data (responses) can be collected, and an answer can be found. Finding the answers to specifics related to mandating a uniform can help a district determine whether it should implement a similar policy. Making minor adjustments to a problem topic can often make it into a researchable question.

An important consideration in developing a researchable topic is the ethics involved with the question. We will discuss specifics about mandated ethical guidelines as they pertain to human subjects as they arise throughout the book; however, for now, keep in mind that you cannot do anything that would potentially harm any participant in any way. Usually potential harm is obvious. You wouldn't want to test the effects of second hand smoke on student achievement by having students work in a room full of smoke. Sometimes potential harm is more subtle. Would asking questions about self-esteem make a student despondent? Particularly as a new researcher you should always err on the side of caution and get counsel from your advisor or your human subjects review board if you are unsure.

WHAT KIND OF PROBLEM IS IT?

Once you have a problem in mind, the next step is to frame it in an appropriate format. How you do that depends on whether the question calls for qualitative data, quantitative data, or both. So let's examine your idea.

Will you be doing a more qualitative study? Are you interested in examining a topic from the viewpoint of those involved? Based on Borg and Gall (2007), the following broad categories of questions lend themselves to qualitative investigations:

- Theory developing; e.g., you are working on a grounded theory; you want to generate a hypothesis to explain an ongoing phenomenon.
- Understanding a complex process; e.g., you want to get to the root of misconceptions; you want to get a deeper understanding of students' thought processes.
- Identifying variables; e.g., what teacher behaviors affect student learning; why do students dislike math; why are some students reluctant readers
- Why something does or does not work; e.g. why a cooperative learning activity fails miserably with one particular class while it is successful with others; why students oppose inquiry-type learning activities

– Examining organizational structures; e.g., how do site councils function effectively; how does participating in professional learning communities affect staff relations
– Examining new constructs; e.g., block scheduling; blended classrooms; inclusion.

If, on the other hand, you are looking at a problem that can be solved by collecting numerical data, your question is better suited to a quantitative methodology. You have a specific hypothesis in mind to prove or disprove. You have variables that you can measure; for example, student achievement, gender differences, relationships among variables. You may want to determine the effect of something on something else—the use of a new curriculum on standardized test scores, a new teaching methodology on student achievement, different study skill techniques on homework completion rates.

You might have a study that requires a little of both methodologies. Perhaps a school district has placed Smart Boards in all classrooms. You might want to determine whether the students' scores on year end exams increase (quantitative) and whether students felt the Smart Boards enhanced their learning (qualitative). Or you might want to not only measure how frequently teachers used the Smart Board in their teaching (quantitative), but also ascertain how they felt about using this new tool (qualitative). In these cases, you would be using multiple types of methodologies. Be cautious about deciding to approach your research problem as a mixed methods study. You need to decide if your problem is best addressed by doing a quantitative study first followed by a qualitative study (or vice versa), or does your problem really need to use both research strategies simultaneously. The more complex your research problem becomes, the more work it will take to gather and analyze data around your topic. Mixed methods studies are often done better as two studies, and you may want to choose only one of those to pursue for your own research, leaving the other for another time or another researcher.

Remember, the type of methodology you ultimately choose to use is determined by your question. Because you are in the "driver's seat" right now with your question, there are a few things to consider: time, interest, and math self-confidence. Quantitative methodologies require mathematics skills or at least quantitative reasoning skills. Some new researchers tend to shy away from questions requiring numerical data, thinking qualitative studies will be easier. Let us assure you that in later chapters we will lead you through a variety of standard statistical tests in a simple fashion. We won't let you get lost. Do not let any qualms about working with numbers sway your decision about what type of question to pursue.

Qualitative studies require a great deal of skill and time. Interviewing is an art that gets better with practice. Writing "essay-type" questions that prompt subjects to focus on a topic and provide solid information without biasing them is not simple. Reading responses to open-ended questions and making sense of multiple data sets are time consuming processes. Often times, studies using qualitative methodologies are more labor intensive than those requiring quantitative methodologies. If time is a serious limiting factor, keep that in mind.

The cardinal rule in choosing a study, however, is ultimately what is of the greatest interest to you. Remember, if you do not have a vested interest in your question, your research journey will be more like a trip to the dentist for a root canal than a trip to the ocean to watch the sun rise.

WRITING YOUR QUESTION

Once you have your research topic in mind, it is time to write your problem statement. The format of a problem statement or research question varies depending on whether the study involves qualitative, quantitative or mixed methodologies.

QUALITATIVE QUESTIONS

Qualitative research is useful for describing or answering questions about particular, localized occurrences or contexts and the perspectives of a particular group toward events, beliefs or practices. The general form of a qualitative problem statement is: what are the patterns and perspectives of a group about something in a particular setting. For example:

The purpose of this research project is to find out from the perspective of our parents how our school can provide children access to a broad range of engaging reading materials through home, school and community programs.

How do middle school teachers feel about being required to use Student Response Systems in their classes?

QUANTITATIVE QUESTIONS

Quantitative research is based on the collection and analysis of numerical data. Underlying quantitative research methods is the belief or assumption that we inhabit a relatively stable, uniform, and coherent world that can be measured. For descriptive and historical studies, the general form of quantitative questions is: what are the descriptions of the characteristics of a group. For example:

What is the socio-economic status of students enrolled in a self-contained seventh grade classroom in a school where other students are in rotational classes?

What is the level of community participation in service projects in a community where service learning is being integrated into the elementary curriculum?

For studies in which groups will be compared statistically, the general form of a quantitative question is: what are the comparisons of characteristics of groups based on an intervention. For example:

Do students in a self-contained seventh grade classroom score higher on stand-ardized language arts tests than seventh grade students in other instructional settings?

27

Does the integration of service learning in elementary curriculum affect teacher self-efficacy?

MIXED STUDIES

Because mixed studies are looking at two questions, one to be answered with a quantitative methodology and one with a qualitative methodology, the question must be a compound statement. This is the only time we recommend the use of the word "and" in writing a problem statement. You can also write your purpose in two sentences, or in a list. For example:

The purposes of this study are to determine: (a) if looping in lower elementary grades result in greater learning gains for students, and (b) how parents feel about their children being looped.

The purpose of this study is to measure fifth grade student attitudes toward classroom science. It will also examine the factors that students feel influence these attitudes.

GENERAL COMMENTS ABOUT PROBLEM STATEMENTS

Regardless of the type of problem statement you have decided on, here are a few guidelines to consider in writing your statement:

The statement typically starts with "The purpose of this study…" Some researchers prefer to use a question rather than a statement. Either is fine. Using one of our prior examples, you can say "The purpose of this study is to measure fifth grade student attitudes toward classroom science" or "What are fifth grade student attitudes' toward classroom science?" We prefer the former just because it makes it very clear what the purpose of the study is.

Write for clarity. Avoid technical jargon or complicated grammatical construction.

Unless you are using a mixed methods design, you make your research work much more complicated if you include more than one question in a study. Especially for new researchers, avoid the use of the word "and" in a problem statement.

ETHICAL CONSIDERATIONS

Every university has a human subjects review committee, often called an **institutional review board (IRB)**, on its campus. While in the United States its function initially is to review any federally funded grant to consider the risks involved to the subjects participating in the research study, in most universities any research project involving human subjects (regardless of funding) needs to be reviewed by the IRB. Depending on the nature of the study, the research project may fall into one of three categories: full review, expedited review, or exempt from review.

The category is determined by the degree to which the study will involve and impact the subjects. Those projects that have greater risks, stress or discomfort to the subjects require greater scrutiny. We encourage our students to design their studies so they will be deemed exempt. This does not mean the proposal is not required to be reviewed and approved by the IRB, but the number of members that must review the proposal is reduced. In our institution, examples of types of proposals generally determined to be exempt can be found in Table 2.1. A complete listing of exempt categories is available in the Code of Federal Regulations (45 CFR 46.101); the URL is located in the reference section of this chapter. You will need to check with your institution to get the specific guidelines to follow to get your research proposal approved.

Table 2.1. Samples of an exempt proposal

- Investigations of commonly accepted educational practices in established or commonly accepted settings (e.g., a faculty member or teacher is examining a new method of teaching instruction to determine educational effectiveness)
- Analysis of information from educational tests that will be recorded in such a manner that subjects cannot be identified
- Surveys or interviews in which responses will be recorded in such a manner that a subject cannot be identified directly or through identifiers linked to a subject. To qualify for exempt status, the surveys would not involve vulnerable populations (e.g., juveniles) or ask questions about sensitive aspects of a subject's behavior (e.g., criminal behavior)
- Observations of public behavior (participant observation)
- Collection or study of publicly available existing data, documents, records or specimens
- Collection or study of existing data, documents, records or specimens in which information will be recorded or reported in such a manner that a subject cannot be identified directly or through identifiers linked to a subject

Source: University of Portland, 2008. Reprinted with permission.

In expedited and full review studies, there are two important criteria that must be met concerning the use of human subjects: their privacy must be maintained and you must have **informed consent**. Privacy of individuals is maintained through the use of anonymous data collection or confidential means such as coding. Although this is not always possible, participants must be assured that they cannot—even through their responses—be identified by a third party.

Subjects must also be willing participants in the research project after being briefed about the purpose of the study and any risks. This consent is written. If the subjects are under 18 years of ago, consent must be obtained by the parent/legal guardian of the minor.

Generally, exempt studies do not require written consent forms. Many action research projects do not require written consent because the data being collected are those which would normally be collected or available to the researcher outside the context of the study. For example, in the regular course of duties, a teacher may try new teaching methodologies, curricula, testing strategies, and the like. Having students participate in these classes and collecting data to determine the effectiveness is something the teacher would normally do. No special consent is required. Likewise, using already collected and available testing data (e.g., state test scores) requires no written consent, provided confidentiality can be assured. If a teacher plans on interviewing a student about things other than what is in the curriculum or studying students with whom they would not regularly interact, however, this is not typical and does require informed consent. The IRB has the final say on whether informed consent is required in specific situations. Written informed consent does need to include certain items. These are:

- Description of the purpose of the research
- How and for what length of time the subject will be expected to participate
- Any risks or benefits associated with participating in the study
- How confidentiality will be assured
- Contact information if the subject has questions about the study or his/her rights as a subject
- Statement that participation is voluntary, and participation may be discontinued at any time without any consequence
- What will be done with the findings of the study

A sample letter of informed consent can be found in Figure 2.1. The subjects (or the guardians if the subjects are minors) receive a copy of the written letter. If the data collection instrument is an anonymous questionnaire (with non-sensitive questions), a cover letter that includes the information can be provided. Submission of the completed instrument would be sufficient for "written" consent. A sample cover letter for that type of data collection is in Figure 2.2.

If you are interested in using a survey in which you will not be able to collect a consent form separately from the survey (online surveys are almost always in this form), there are models for writing consent forms in which completing the survey is implied consent (see Figure 2.2). The form of the letter is essentially the same and is shown on the first page of the survey before any questions are answered. The final line of the consent form reads something like: *Completing this survey constitutes your informed consent to use your responses in our study.* Some IRB committees are nervous about doing this because it is difficult to ensure anonymity. Be sure you know how your institution approaches this before you do a survey of this kind.

You should also be aware of any district guidelines for conducting research in your classroom, school or district. In some cases, a discussion with the principal is all that is required. In other districts, you need to go through a process similar to the IRB at a local level.

PARENTAL/GUARDIAN CONSENT FORM

Your child is invited to be in a research study about test anxiety and academic self esteem. I am asking for your child's participation to assist in my research for the completion of my Master of Education degree as your child is currently enrolled in my class. I ask that you read this form and ask any questions you may have before agreeing to have your child in this study. I can be reached at the school at 555-1234 or at home at 555-1111 (please no calls after 9:00pm).

The study: The purpose of this study is to determine if there is a relationship between a students' academic self-esteem and the presence of test anxiety. If you agree to have your child in this study, your child will be asked to complete two questionnaires. Your child will be asked to rate to what degree they feel anxiety coming into a test situation (on a rating scale of never, almost never, almost always and always) and the second will evaluate their level of academic self-esteem (by responding yes and no to different items). The questionnaires will take approximately 20 to 45 minutes to complete.

Risks/benefits: I feel there is little risk to the students. They are merely reporting their feelings in an anonymous setting. Individual students may feel like I will be scrutinizing them, but after explaining how the anonymity of the study works, hopefully their fears will be put to rest. Each student participating in this study will receive a fun pen or pencil, regardless of whether or not she or he completes the questionnaires.

Confidentiality: The records of this study will be kept private. Questionnaires will be coded to maintain anonymity and only I shall have access to the information. The coding is only done so that the data from the questionnaire can be sorted based on different demographic criteria. In the finished project, it will be impossible to identify subjects by name. Consent forms will be kept securely along with question-naire results for 1 year after the completion of this study.

Voluntary nature/questions: Your decision whether or not to participate will not affect current or future relations with me or the school. This is a personal endeavor to help me better understand how my students think. If you decide to allow your child to participate, I would greatly appreciate the assistance. Again, I welcome any questions or concerns and look forward to getting started, so please feel free to contact me if you have concerns.

Tia Martini

Name of Child _____

Signature of Parent/Guardian _____ Date _____

Figure 2.1. Sample letter of informed consent that needs to be signed.

You are invited to participate in a research study conducted by Patricia Morrell and James Carroll, School of Education, University of Portland.

This study is being conducted for several purposes:

1. Initially to help determine what kind of support, training, or resources you need or would like to have to help you in integrating the Smart Board and Student Response System into your teaching;
2. To evaluate, at the end of the school year, the professional development delivered and determine what you may still want help with in the future;
3. To see what affect, if any, the use of the technologies has had on student achievement;
4. To learn how teachers infuse these technologies into their teaching; and
5. To shed light on the benefits and problems associated with a school-wide adoption of new technologies.

To help with objectives 1, 2 and 5, we are asking for your assistance by completing this survey. Your participation in this study is voluntary. Your decision whether or not to participate will not affect your relationship with the researchers or the administration at XYZ Middle School. If you decide to participate, you are free to withdraw your consent and discontinue participation at any time without penalty. All responses you make will be confidential. Only information in the aggregate will be reported. We will have two survey collections: one now and another at the end of the school year. We ask for an identification number (the last 4 digits of your phone number) just so we can track responses from the same individual over the two survey administrations.

We do not foresee any risks in your participating in this study. You would benefit from this study by helping to shape the professional development offered regarding use of the new technologies, by allowing us to trouble shoot any problems that might have been unforeseen with the integration of these technologies into your teaching, and by learning what affect, if any, the use of the technologies has had on student achievement.

If you have any questions about this study or the survey please contact Tisha Morrell at morrell@university.edu (123-456-7890) or Jim Carroll at carroll@ university.edu (123-456-7890). If you have any questions regarding your rights as a research subject, contact the IRB at the University of Portland.

Your submission of the survey indicates that you have read and understand the information provided above, that you willingly agree to participate, that you may withdraw your consent at any time and discontinue participation without penalty, that you received this form, and that you are not waiving any legal claims.

Thank you!

Figure 2.2. Sample of letter of informed consent to accompany an anonymous survey.

ORGANIZING AND WRITING CHAPTER ONE

Once you have your problem statement, you are ready to begin writing your research paper. You have what you need to write Chapter One, The Introduction. An introduction is a narrative in which you make the case that your research question is worth asking. As an exercise, select a published research study or use one of those included in this book and try to write a short phrase or sentence that summarizes the main point(s) of each paragraph in the introduction of the paper. More often than not you will discover that the notes you have made form a logical argument. Each point or paragraph works toward making the case that the research study needs to be done. For this reason, problem statements usually appear at the end of the introduction.

A simple way to structure an introduction is outlined in Table 2.2. Once you structure your argument, take each point and expand it into one or several paragraphs. This will provide you with the bulk of your introduction. Let's look at an example. Suppose you think some of your students suffered from test anxiety. You want to see if you can reduce this test anxiety and get a better measure of your students' actual learning. Your introductory outline might look like this:

I. History
   What prompted the study
   Types of assessments generally used

II. Context
   Where do you teach (brief description of school/community)
   Description of students
   (Note: descriptions are kept anonymous)

III. Theoretical constructs
   Purpose of assessment
   Why test anxiety is an issue
   Theories that shed light on the issue of test anxiety
   Strategies that exist to reduce test anxiety

IV. Why is it important?
   Importance in terms of accurately measuring student learning
   Improved test scores
   Personal teaching goals
   Meaning of scores for district/federal funding

V. Problem Statement
   Write the problem statement
   Which strategy will you implement to try and reduce students' test anxiety

VI. Terms
   Define test anxiety

Table 2.2. Components of chapter one

Chapter One typically includes the follow pieces:
- History of the problem
- Description of the context
- Theoretical constructs
- Why the problem is important
- Problem statement
- List of terms

Let's look at this in more detail. Readers of research reports expect to find certain information in the introduction in addition to support for the need for the study. They would expect to find a description of the history of what prompted you to study the problem. In our example above, the opening paragraph might include talk of how the results of on the tests you have been giving do not seem to match your predictions of how well you expected some students would do. Or, that you have noticed a high rate of absenteeism on test days. The introduction would include some narrative that helps the reader understand how you became aware of the problem.

Readers will expect to find information about the context in which the study is being done. A sense of the setting/context of your problem is necessary to understand why the problem exists and why it is important to research. For this next part of your introduction, you would briefly describe the type of school in which you are working and the students in your class. Provide demographics of the community if they are relevant. Do not include identifying information in your description. For example, when discussing a specific high school in Portland, Oregon, you would say a large, public, urban high school in the Pacific Northwest. Do not use actual names of schools or subjects. You may assign pseudonyms as needed. Perhaps the most confusing thing to beginning writers of research reports is the idea of a theoretical construct (ways in which the research community views the problem). See section III of the outline above. This includes some set of studies or the work of a specific author that defines the space in which your study fits into the larger body of educational research. This prior work helps define the way you will proceed with your study.

Readers will look for the reason your question is an important problem. Discussion of this would include number IV above. And, finally, they will want to have some idea of what you intend to do in the study. In our case, that would be a short description of why you chose a specific strategy (say playing soft music) to try with your students to reduce their test anxiety. If the progression of the argument makes sense, the introduction would end with the problem statement.

Also included in Chapter One are definitions for terms that either have multiple meanings or whose definitions may not be understood by all readers. These words are either defined within the Chapter as they appear in the text or under a separate heading at the end of Chapter One in a list format. Note that this listing is not a glossary or a dictionary. It should only include salient terms that may cause confusion because of their use. "As has been demonstrated in the literature many times, sometimes seemingly familiar terms develop a life of their own as a diversity of definitions, understandings, and interpretations emerge over time" (Loughran, 2006, p. 1). Some examples of these are reflection, looping, blended, inclusion, cooperative learning. The purpose of including the definitions is so the readers will understand the meaning of the terms as you intend them to be understood.

Examples of introductory chapters for several of students are located in Appendix 2-A, located at the end of this chapter. Reading through them may help give you a more solid understanding of what goes into Chapter One.

NEXT STEPS

You are taking the hardest step. You are examining your professional life and determining what problem you would like to solve. After you decide on a purpose for your study, you have what you need to craft your question into a researchable problem statement. Chapter One of your research paper will lay the groundwork for what you want to do and why. It's now time to examine what others have to say and have done in the same area. On to the Literature Review!

CHAPTER SELF-CHECK

Having completed this chapter, you should be comfortable discussing the following:
- considerations in deciding on a problem statement
- requirements of a researchable question
- characteristics of qualitative and quantitative questions
- guidelines for writing your problem statement
- ethical considerations when designing a study
- regulations affecting studies with human subjects
- organization and writing Chapter One

CHAPTER REVIEW QUESTIONS

1. What makes a question researchable?
2. Frame a question for the following problems:
   a. You are interested in discovering how the teachers in your building feel about the new reading curriculum.
   b. You are interested in determining whether the implementation of the new reading problem will affect student scores on the annual statewide reading test.
   c. You want to know both how teachers feel about the new reading program and if the reading program will affect student achievement scores.

3. What is an exempt study?
4. What is a letter of consent, when is it required, and what must it contain?

REFERENCES

Bogdan, R. C., & Biklen, S. K. (2006). *Qualitative research for education: An introduction to theory and methods* (5th ed.). Boston: Allyn & Bacon.

Borg, W. R., & Gall, M. D. (2007). *Educational research: An introduction* (8th ed.). New York: Allyn & Bacon.

http://www.hhs.gov/ohrp/humansubjects/guidance/45cfr46.htm#46.101

http://www.up.edu/irb

Loughran, J. (2006). *Developing a pedagogy of teacher education: Understanding teaching and learning about teaching*. London: Routledge.

APPENDIX 2-A: SAMPLE CHAPTER ONES

EXAMPLE 1 (REPRINTED WITH PERMISSION OF CHRIS STILES)

THE POTENTIAL POWER OF TESTWISENESS

CHAPTER ONE: INTRODUCTION

As an educator, nothing is more frustrating than handing a wretchedly low test score to a student who works diligently and tries his hardest. This is the student who puts in 110%, hands in all assignments, works well in collaborative student groups- yet still fails one examination after the other. These types of students seem to have two different learning tendencies. On one hand, the students possess skills that enable them to interact well with others and demonstrate sound work ethic, while on the other, they are simply not able to convert these abilities into successful test grades. It is disconcerting to hand back exams to these students when their effort and in-class contributions seem to be inversely proportionate to their overall test performance.

The ability to write a sound exam is a vital learned skill for any successful student. Whether to demonstrate proficiency in core subjects, complimentary courses, or for a government issued driver's license, exams are a common fact of life that we are all forced to face. Many factors may affect students' ability to achieve high grades on an exam. At some point or another, we have all been faced with these stressful hurdles. The stumbling blocks test takers often encounter usually encompass some level of test anxiety. Any activity which measures a person's competencies with a score which reflects pass or failure, ultimately raises the stakes of that evaluative activity. Whether it be due to lack of preparation, inability to recollect requisite facts at the crunch time, or simply tripping up in the format of the exam, a test can present students with the opportunity to feel like a learned success story or an inept failure.

From an early age, students are coached to take a better exam. In the province of Alberta, students are required to complete a standardized exam as early as nine years of age. They then continue to write them in three year intervals culminating in the completion of diploma exams throughout their graduating year. While all educators surely agree that written exams are only one of a myriad of acceptable assessments, they seem to garner the majority of weighting and emphasis throughout a student's educational career. The key, then, is to prepare students to assist them to enhance their scores on any given exam.

The buzz word that describes this process involves enlightening students in developing a competent aptitude to demonstrate "testwiseness." Operationally defined, this involves training students to utilize strategies to improve their results largely independent from the material being assessed. Case in point, this means being able to write a better exam on the French Revolution without having to know anything about the information from that period. In essence, most testwiseness skills lie in the ability to recognize faults in question design, helpful patterns, and well established strategies. Others emphasize the pre-test preparation that must occur, or skills to overcome reading comprehension, or to alleviate test anxiety. At the high school level, the question that arises is whether or not students have received ample amounts of coaching in order to be well versed in the art of testwiseness.

Standardized exams ultimately determine the suitability for seniors in high school to qualify for post-secondary admission. With their future weighing in their minds, the stakes certainly could not be higher. Not only do grade twelve standardized exams determine success or failure for students, undeniably by extension, they also are perceived to indicate the quality of the instructor. Staffrooms in every school are often filled with the moans of teachers stressing about their students' test performance and, by extension, the image that it will relay on their methodologies. Testwiseness also forces teachers to tiptoe the precarious line of morals and ethics while preparing students for exams. As a result, teaching testwiseness to students may run the risk of spoon feeding information to our students, or simply teaching to the test. Ultimately, because of high stakes exams teachers feel constricted to "lock down" the curriculum and feel unable to explore areas of interest that do not directly apply to the content of the exam. As aforementioned, there are definite problems that arise from issues that pertain to testcoaching and testwiseness.

The focus of this study then, is to attempt to affect positive academic improvement upon grade 12 social studies students through providing them with moral and helpful testwiseness tips. Students must be reminded on a continual basis of the importance of writing an exam with a critical mind. Often, as classroom teachers, we mention these skills in passing somewhere at the beginning of the semester. Or worse, we assume senior high students have already acquired the aforementioned test taking cleverness. Why not provide students with reminders of these skills on the day of the exam? Why not revisit these skills without the subject becoming overburdened or obtrusive upon the students? Through the comparison of student performance on the exact same exam before the implementation of an "improved testwiseness workshop" and after it, this study will correlate test writing skills with achievement.

The purpose of this study is to determine if providing a testwiseness reference sheet for use during the examination will elicit significant improvement in students' test scores. If students are refreshed of these test-wise skills immediately before writing an exam, the hope is that it will better serve them in experiencing future success. Will the current class of students who have received the testwiseness intervention perform significantly better than their past counterparts who did not receive it all?

EXAMPLE 2 (REPRINTED WITH PERMISSION OF SHARON CLARK)

PROJECT: COLLABORATION

CHAPTER ONE: INTRODUCTION

As an administrator on our school's instructional leadership team, looking at collaboration has become the driving force of our team's conversations. We have found that, as a staff, we need to find the time for collaboration. Collaboration is a difficult goal to achieve because our staff must perform a myriad of diverse activities in a challenging working environment. Our challenging working environment is a function of the combination of the logistics of the large building we work in and our teaching assignments that necessitate working in many department areas. Finding opportunities for collaboration will require both sound planning and a commitment from all staff members.

Before proceeding to clarify the definition of collaboration, some background information about our school will be helpful. Our school is an elementary and junior high school (grades 5 to 9). We have approximately 300 students, 15 teaching staff and five teaching assistants. Our front office consists of two administration assistants, an assistant principal and a principal. Our school offers students four programs: a Community Learning Skills Program that works with mentally handicapped students; a Logos program that is an alternative Christian program; a Strategies program that provides support for students who have learning disabilities; and a regular academic program that provides students with a strong academic emphasis. Within these programs we offer students a variety of complimentary courses. Clearly, our school programs cover a wide spectrum of areas demanding a diverse assortment of expertise from our staff members.

Four years ago, based on the influence of our Superintendent, each school developed a team of lead teachers that made up an Instructional Leadership Team. This group of lead teachers has the responsibility of leading the rest of the staff through a variety of best practices. The lead teachers on the team are department heads, rookie teachers, experienced teachers and any keen staff members that want to enhance the best practices of our staff members. The team is made up of five teachers. My role on the Instructional Leadership Team is a lead teacher representing the school administration. An example of a best practice pursued is teaching strategies that help improve reading comprehension skills of our students in keeping with our school instructional focus on reading comprehension. Our focus emerged by interpreting the Provincial Achievement Test Results to target specific needs of our students.

For the last three years, we have worked very hard at developing these best practices for teaching reading comprehension skills. Now our staff is at the next stage of this process that includes looking at student work and reflecting on this process. Our Instructional Leadership Team recognizes the importance of these two tasks and that staff collaboration needs to happen in order for this process to be successful.

39

Collaboration is not a precise area of study. For the dual purpose of completing this research project and supporting the work of our staff members, my part will be to work with the Instructional Leadership Team to further staff awareness of the importance of and benefits gained from collaboration. Also, considering the conversations that our instructional leadership team had at our year-end retreat, I will be looking at the comfort level of the Instructional Leadership Team in fostering collaboration among the teaching staff. We will be able to engage successfully in collaboration if the staff does not become caught up in the traditional style of individualistic teaching and focuses instead on cooperative teaching. The success of our effort to foster collaboration will be enhanced if our teaching staff respects the initiatives of the Instructional Leadership Team. If the staff buys into the initiative of our leadership team, collaboration among teaching staff will grow. How comfortable is the Instructional Leadership Team in fostering collaboration among staff members in our school?

DEFINITIONS:

I decided to use da Costa & Riodan's (1998) definition of collaboration: "work done among two or more teachers in a climate of trust and openness to scrutiny and criticism" (p. 3)

Instructional Leadership Team is a group comprised of teaching staff representing various curricula areas or specialized areas that role is to provide leadership in the area of instruction.

EXAMPLE 3 (REPRINTED WITH PERMISSION OF STEVE COLKITT)

A LOOK AT EIGHTH GRADERS' ATTITUDES AND ACHIEVEMENT IN MATHEMATICS

CHAPTER ONE: INTRODUCTION

American Psychologist Professor William James once said, "It is our attitude at the beginning of a difficult task which, more than anything else, will affect its successful outcome." As a mathematics teacher I enjoy math and learning in general. I like to discover, explore things, and work with numbers. However, I know that not all my students share this same enthusiasm for education and particularly mathematics. In the classroom I commonly hear students mumble (and occasionally yell in frustration) about how "stupid" math is and how much they dislike math. In turn, some students become very frustrated and decide to give up on whatever task we are trying to work on or accomplish.

Many school districts across the United States are reforming their mathematics curriculum in an attempt to help students see the applications of math in the real world and focus more on higher thinking skills rather than rote memorization of algorithms. Programs such as Connected Mathematics, Investigations, and Everyday Mathematics are based on of the idea of showing students the usefulness of math in life, getting them to discover how it is used, and encouraging students to link concepts and ideas together. My school district has restructured the K-8th grade math curriculum to incorporate these problem-solving based curricula in hopes of raising state test scores and helping students stretch their thinking and problem solving skills. This is the fourth year the school I work at has used the Connected Math Project (CMP). The 2004–2005 school year was the first year where substantial growth occurred at the eighth grade level at the school I work at since the school-wide implementation of CMP in 2002–2003 school year. Roughly 15 percent more of eighth grade students passed the Oregon State Assessment Test (OSAT) than the previous year by meeting the eighth grade benchmark score set by the Oregon Department of Education.

Despite the growth that occurred with last year's tests results, over half of the 8th grade students at the school in which I teach have below average math skills (according to RIT scores based on Oregon State Assessment Tests), and roughly 35 percent of math students in my class receive a quarter grade of D (59 to 69 percent) or F (58 percent and below). I am interested in analyzing students' interests, successes, and failures in mathematics to give me a better picture of where they are coming from and use the information collected to help improve their chances of succeeding in my classroom. The information will also give me help with how I should alter the current curriculum to better meet the needs and desires of my students. I also hope to use my research findings to help me apply for various math, science, and technology grants that will allow me to integrate more technology and classroom projects into the curriculum.

The purpose of this study will be to discover what my eighth grade students' attitudes towards mathematics are and if those attitudes are related to achievement in mathematics. It is hypothesized that there is a positive correlation between attitude and achievement in the area of mathematics. If a correlation is discovered between attitude and achievement I can look for ways to improve students' attitudes towards mathematics as a pathway to help increase students' math scores. If a correlation does not exist, I can analyze other aspects of my math pedagogy and focus on those areas to help increase student achievement in mathematics.

THE LITERATURE REVIEW

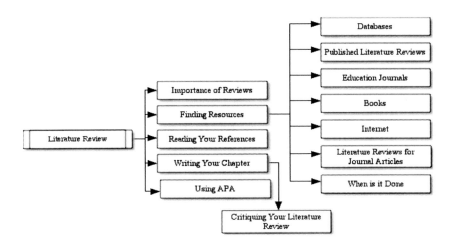

CHAPTER OVERVIEW

Chapter Three will continue with the five-chapter format by providing instruction on literature reviews. It will discuss the need for a literature review and detailed instruction on how to go about conducting a literature review. It will build on the information provided in Chapter One on being an informed consumer and provide more details for critiquing published research. Finally, the chapter will provide guidelines for writing this portion of a proposal and study.

INTRODUCTION

Now that you have some idea of a problem to research, the next step is to mold it into a "great notion." You do this by finding out what others have written about your issue; that is, you carry out a literature review. There are several reasons why this is an important step in your research journey.

THE WHYS OF LITERATURE REVIEWS

First, by reading about your topic, you will become more versed about your problem. A literature review will provide you with background information and, if you don't already have one, also suggest a theoretical base upon which to build your research design. A theoretical base/framework is helpful in guiding your research. It can be used to focus your problem statement, assist in finding relevant past research, and provide a rationale for collecting data and interpreting your findings. Theoretical frameworks are larger, established constructs within which your work can be based. Some examples might be cognitive dissonance, conceptual change theory, or feminist ideology.

Second, by examining related research studies, you can get an idea of whether your question has been "studied to death" and is unnecessary, if there is a dearth of information on the topic, or if there is an off-shoot of the problem that you might find more intriguing to study. Does research that has already been done need to be re-examined in the context of your school or classroom? Looking at implication sections of others' studies often provides new ideas for research that you may not have already considered.

Third, it can prevent you from "reinventing the wheel." Has someone used a methodology you could emulate? Are there instruments and/or interview questions that have already been tested that you could employ? What have others seen as limitations to their studies? What suggestions do they have for strengthening the work? Are there ideas for future studies that you can use to sculpt your question?

Finally, by reading what others have already discovered, you have a basis for comparisons of your research findings down the road. Will your conclusions match what other researchers have found? If they don't, why might what you have found be unexpected? Are your findings an extension of something already known? What does your work add to the current literature base?

Conducting and writing a literature review is a crucial piece of a research study. A well-done literature review leaves the reader feeling informed about your topic, knowing enough to decide if you have proceeded appropriately, and believing you can support all of the points you will make.

Something to note: when you are writing an educational research paper you will include a list of references at the end which is a precise list of all of the materials which are **cited** in the paper. This is different from a **bibliography** which includes all relevant materials you have read whether they are actually cited or not. While you may read many resources that help you with understanding your topic, you will probably find when you are writing that you don't need to cite something from everything that you have read. New researchers are often tempted not to *waste* anything they have read but this is seldom a good strategy. Only cite what needs to be cited—what statements are you making that need support? What is not general knowledge and needs a reference? What are the highest quality references for each of the points you are making? The quality of your literature review - not the number of citations - will "prove" that you are well versed in your topic area.

FINDING RESOURCES

Now that you are convinced that a literature review is the next important component, how do you go about conducting a literature review? A first step is to make an

I. Grouping – Background information on grouping (defining terms)
    A.   What kinds of grouping structures exist (collaborative, cooperative)
    B.   How are groups formed (randomly, by ability, by personality, by teachers, by students)

II. Grouping and achievement
    A.   Is there evidence showing a link between grouping and improved achievement?
    B.   Do any studies show a decrease in achievement when grouping is used?
    C.   Do different types of groups have different effects on achievement?
    D.   Are there other indirect benefits of grouping that may lead to increased achievement (i.e., better communication skills)?

IV. Other things to look for in the literature
    A.   What suggestions for future studies have been made?
    B.   What limitations to studies have been listed and how can you avoid them?
    C.   What methods for gathering data have been used that might be appropriate for your study?

Figure 3-1. Sample outline for grouping question.

outline of what you think needs to be reviewed. For example, if you are thinking of determining whether small group work improves student achievement your outline may be as simple as that shown in Figure 3-1.

While this may seem obvious, actually having a written outline helps in focusing your search and, later, in writing this section of your research paper. Often, when we start delving into the literature, we get "sidetracked" and begin reading articles that are not relevant to our current study. While reading is always a good thing, going astray when time may be limited can turn out to be more frustrating than beneficial in the long run. A good question to keep asking yourself is, is this article relevant to my study?

Databases

Using your outline as a guide, develop a few key words; for our example (Figure 3-1), perhaps we would start with grouping and achievement but also pay attention to cooperative groups, homogeneous groups, or ability grouping. The **Education Resources Information Center (ERIC)** is probably the most commonly used database in education and can be accessed by anyone via the internet. ERIC is accessible in two forms: one is through subscription with EBSCO (to which many libraries subscribe) and another is a free Internet version (www.eric.ed.gov). It contains well over a million educational citations and is easy to navigate.

Searches are generally carried out initially by using the key words. Also, ERIC has its own thesaurus making it easy to generate a list of words you can use to find articles related to your area of interest. Rather than go into detail now, when you are ready to start your ERIC search, refer to the Search Tips link from the ERIC site (eric.ed.gov), which provides an overview and detailed instructions of how you can access and search the ERIC data base. Once you find an article on your topic, be sure to note down authors who may have written other things on this topic, productive looking keywords that you hadn't thought of before, or publications that might have other articles relevant to your search.

It is important to realize, however, that not all articles found through ERIC have been peer-reviewed. Aside from providing citations to articles that have been published in journals (and thus peer- reviewed), ERIC also acts as a clearing-house for a variety of papers, presentations, conference proceedings and the like (which have not necessarily been through any review process). While many of the second category of references are very useful, the quality of the research has not been determined prior to being included in the ERIC database. As electronic access through our libraries to more and more material becomes possible, ERIC has lost some of its importance to our work. Use it as a first stop to easily get a sense of your topic and collect some keywords that will be useful. Then look further.

Educational databases in addition to ERIC also exist; these do require subscriptions, but many local and most (if not all) college and university libraries have subscriptions to a variety of databases. Do not discount them; rather, ask a local librarian for assistance in using these. You are likely to find valuable articles that are accessible through sociology (e.g., SocINDEX) and psychology (e.g., PsychINFO) databases that might not appear in ERIC. Be creative in imagining what other disciplines might be interested in the same topics you are investigating. Many libraries also hold subscriptions to databases such as Wilson Select Plus and Education Abstracts. Again, do seek out the advice of experts (i.e., reference librarians) for assistance in finding what sources are available for your use.

Currently the quality of access to scholarly material through conventional search engines is increasing. A prime example is Google Scholar (http://scholar. google.com). Google Scholar uses the WorldCat database as the initial source for references, but adds a number of services that might be valuable to you as a researcher. The most important thing to consider regardless of the sources you use is whether the material you are reading has been reviewed by experts in the field of study. Sometimes you will have to look closely to be sure this is the case. Is it a journal article or a book from ERIC? If it is from ERIC, is it EJ or ED? EJ refers to journal articles; ED does not. Journal articles are peer-reviewed prior to being accepted and published. ED articles are submitted by the author and have not necessarily undergone any review process. To help you search databases, Appendix C provides some general comments about libraries and the online interfaces that they provide, other interfaces available for your use, and some basic search tips.

Published Literature Reviews

Some books and journals are dedicated to publishing literature reviews. Typical journals that publish literature reviews include the *Review of Research in Education* and *Review of Educational Research*. For instance the *Review of Educational Research* is a quarterly publication of the American Educational Research Association (AERA), which describes itself as "a forum for reviews of previously published work in a field that is populated by scholars from diverse traditions." (http://ojs.aera.net/journals/index.php/rer)

Numerous books that publish comprehensive reviews of literature around specific topics in education also exist. Most of these have a title that begins *Handbook of Research on ....* They range from general areas (*Handbook of Research on Teaching*) to works that cover more specific topics (*Handbook of Research on Teaching Literature through Communication and Visual Arts*). These are valuable first places to go as you begin to review the literature around your topic because the articles in them are very comprehensive and will help you identify the key issues around your topic, not to mention that someone else has already done much of the initial reference searching that you would need to do. You will have to go to the library (not a bad thing) to read these.

ERIC Digest contains short essays on a variety of educational concepts and practices. Their website describes the *Digest* as "designed to provide an overview of information on a given topic, plus references to items providing more detailed information" (http://www.ericdigests.org). ERIC finds authors who do short reviews of the literature that is available through ERIC. Even though these digests are not nearly as comprehensive as what you would find in review articles and handbooks on research, they are often a good way to get started.

Some journals, although not literature review journals per se, tend to publish articles that include extensive literature reviews. A prime example is the *American Educational Research Journal.* Keep an eye out for articles in this and other journals that seem to be longer than normal journal articles. That is usually a clue that a long list of references is included.

New researchers often feel like they are not doing the work required if they use review work that is done by others. All good researchers take advantage of these reviews and your work will get better as you discover the reviews that are most closely related to your topic. However, the purposes of these reviews are to help you develop a solid grounding in your area of study and to provide insight into which articles and authors you may want to read. They are for personal background and use as directional tools. The problem is that people who are getting started doing research are tempted to cite articles based on abstracts or the reviews that others have written without actually reading the original work. Do not allow yourself to succumb to this temptation. Retrieve and read the article described in the review if you believe it will be a good reference for your study. Only if you cannot find the original article after a sincere effort (have you talked to your local reference librarian?) should you cite from a review.

Because we know that you are new to literature reviews and because your time is limited for completing your projects, it is important to know how to cite these secondary sources in your paper. As an example of how this would appear, let's say you cannot find an article by Jones cited in a review by Smith. In the body of your paper, the sentence may say "Jones (as cited in Smith, 2007) found…" In the literature cited list, you would include only the Smith citation. Talk with your advisors to see whether this strategy will be allowed in your paper, remembering that it is always a course of last resort.

Education Journals

Do pay attention to journal types. Journals can be categorized in a number of different ways. Generally, for our purposes, there are three basic categories of journals: practitioner, policy and research.

Practitioner journals are published to help teachers solve specific problems in their own classrooms or schools. Some are general (e.g., *Instructor*), while others are oriented around specific content areas (e.g., *Science and Children*). These journals have articles which are not necessarily based on research and are intended more to provide helpful ideas and collaboration than to communicate generalizable truths. While these types of articles may help you in practice and in refining your problem statement, they are generally not the types of articles you want to focus on for your literature review. They tend to promote ideas based more on opinions or supposition rather than ones supported by evidence.

Policy journals are intended to review important issues in education. These journals often have theme-based issues and try to present well-known authors in the particular area. Although the authors often cite current research on their topic, the point of an article is usually not to focus on the related research but to outline the broader issues. Examples of this type of journal are *The Kappan* and *Educational Leadership*. These are useful in providing a framework and basic understanding of underlying principles.

Research journals present peer- reviewed current research. There are literally hundreds of these in education. Because subscriptions are often expensive, most libraries can not maintain too large a collection of these journals. Some journals make older issues available online. Often you have to hunt and avail yourself of interlibrary loan capabilities to find all of the ones you might want to read if they are not available electronically. If journal articles do not appear in the online databases you have available, first go the website for the journal in which the article was published to see if older issues are archived. If that does not provide the access you need, try searching for the website of the author, who may provide access directly to articles, or drafts similar to the published versions of the articles he or she has written. Each of these journals will be useful to you for one reason or another; you are unlikely to find current research or seminal articles that describe theoretical constructs in anything but research journals. Reviewing articles from these will make up the bulk of your literature review. Like the practitioner journals, research journals come in a general interest category (e.g., *American Educational Research Journal*) and content specific areas (e.g., *The Journal of Research in Science Teaching*). Both arenas should be explored.

Something you might come across that you are unfamiliar with is a **meta-analysis**. What this means is that someone studied a number of studies; that is, the data presented in published studies are used as the data sources. There are many criticisms of this type of research/article; however, meta-analyses can be useful. Besides providing conclusions based on the accumulation of a number of research studies, meta-analyses can be great bibliographic sources. Try adding "meta-analysis" as an additional search term in your next database search.

Books

Books are helpful in providing theoretical constructs. However, materials in books tend to become even more dated than those in journals and often involve more reading than is necessary to find the ideas that are most important to your search. Typically you may find that you use books sparingly as reference sources. Some books are compilations of chapters by a number of authors around a common topic. These tend to get to press faster than single author texts and may provide you with a broader range of views on your topic.

Internet Finds

With the Internet becoming commonplace, many people like to just use any search engine (e.g., Google, Yahoo) to find articles related to their interests. A word to the wise: this is an easy way to get some hits. It is the quality of the hits that is suspect. Because anyone can post anything to a website, what you read is probably not peer-reviewed and probably not the type of reference you want to cite in your paper. We recommend that if you take this route, use it as an initial segue into finding more substantiated documentation of your issue. Check out the author or citations on a reputable educational site to validate its use. There are, of course, exceptions. Many solid, research journals are available online, with older issues available without a subscription.

Literature Review from Journal Articles

You will find as you start searching that the bibliographies and literature citations of the articles you read will lead you to more articles. Depending on your topic, this may seem like either a closed loop or a hierarchical branching to infinity. Using others' reference lists to guide you is a great tool. However, be careful to stay focused on your topic and, unless the reference seems seminal, pay attention to timeliness. As you go back further and further into the literature, you may start finding outdated studies. Focusing and timing will help limit your search.

Many inexperienced researchers come to the task of gathering materials for a literature review thinking that it can be done relatively quickly and in one sitting. This is almost never the case. You will need to go through a cycle of finding materials, reading and reviewing them, using that knowledge to go back for more materials and continuing to develop broader knowledge of your topic. You may need to begin reviewing research even before you have a problem statement and it is likely that you will continue to find additional references well after data are collected. Often literature reviews require the greatest proportion of effort in a research study. Start the literature review process as early as possible in your research work in order to become as informed as you can about your topic as you are developing your study, and to be sure you have enough time to do a quality job on your paper.

When Do I Know When I Am Done?

The question most asked by students is "when is enough, enough?" Let's go back to the example presented in Figure 3.1. If we enter the general expression of "grouping" into an ERIC search, 196,048 possibilities are found. If we choose to instead type "cooperative learning" into an ERIC search, we get a mere 23,646 matches with potential resources. If we narrow that search, sorting through those that also deal with "elementary," the number is reduced to 8,941. While this is much more manageable than over 23,000, these are still too many references to even scan! Looking at descriptors for any of the articles will provide some terms to use to further narrow the search (e.g., "grouping (instructional purposes)" or "ability groups"). This may also provide some insight into the problem, itself. Since the problem focuses on trying to decide if small group work improves student achievement, you might want to narrow your scope. Read some articles about different ways to group. Maybe you will want to compare the effects of grouping by ability groups in mathematics as compared to grouping by ability groups in social studies. Maybe you will want to compare heterogeneous and homogeneous groupings in reading. Or is it student achievement of student-made groups to teacher-made groups (and what kind of teacher made groups) that you would like to compare? By doing some background reading, you may be able to decide just what it is about grouping and achievement that you are truly interested in exploring. This will help you both sharpen your problem statement and narrow the rest of your literature searching. Keep thinking about the relevancy of the articles you are reading to your study and remember that more recent work is likely to supercede work done some years ago.

Conversely, let's say you are taking a teaching position in the Australian Outback. Let's further suppose that you are not familiar with the specifics of that culture, but wonder if you would be successful in using groupings with that classroom population. So, you do an ERIC search of "Australian Aboriginal Groupings." You will get 0 hits. This is "virgin territory" so to speak! However, while it may excite you that you will be the first to publish in this area (at least as far as those terms in ERIC are concerned), this does not help provide you with the background you need to proceed with your research project. In that case, you may need to widen your search terms. Perhaps you want to look at "Australian Aboriginal Education and Cooperative Learning." This will provide 24 possibilities. You might want to broaden the search by also searching with the newly found descriptors of "culturally relevant education" or "indigenous populations." You may even go to a sociology index and learn a bit about Australian aboriginal cultures to see how they feel about group versus individual work. The point here is that you may find important information about your topic in papers that have been written to focus on other, possibly related, topics.

You will know you have sufficiently researched your topic when the same authors and articles keep being cited and you are finding no new information. If an author/article is referenced a number of times, that is a beacon telling you that you need to find and read that original document. Articles that are referenced by multiple authors often turn out to be those references that form the theoretical foundation of your work. Sometimes identifying the older references in a reference list can point to foundational work. Additionally some authors are primarily associated with a particular educational concept and you would be remiss not to read about the topic from the guru himself/herself. You can often identify this person by the number of times that particular name is connected to a concept. For example, speaking of Multiple Intelligences without reading something written by Howard Gardner or Cooperative Learning without directly citing Johnson and Johnson would make the reader wonder if you, yourself, truly had a solid grounding in the topic. Not all concepts do have a "mastermind" but if you are seeing repetition in citations, do not brush it off. Additionally, as another rule of thumb, any time you find an interesting and seminal article being discussed, do not settle for the secondary review of the article—go to the primary source and acquaint yourself directly.

Unfortunately, there is no magic number of references you need to make a solid literature review. It really is topic dependent and a judgment call on your part. Is it really not worth your time to read more? Have you identified what appear to be the major themes? Have you adequately represented all points of view on your topic? Is there an article or author that is frequently referenced? Have you read that article or work by that author? If you have answered "yes" to all of these, you are probably done collecting sources. Keep an open mind, and do add to your literature review down the road should some new article get published while are you progressing with your research.

READING YOUR REFERENCES

When you are doing a literature search, it is important to take notes in a systematic fashion. That will help save you time later when you begin to write your Literature Review chapter. There are many ways that you can organize your note taking to be efficient. We will suggest just one. Regardless of how you take notes while you read, however, there are some pointers that we would like to highlight:

1. You must have complete citations. You will need to include a reference list at the end of your research paper. The best time to be sure you have all the information you need for the reference listing is while you are reading the article; not going back later to find a "missing" volume or page number. It may be useful to keep a separate document on your computer that includes all of the full references for everything you read as you are reading. It is easy to cut and paste

these into your final paper when you decide on the exact references you will use. You will be surprised at the amount of time it takes to type references if you wait until the end of your writing to put these into APA form.

2. If you have a direct quotation from a source, be sure and note the exact page number after your quote in your notes. Forgetting to do this is very time consuming to correct later.

3. When reading an article, decide whether you can do with just taking notes or if you feel the piece is important enough that you might want to refer to the original. If the latter is true, then download a copy of the article or make a photocopy. Do not download or photocopy articles when just a few notes or excerpts will do. Do be sure and include complete citation information if you take notes from the article.

OK. So, let's assume you have a list of journal articles you want to read for your literature review. Before you begin reading, decide how you feel most comfortable taking notes. Are you a computer person? Do you go nowhere without your laptop and couldn't imagine taking notes on anything but? Are you more a pencil/paper kind of person, putting things in electronic format later, after you have processed it by hand? Do you prefer taking notes on index cards so you can manipulate them to organize your thoughts before you start writing your literature review? Any of these ways would work just fine. Do what is most natural for you. There are some slight differences that will be recommended depending on which method you decide to use, but for the most part, note taking is note taking.

We know some of you have had a lot of experience in researching a topic and writing a literature review. We also know that for other readers, this is an experience that is relatively new or something you have not done in a long time. We will gear the rest of this section to the latter.

Assuming you are doing an ERIC or other database search, you will have a list of possible studies. First, read the abstract of the article that is shown. This should give you a strong indication of whether the article is worth reading for your purposes. (You may need to click on "details" to see the full abstract.) If the abstract does not seem on target, move on to the next citation. If it does, mark the "add" so you save this entry to a clipboard that ERIC starts for you. Continue this process until you are done with this preliminary review (More detailed instructions on what to do with your clipboard of information is available on the ERIC site). If you had a starting point other than a database (perhaps someone recommended specific articles to you or you used a published literature review), we still recommend reading the abstract of the article, if one is available, to try to judge the possible usefulness of the study. When you are done with this abstract scanning, you will have a list of presumably pertinent research studies to review.

Retrieve the full text of your first article (never rely just on abstracts!). Before you take notes, whether by computer or by hand, be sure to copy the complete citation of the article, either by hand or electronically, first! (If it is a book, you might want to include the call number in case you need to find it again in the future.) If you are reading the article online, it is easy to cut and paste pieces of the article you feel are important, following the article heading. Also, do not forget to note page numbers of the passages, if possible. If you are taking notes by hand, do use quotation marks when you are copying directly and not paraphrasing, and do include page numbers for those direct quotes. As you read, pay attention to references the authors use; are these articles you should also read? If so, add the complete citations to your possible reference list so you can access them later.

When we read research articles we do not necessarily read them from front to back. After you have read the abstract you will realize that there are certain parts of the article that are most important to you. If you are interested in the instrument an author used you may want to go directly to the methods section. If you are trying to figure out if the work is really something that is close to what you are studying you may want to go directly to the conclusions. Because you are likely to be reading a lot of research, it is valuable to find the information that will tell you if the article is worth more time as quickly as possible. If it turns out to be on target then go back and read the entire work thoroughly. If not, you can eliminate it from your reading list.

This is a good time to reinforce the importance of five chapter design as a way to organize research reporting. Because that design is part of the culture of educational research reporting (as it is in many other fields as well) you as a reader of research will know exactly where to find the specific pieces of a research study very efficiently. When others read your research paper they will expect to be able to do the same thing.

Besides getting information from the studies as you read them, your job is also to evaluate what you are reading. Make your own notes (in a separate color or font if using a computer) about your thoughts as you read the articles. Are there questions that are raised in your mind as you read? Are there concerns with the methodology used? Do you feel the conclusions are warranted? Ultimately, a literature review is not just a summary of known information, but includes an evaluation piece, as well. Do not accept everything you read. You may need to process it in terms of prior and new knowledge and in terms of what others are finding about the same topic. Making "side-notes" to yourself as you read is a way to record these ideas as they arise.

When reviewing your selected references, keep your outline handy. As you review the literature, you may want to add detail to your outline or refine it. Depending on your ability to multi-task, you may want to organize your notes as you read as well. As you take notes (or chunk things to your computer file), code them based on your outline. For example, again using the grouping template from Figure 3-1, if a piece of an article has to do with improvement in achievement and grouping, put the Roman numeral and letter that matches that piece of your outline in the margin of your notes; in this case, IIA. If a portion adds to background information on type of group formation, code it with IB. If you do not feel comfortable doing that as you read, once you are done taking your notes, go through them and code them. We find this greatly helps us with the next step, which is writing the actual literature review.

WRITING YOUR LITERATURE REVIEW CHAPTER

While reading the literature has its advantages, the actual writing of the chapter provides additional benefits. This chapter of the research paper is used to help

Example 1 (Reprinted with permission of Caroline Missal)

The purpose of this study is to determine if teacher beliefs around inclusion of students with special needs in regular classrooms in the three Edmonton Public Inclusion Pilot Project schools vary according to the different coding categories of students. There is increasing demand for inclusive educational settings, yet many barriers still exist in our present delivery models (Buell, Hallam, Gamel-McCormick, and Scheer, 1990). This literature review focuses on beliefs of teachers towards inclusion of students with disabilities in the 'regular' classroom. The review is organized using the common themes that emerged from the research articles reviewed; namely,

> Adequate training and lack of knowledge about students with disabilities;
> Attitudes toward different disabilities of students;
> Collaborative work environments;
> Leadership;
> Lack of exposure to individuals who have a disability; and
> Balancing the needs of one student with the needs of all students.

Example 2 (Reprinted with permission of Carolyn Cameron)

This research will focus on what teachers perceive as the benefits, drawbacks and limitations when teachers share a common space and share their students in a collaborative environment. The research I reviewed on the subject of team teaching revealed several common themes: information on educating the whole child, the complexity of the teaching profession and the need to establish a community of learners. The literature indicated several areas that are strengthened by collaborative approaches to teaching. Several studies also included suggestions for successful collaboration. Finally, the literature reviewed examined open areas and flexible classroom spaces as supports for collaboration in a shared learning environment.

Example 3 (Reprinted with permission of April Crysler)

Student success in school is an important issue to educators. Our hope is to have actively engaged students in our classrooms and to have these students become successful and involved citizens in our communities. Unfortunately, there are a number of students who do not experience success in their schooling, do not complete high school, and are at-risk to experience adversity. The literature reviewed addressed many common mechanisms to assist students not encountering success in school. This paper will focus on three main themes to increase student success rates: improving communication between students and educators, increasing school to work relevance for students, and creating appropriate learning environments.

Figure 3-2. Examples of introductory paragraphs to a literature review chapter.

organize your thoughts, synthesize what others have found, and provide your evaluation of those findings. Literature Reviews typically follow one of the following two approaches:

1. Identifying the main themes/ideas, following the format of your outline, and referencing all appropriate documents as you discuss these; or
2. Reviewing the content of each article individually, stressing the important pieces, and then showing a relationship among the group of articles.

Which approach you use depends on personal preference and comfort. The first approach generally helps you to really critique and analyze what you've read when you look at your notes as a whole, versus article by article. It ensures your literature review will provide a synthesis of main ideas, points, and discrepancies on your topic rather than being a collection of article summaries with concluding critiques and analyses. Regardless, you may discover that even though your review is organized around themes, one or two studies are so important that they merit individual attention. The final result may not be a literature review that is all one way or the other.

So, let's get down to the nitty gritty. Generally, at the start of your Chapter Two: Literature Review, you begin with a restatement of your problem. If you have limited your literature search for specific reasons, this would be the time to explain what you did and why. If you will be organizing your literature review around certain themes, describe your plan. These would comprise your introductory paragraph. See Figure 3-2 for examples. Now you can focus on the literature you've read.

If you use the numbering format suggested earlier (where you assign outline markers to pieces of articles), it is very easy to write your literature review based on themes. Simply look at all the I's, the IA's, IB's, etc. Because your outline has a natural flow, the literature review section will have that same logic. Summarize all the salient points about that piece of the "literature puzzle," citing particular studies as you go along, providing a critique if warranted (i.e., the sample size is too small, no studies are done at the middle school level, etc.—look at those "side notes" you wrote as you read the article), and being sure to note what the articles have in common and where they may differ. Although it is important to point out concerns that you may have about a particular study, you should be humble in your criticism. For instance, it would be better to point out that an author may have been unable to use random groups in his study than to say the lack of random groups is a major flaw in a study. To help you in critiquing studies, you might want to consider the following. You may have trouble with some of these points so early in this text because you do not yet have the background needed; e.g., appropriateness of methodologies or analyses—but you will!

- Is the problem statement clear?
- Is the literature review in the paper current?
- Is a theoretical framework presented?
- Is the methodology fully explained and does it seem to fit the question?
- Are the instruments valid and reliable?
- Are any researcher biases noted?

- Are the results clearly and fully presented?
- Are the methods used to analyze the data appropriate?
- Are the conclusions supported by the data?
- Are limitations acknowledged?

End each section of your literature review with a short statement that ties the section all together. As an example, you might write:

A considerable number of basic models of cooperative learning are generally used (DeVries & Slavin, 1978; Johnson & Johnson, 1975; Slavin, 1983).

OR

Johnson and Johnson (1975) developed the Learning Together model of cooperative learning in which all participants are responsible for all of the group work. Slavin (1980) expanded this work in a model called Jigsaw II by suggesting ways that groups could break down the task among group participants. DeVries and Slavin (1978) discussed how students work together to master content in the Teams-Games-Tournament approach.

Regardless of your writing style, do use direct quotes sparingly. Quoting excessively makes the reader think you really have not processed the main points of the authors. We recommend using a quote only when paraphrasing will reduce its strength. Occasionally an author will write something that is so well said that any attempt to summarize the point will lessen its impact. Our experience is that that does not happen very often. Do remember that even when paraphrasing, you do need to cite the source! Page numbers are only needed for the direct quotations, however.

The point of a literature review is to present a summary of what is already known about your topic from literature that has already been published. You are summarizing the findings and opinions of others who have used good research to form their opinions. Readers do not expect to find your opinions in the literature review. The research you are doing will form the foundation from which you can proclaim your own point of view, and the best place for that is in the conclusion section of your paper. Generally, the words *I* and *me* (and especially *this researcher*) do not belong in a literature review. The bulk of this chapter is written in past tense since you are reporting on what has already been found.

At the close of the chapter, conclude with a brief summary of what is known. Briefly discuss how what you have read is related to your specific study. Are you looking to see if what others have found holds true for your students, as well? Are you looking to refine what is known—maybe trying to determine if what works at the elementary level will also work at the high school level, or if applying a traditional reading methodology to a mathematics lesson improves instruction? Are there ideas that you want the reader to particularly remember as you proceed with your report? This helps to make a transition to your next chapter which is a description of your methods. Figure 3-3 presents a sample of the closing of a literature review chapter. Samples of complete literature reviews can be found in Appendix 3-A.

Example 1 (Reprinted with permission of April Crysler)

Collectively, the literature reviewed stated that helping at-risk students achieve success by overcoming their barriers to high school completion is a complicated, multi-faceted problem that involves looking at the issue from many angles. Improving student communication in educational relationships, increasing student perception and awareness that their learning is relevant to their lives, and providing innovative learning environments appears to be the three main themes in the literature. The characteristics of the students in my classes are similar to the at-risk populations described in the literature. I will be conducting a study to determine what students feel they need to be successful in my grade 12 chemistry classes.

Example 2 (Reprinted with permission of Emily Ferguson)

Exercise is an integral component in health for reasons regarding obesity, brain function, the immune system, metabolism, physical strength and depression. These positive effects of exercise are widely regarded as true, and although the effects of exercise on academic achievement are positive in a number of studies, the strength of the relationship is still being studied. This research study will examine how exercise affects academic achievement of high school students using sport and extracurricular activities that involve exercise.

Example 3 (Reprinted with permission of Carolyn Cameron)

In summary, the research I reviewed supports the notion that teachers benefit by growing and learning together in a collaborative environment. Learning theory suggests that students possess multiple intelligences and an integrated approach to educating the whole child is the most engaging way for students to learn. This kind of educational environment requires the expertise of a variety of teachers teaming up to provide an interdisciplinary program of studies. This may be the most effective way to make learning meaningful for students. The complexities of the teaching profession make it difficult for teachers to be effective working in isolation. A learning community where trust is established and relationships between teachers, students and their families are built over time can provide a sense of belonging and commitment. Learning communities can be established when teachers team up and collaborate to provide effective instruction and learning opportunities for students. Collaborative teachers are empowered to engage in innovative teaching practices and feel supported as professionals. Furthermore, the kind of collaboration that is possible when teachers are students and work space gives teachers the opportunity for professional growth through regular dialogue, coaching opportunities, and common experiences. Sharing teaching space with colleagues embeds the benefits of team teaching into the every day work of teachers. This leads me to the research question: Do teachers who have worked in team teaching learning environments feel collaborative team teaching environments enhance their professional growth and create opportunities for innovative teaching practices?

Figure 3-3. Example of summary paragraphs to a literature review chapter.

Critiquing your Literature Review

After you are done drafting your literature review chapter, use this checklist (adapted from McMillan, 2008) to help you determine whether it needs any refining. You can also use this list to assist in evaluating research that you are reviewing.

1. Did you find a theoretical framework for your study? Your review should include a theoretical context that helps you frame your study.

2. Did you do an adequate job of reviewing the literature published on your topic? You should have sufficient coverage so your topic is fully explored and includes any important studies and/or prominent authors. The readers should feel that both you and they have a firm understanding of the current thinking/findings on your problem area.

3. Is it based on research versus opinion-based articles? Your review should be based on empirical studies, not what someone thinks or feels. This is a common flaw. We are so used to reading practitioner articles that we tend to overlook that statements or suggestions are not always supported with data.

4. Is your review of current research? Be sure you have read the most current research available on your topic. Do not rely on just older studies if more recent work has been done.

5. Have you synthesized and evaluated what you have read? Remember, this is a review, not just a summary. Your literature review should show that you made sense of others' work, ascertained connections among the pool of findings, and identified any problems or "holes" in the existing research.

6. Is the literature reviewed tied to your study? There should be a clear line of thought from what others have done to what you plan to do.

USING APA FORMAT

Every discipline has a designated format to use for writing journal manuscripts. Education, as most of the social sciences, follows the format of the American Psychological Association, more commonly known as APA. The *Publication Manual of the American Psychological Association* is updated regularly and contains all the rules to be followed in preparing your research paper. The *Manual* describes things like punctuation, headings, tables, citations, and the like. While the most current *Manual* should be consulted when you finally prepare your paper, we have included in Chapter 10 a summary of what we find to be the most common rules we and our students tend to need. Most college and university libraries keep the latest copy of *The Publication Manual of the American Psychological Association* in their reference sections and probably a faculty member in Education or one of the other Social Sciences has a copy you can reference. Additionally, the APA web site (www.apastyle.org) has links to "frequently asked questions" and "APA style tips" that you might find handy.

Some researchers use software that automatically formats citations and references. If you search the web for "citation tools APA" you will see that there are quite a few available and some are free. Applications like ProCite and Endnote are high-end tools that will accommodate most bibliographic research needs, but they have a hefty price tag for the privilege. A little searching online might help you find free or low cost software that does some of the referencing job for you (e.g., Zotero). In addition, some college and university libraries subscribe to on-line bibliographic tools as well (e.g., RefWorks), that are made available as a service to their students. Regardless of any software that you might use you still need to learn the rules for citations and references because most of the software packages do not format everything absolutely correctly. So, unless you intend to do quite a bit of research writing, the most cost-effective way to go is to teach yourself the basic rules and type in the references correctly in the first place.

There is enough leeway in the rules of APA that different schools, different faculty or different journals may have some specific requirements in how APA style is to be accomplished. Be sure you ask about this so that you do not have to go back and redo work that you have already completed.

NEXT STEPS

Remember, the purposes of doing a review of the literature included grounding you in the constructs you would be working with and helping you with your problem statement. As you read the literature, do work on your question. Does it need to be refined? Is it too narrow? Is it too broad? Is there a related question that you actually find more interesting and meaningful? Do sculpt your question as needed. Finally, what have others done to gather data? Are they using methods and/or tools that you might be able to use? Having read what others have done, having tightened your own question, you are now ready to start thinking about how you will collect your own data.

CHAPTER SELF-CHECK

Having completed this chapter, you should be comfortable discussing the following:
- purpose of a literature review
- finding resources: ERIC, published literature review, journals, books, internet
- how to organize your reading and take notes
- organizing and writing Chapter Three
- critiquing your own and others' literature reviews
- APA guidelines

CHAPTER REVIEW QUESTIONS

1. Why are literature reviews important?
2. What types of resources are found in ERIC?
3. Differentiate among practitioner, policy and research journals.
4. How do you decide your literature review is "exhaustive?"
5. Why and how would you take notes when you read your references?
6. What is APA?

CHAPTER 3

REFERENCES

http://www.ericdigests.org
http://ojs.aera.net/journals/index.php/rer
http://scholar.google.com
http://www.ericdigests.org
http://www.apastyle.org
McMillan, J. H. (2008). *Educational research: Fundamentals for the consumer (5th ed.)*, Boston, MA: Allyn & Bacon/Merrill Education.

APPENDIX 3-A: EXAMPLES OF LITERATURE REVIEWS

EXAMPLE 1 (REPRINTED WITH PERMISSION OF STACEY BOATRIGHT)

LITERATURE REVIEW

The purpose of this study is to investigate the personal and academic needs of nursing students in the Direct Entry Master's Program (DEM) and the more traditional Master of Science in Nursing Program (MSN). Scholarly research about graduate students generally focuses on the areas of student attrition and persistence, learning experiences, socialization and programmatic interventions (Nesheim et al., 2006). Literature about adult nursing students usually investigates traditional, non-traditional and adult students in accelerated or second-degree undergraduate nursing programs rather than adults in DEM or traditional master's programs (Bankert & Kozel, 2005; Borges, Richard & Duffy, 2007; Cangelosi & Whitt, 2005; Miklancie & Davis, 2005; Utley-Smith, Philips & Turner, 2007). Research about adult students, graduate students, and nursing students in accelerated, second-degree and traditional programs does shed some light on the more specific area of the academic and personal needs of DEM in nursing and MSN students. What follows is a review of literature related to (1) program types, (2) student types, (3) frameworks for understanding adult learners, (4) the personal needs of adult students, and (5) the academic needs of adult students.

Program Types

Literature related to adult students in graduate school tends to investigate adult students from the perspective of particular program types. Research pertinent to the present study focuses on accelerated and second-degree undergraduate programs and traditional master's programs. It is important to understand the definitions, formats and designs of these different program types because the program type an individual chooses tends to be based on one's personal and academic needs.

Accelerated and second-degree programs. The concept of a DEM program, defined earlier as an efficient way for an individual who holds a baccalaureate degree to earn a master's degree in an unrelated field, is relatively new in academia. The DEM in nursing program at my institution is similar to an accelerated under-graduate nursing program for individuals with prior degrees; the difference is that we grant a master's degree in nursing rather than a BSN. We provide coursework that is equivalent to a baccalaureate nursing education in an accelerated format, which qualifies the DEM student to become a registered nurse. Rather than awarding a BSN at this point, our students continue on to study a master's-level curriculum for two years while working full-time as RNs and they graduate with their first degree in nursing at the master's level.

Literature about DEM programs like ours is virtually non-existent. But, research about accelerated and second-degree programs is beginning to emerge due to the increased prevalence of and demand for these program types in the United States. Because DEM in nursing students at my institution essentially receive baccalaureate-level nursing education in an accelerated amount of time and each student has a prior degree, research about these two program types are relevant to the current study.

Accelerated learning programs, as defined by Wlodkowski (2003), provide a way for adult students to earn college credit, certificates or degrees in a shorter amount of time than traditional programs. In other words, due to their "fast-track" structure, accelerated programs allow students to graduate sooner than students in traditional programs. These programs tend to use a cohort model, require less in-class time and use weekend, evening, intensive, or distance learning formats (Kasworm, 2001; Wlodkowski, 2003; Wlodkowski, Mauldin & Gahn, 2001). The time frame for learning in each course is abbreviated under the assumption that adult learners are able to learn course material in a shorter amount of time than traditional undergraduate students due to the richness of their prior personal, academic and professional experiences (Kasworm, 2001). It appears from the literature that accelerated programs are most commonly offered at traditional, often faith-based institutions at the undergraduate level (Wlodkowski, 2003).

The distinction between accelerated and second-degree programs is somewhat vague. Often second-degree programs are, by nature, accelerated because they acknowledge an individual's prior degree by accelerating the learning that is required to earn a second degree in an unrelated field (Utley-Smith et al., 2007). Conversely, accelerated programs do not necessarily require students to have a prior degree. Rather, the learning or coursework in an accelerated program is simply completed faster than it would be in a traditional program. In any case, second-degree programs attract adult learners seeking a degree at either the undergraduate or graduate level as an entry point to a desired new career or profession (Cangelosi & Whitt, 2005; Miklancie & Davis, 2005).

Traditional programs. A traditional program can be defined according to what an accelerated or second-degree program is not. In other words, a traditional program requires regular on-campus attendance with typical course scheduling options as opposed to distance-learning, intensives, weekend, or evening formats. Traditional undergraduate programs are four years long and consist of approximately two years of foundational liberal arts (sometimes referred to as "core") coursework followed by two years of coursework related to a student's chosen academic major. A traditional master's program requires a baccalaureate degree in the same or similar field, takes between two and three years to complete and often ends with a culminating learning experience such as a thesis or capstone project. Students in traditional programs are known to have a stronger preference for their chosen career field and vocational identity than students in accelerated programs (Borges et al., 2007).

Student Types

The literature suggests that there are three different student populations on college campuses today: traditional, non-traditional and adult students. A student is commonly categorized as "traditional" if he or she is a recent high school graduate, a full-time student and resides on the college campus (Sissel, Hansman & Kasworm, 2001). In general, a non-traditional student is a student who is 25 years old or older (Compton, Cox & Laanan, 2006). According to this definition, adult students are non-traditional students simply because of their age. However, depending on the definitions being used, a non-traditional student is not necessarily always an adult student.

The distinctions between non-traditional and adult students are becoming increasingly apparent and delineated. According to the National Center for Education Statistics (2002), a non-traditional student is defined as someone who possesses one or more of the following characteristics: delayed college enrollment until one or more years after high school graduation, is a part-time student, is employed full-time, is financially independent, has dependents besides a spouse, is a single parent or does not have a have a high school diploma.

Adult students, on the other hand, can be defined according to their own unique set of characteristics. Adult students (1) are likely to be enrolled in a vocational certificate or degree program at a community college, (2) are highly focused on their educational goals as a means to improve their work skills and transition from one professional phase to another, (3) often think of themselves first and foremost as workers rather than students, (4) are commonly enrolled in distance-learning programs in order to accommodate their full daily lives, (5) are likely to primarily speak a language other than English and (6) are prone to leaving postsecondary education without earning a degree (Compton et al., 2006).

In relation to the present study and according to my experience, DEM in nursing and MSN students may have some of the characteristics of non-traditional students, but they are more closely aligned with the characteristics of adult students. For this reason, I have chosen to study the personal and academic needs of DEM in nursing and MSN students by using adult learner frameworks (andragogy in particular) and reviewing literature related to adult student needs, characteristics and attitudes and how they can be addressed.

Frameworks for Understanding Adult Learners in the Classroom

There are several theoretical frameworks in the area of adult learner research that may be applicable when investigating the needs of adult college students. There is no particular theory or model that is suitable to explain all adult learners. Rather, there is a mosaic of theories that, when combined, form a foundation from which an understanding of adult learning can be derived (Merriam, 2001). The specific adult learner theory that seems most appropriate in the present study is called andragogy, which is explained below. In addition to andragogy, the following models seem to inform the current study: the conceptual model of adult accelerated programs and the returning-to-school syndrome model.

Andragogy. When Malcolm S. Knowles began examining adult learning in the late 1970s, he was stunned to find that the usual approach to adult learning was based on pedagogy, a framework that literally means "the art and science of teaching children" (Knowles, 1978, p. 10). In response, Knowles developed andragogy, which he defined as "the art and science of helping adults learn" (Knowles, 1980, p. 43). Knowles argued that, according to the theory of andragogy, the climate of an adult classroom should be one in which adults "feel accepted, respected and supported," (Knowles, 1980, p. 47). Additionally, there should be "a spirit of mutuality between teachers and student as joints inquirers" (Knowles, 1980, p. 47) and an adult's capability to direct their own learning should be recognized (Merriam, 2001).

Andragogy sets forth five assumptions about adult learners. First, adult learners appreciate the ability to direct and make choices about their own personal and academic paths. Second, adults have a large repertoire of life and professional experiences to build upon and they embrace opportunities to "learn by doing." Third, adult students are eager and ready to learn, often because they recognize a deficit in their knowledge or performance level. Fourth, adults generally have a task- or problem-focused orientation to learning. Fifth, adult learners tend to be internally motivated rather than motivated by external factors like increased pay (Knowles & Associates; as cited in Ross-Gordon, 2003).

Conceptual model of adult accelerated programs. Carol Kasworm (2003), a noted scholar in the field of adult learning, has offered one answer to the question of why adults are attracted and motivated to enroll in accelerated degree programs through the development of the conceptual model of adult accelerated programs. The model is comprised of three components: adult competence, adult action and adult work identity.

Adult competence as a key attractor to accelerated programs refers to the emphasis such a program places on adult students as "skillful workers and know-ledgeable contributors to society" (Rossiter, 2007, p. 24). In other words, adults appreciate that their rich repertoire of professional and educational experiences is recognized and capitalized on in accelerated programs. They are drawn to course-work that fosters active engagement and reflective learning.

The daily lives of active adults are no doubt busy and full of competing demands. Adding the pursuit of a degree to an already full schedule adds even more stress, complexity and role conflicts. Because they embrace adult action – the intricate web of real-world commitments to action and learning experienced by adult students – accelerated programs are attractive to adult students. Adult accelerated programs seek to accommodate students by offering convenient, accessible, flexible and customer service oriented program formats. Cohort grouping, active learning strategies, and group projects are some of the special support structures that allow adult students to flourish in both their personal and academic lives.

Related to adult work identity, Kasworm (2003) states "Adults value the accelerated degree programs because they desire advanced career development, targeting key knowledge and skills for improvement of their profession and their workplace" (p. 25).

Adults who enroll in accelerated degree programs have identified a specific professional goal and expect that coursework will require more than memorization and conventional testing as learning techniques. Opportunities to apply coursework to the real world and to construct new knowledge and understandings are cited as motivating factors involved in choosing an accelerated program (Kasworm, 2003).

Returning-to-school syndrome model.   The returning-to-school syndrome model, developed by Dr. Donea Shane in the late 1970s, is a nursing education model that was originally designed to address the issues associate-prepared nurses were experiencing when they returned to school to earn their BSN (Utley-Smith et al., 2007). Utley et al. (2007) propose that the model is also applicable to students in accelerated second-degree BSN programs. The model involves three stages. First, there is the honeymoon stage, which is characterized by a "positive glow," a "sense of satisfaction" and an "optimistic outlook" (Utley-Smith et al., 2007, p. 425). This stage may last a few hours or several months. Second, in the conflict stage, students start to feel a sense of inadequacy and a lack of understanding of the nursing rules and concepts; they may even experience depression, lethargy and overall exhaustion. Reintegration, the final phase, usually begins with hostility and unfair stereotyping. This phase may either end with biculturalism, which means that the student's original work culture is successfully integrated with the new nursing culture, or with chronic hostility and maybe even vacating the program. Utley-Smith et al. (2007) purport that teaching accelerated second-degree nursing students and faculty about the three stages of the returning-to-school syndrome model helps students validate and understand their feelings, which leads to better student and program outcomes.

Personal Needs of Adult Students

It has been noted elsewhere in this review of literature that adult students have unique characteristics and considerable non-academic commitments and obligations. To position them for success, it is important to recognize and serve their personal needs. A personal need is different from a scholastic or learning need such as the opportunity to work in collaborative learning groups. In the present study, personal needs are the things that must be met or provided in a student's personal life in order for he or she to be successful – they provide the infrastructure for academic achievement. Scholarly research (Borges et al., 2007; Cangelosi & Whitt, 2005; Compton et al., 2006; Mauldin & Campbell, 2002; Nesheim et. al., 2006; Wlodkowski et al., 2001; Wlodkowski, Mauldin & Campbell, 2002; Wlodkowski, 2003; Ross-Gordon, 2003) suggests there are three personal needs in particular that beg the attention of college program administrators, faculty and student services personnel. They are: (1) financial aid, (2) flexible, convenient scheduling and (3) advising and counseling. These three personal needs are elaborated on below.

Financial aid.   In a study that investigated adult learners' persistence and success, researchers found that "tuition aid is significantly related to persistence and grades" in both accelerated and traditional programs (Wlodkowski et al.,

2001, p. 26). When there is less of a financial burden, it appears that students in both program formats are more likely to graduate (Wlodkowski et al., 2001; Wlodkowski et al., 2002). Unfortunately, as confirmed by a different study in which researchers attempted to identify what is necessary to develop a quality accelerated nursing program, sources of financial aid for accelerated students are limited and difficult to find (Wassem & Sheil; as cited in Cangelosi & Whitt, 2005).

Flexible, convenient scheduling. The way courses are scheduled emerged in the literature as an important topic for adult students. Courses should be scheduled in a manner that is convenient for the students to attend. For instance, weekend courses reduce the conflicts between job and family obligations, especially for women (Wlodkowski, 2003). Additionally, in a study where students were asked to design their ideal accelerated second-degree program, they stated that it would be year-round, take two years to complete and tailored to their individual needs (Sheil & Wassem; as cited in Cangelosi & Whitt, 2005). Offering clinical courses more than one time each year and increasing the flexibility of course scheduling has also been suggested to increase the successfulness of students in both accelerated and traditional nursing programs (Shiber; as cited in Cangelosi & Whitt, 2005). It appears from these findings that meeting the scheduling needs of adult students in both accelerated and traditional programs may be important to their personal, professional and academic progress.

Advising and counseling. Graduate students are often a small sub-set of the larger student population at colleges and universities. The missions of most traditional institutions are, above all, to educate baccalaureate-level students as a means of entering qualified practitioners and professionals into the workforce. Being so, graduate students may not receive an equitable amount of attention, information, guidance or resources as their undergraduate counterparts. Indeed, graduate students have described a need for information about student housing, health benefits, conflicts with faculty advisors, harassment, discrimination and more (Nesheim et al., 2006).

In addition to providing basic advising and counseling services to graduate students, adult learners have identified teachers, mentors and advisors ("educational helpers") as integral players in the process of exploring new possibilities and forming positive future self-concepts (Rossiter, 2007). More specifically, educational helpers have been shown to prompt adult students to identify new career and educational options, investigate possible careers, and reawaken earlier goals. They serve as role models, enhance beliefs about self-efficacy, help adult students develop clearer images of their future selves and they guide students through the process of achieving their goals (Rossiter, 2007). The role of advisors and counselors – whether faculty, student services professionals, or other higher education employees – is of obvious importance to serving the personal needs of students in DEM and traditional master's programs.

Academic Needs of Adult Students

After reviewing quite a bit of literature about adult students, it is somewhat difficult to draw a distinct line between a personal need and an academic need. For the purposes of this study, an academic need is defined as something a student needs from an academic institution in order for him or her to learn and achieve at the maximum level of scholarship. According to the literature (Bankert & Kozel, 2005; Cangelosi & Whitt, 2005; Compton et al., 2006; Kasworm, 2003; Mauldin & Gahn, 2001; Nesheim et al., 2006; Ross-Gordon, 2003; Rossiter, 2007; Sissel et al., 2001; Utley-Smith et al., 2007; Wlodkowski et al., 2001; Wlodkowski et al., 2002; Wlodkowski, 2003), four academic needs surface to the top as highly important for adult learners: (1) the recognition of prior learning and professional experiences, (2) specific teaching-learning strategies, (3) relationships with faculty and peers, and (4) a supportive learning environment.

Recognition of prior learning & professional experiences.   Adults who decide to pursue a second degree benefit from their prior work and postsecondary experiences. Research shows that adult students who enter an accelerated or traditional program at a four-year college are more likely to persist through graduation (Wlodkowski et al., 2001; Wlodkowski et al., 2002). They are also known to have greater confidence, coping skills and familiarity with learning at the college level. The wealth of knowledge they bring to accelerated and traditional programs brings diversity to classrooms and enables them to form advanced, complex understandings through experiential learning (Rossiter, 2007).

As demonstrated by the conceptual model of adult accelerated degree programs and the assumptions of andragogy, adult students need to feel that their prior academic, professional and personal experiences are recognized, valued and capitalized on (Knowles, 1978; Merriam, 2001; Ross-Gordon, 2003; Rossiter, 2007). Being so, it is becoming more and more common for institutions to explicitly validate an adult's prior learning by offering credit through testing, portfolio reviews, a learning assessment workshop, or a learning assessment advisor (Compton et al., 2006). If adult students can demonstrate that they have achieved the objectives of a particular course through their past experiences, they may be deemed exempt from that course, which results in an individualized and perhaps accelerated curriculum plan. This allows students to spend their time constructing new know-ledge rather than reinforcing prior learning (Compton et al., 2006).

Specific teaching-learning strategies.   Nursing students in second-degree programs are, in general, older, have a heightened capacity to learn, and take initiative in gaining clinical experiences more often than traditional students (American Association of Colleges of Nursing; as cited in Miklancie & Davis, 2005). They strive to maximize their opportunities to practice their nursing skills and are often perceived as more assertive than traditional students (Miklancie & Davis, 2005). Due to their task- or problem-centered orientation to learning, accelerated nursing students appear to need and even demand immediate real-world application of their learning.

Due to their experiential learning needs, it is not appropriate for adult students, especially in nursing, to simply sit, listen, receive information and complete required assignments (Bankert & Kozel, 2005); adult learners require "more interactive and participatory components with few lectures" (Husson & Kennedy, 2003, p. 52). Second-degree nursing students have been found to thrive in programs that take a comprehensive approach to education with unnecessary busywork eliminated (Miklancie & Davis, 2005). Adult students who pursue nursing as a second degree tend to view their nursing education with a critical, business-related, and goal-driven eye (Miklancie & Davis, 2005). Having already researched nursing as a career and committed themselves to this career trajectory, second-degree nursing students are "highly focused on the outcome of their nursing education and how quickly that outcome can be achieved" (Utley-Smith et al., 2007, p. 424). It is important then for nurse educators to provide a mechanism for students to monitor and measure their progress and the achievement of program outcomes.

According to adult learner theory, learner-centered instruction is generally preferred by adult students. Availability, helpfulness, concern and respect for students, the encouragement of discussion, flexibility, clear presentations, well-organized lectures and knowledgeable instructors have been cited as key characteristics of effective teaching for adult students (Ross-Gordon, 2003). Learner-centered instruction, which entails learner-centered activities, personalized instruction, relating course content to student experience, assessing student needs, and flexibility for personal development, is associated with a grater sense of self satisfaction and accomplishment among students who are over 25 years old (Conti; as cited in Ross-Gordon, 1991).

Relationships with peers and faculty. The importance of relationships with peers and faculty is greatly emphasized in literature about adult, accelerated degree, traditional and graduate students (Bankert & Kozel, 2005; Compton et al., 2006; Kasworm, 2003; Miklancie & Davis, 2005; Nesheim et al., 2006; Rossiter, 2007; Wlodkowski et al., 2001; Wlodkowski et al., 2002; Wlodkowski, 2003). For adults in both accelerated and traditional programs, involvement and interaction with peers and faculty significantly and positively impacts persistence through graduation (Wlodkowski et al., 2001; Wlodkowski et al., 2002; Wlodkowski, 2003). Students who feel socially integrated with their peers are more likely to graduate (Wlodkowski et al., 2001; Wlodkowski, 2003).

In a study in which adult students in an accelerated degree program were asked to identify particular areas of support that they felt facilitated their success in their program, the quasi-family relationships with their fellow students was ranked number two, behind a supportive learning structure (Kasworm & Blowers; as cited in Kasworm, 2003). Second-degree programs are often intensive and demanding and, as adults, students are often confronted with unpredictable life-changing events during their program (e.g. divorce, layoffs, deaths). It is imperative that adult students have a support network to work through the stresses of their personal and academic lives. A cohort model in which the same group of students progresses through a program together is especially conducive to the formation of a group friendship and intimacy that supports personal sharing and problem solving (Kasworm, 2003).

The positive impact educational helpers can make in the lives of students was explained above in the context of the personal need for quality advising and counseling. But, faculty play a particularly important role in the lives of adult students. Faculty who are consistently available, treat their colleagues and students with respect and are willing to collaborate with students on publications contribute to a student's perception of a community-oriented organizational climate (Anderson & Swazey, 1998). When a faculty member and adult student share a commitment to being co-participants in the teaching-learning experience, a sense of closeness, unity and shared responsibility emerges and the traditional roles of student and teacher are transformed. This transformation contributes to a rich, caring and meaningful educational experience for both the students and the faculty (Anderson & Swazey, 1998). A learning environment in which adult students and faculty have a collegial as opposed to a superior-inferior relationship is needed for adult students to feel supported and positioned for academic success.

Supportive learning environment. A supportive learning world is of utmost importance to adults, especially in accelerated programs. A supportive accelerated degree program consists of (1) an accessible, relevant and predictable program of study, (2) a structure that pushes students toward their degree, and (3) a caring community in which students are connected with one another (Kasworm, 2003). An environment that is customized for adult learners, a publicly-accessible and pre-determined schedule, personnel who understand and work to accommodate the nature of adulthood, part-time course loads, work-oriented instruction, and a cohort model that facilitates steady progress through graduation and are all necessary elements of a successful accelerated program structure (Kasworm, 2003).

Beyond appropriately addressing programmatic issues like scheduling, course offerings, registration processes, and curriculum plans, adult degree programs should offer a caring learning environment that is specifically designed for adult students (Husson & Kennedy, 2003). The characteristics of a caring learning environment include valuing, genuine dialogue, relations, connectedness, attentiveness, openness, a sense of ownership that comes from contributing to the caring learning environment, meaningful relationships and an appreciation of colleagues (Anderson & Swazey, 1998).

In sum, literature about adult students covers a wide array of topics related to their unique experiences, circumstances and needs. Research that clarifies the differences between program types is helpful in understanding what motivates adults to return to school and why adults choose particular program formats. Being knowledgeable about the characteristics of traditional, non-traditional and adult students helps higher education professionals better serve and understand these student populations. Frameworks such as andragogy, the conceptual model of adult accelerated programs and the return-to-school syndrome model bring to light the particular learning needs of adult students. Personal needs such as financial aid, convenient scheduling and advising/counseling appear to be of particular relevance to the persistence and success adult students. The recognition of prior experiences, specific teaching-learning strategies, relationships and a supportive learning environment emerge from the literature as academic needs worthy of note.

Adult students may experience apprehension, uncertainty and a lack of confidence as they embark on a new educational (and therefore professional) journey (Ross-Gordon, 2003). Being so, higher education professionals should be sensitive to individual differences and be mindful of the need to create opportunities for students to experience success early on, to learn the norms of the institution, and to enhance self-awareness (Husson & Kennedy, 2003). Higher education professionals who serve adult students should keep in mind that older adults desire quality, value, access and convenience (Husson & Kennedy, 2003). Programs that strive to effectively meet these desired ends would be obliged to follow these suggestions offered by Compton et al. (2006):

1. Formally validate prior learning (e.g. testing, portfolios) and therefore reduce the time and effort required for students to complete their program.
2. Offer courses in a variety of formats and give students an opportunity to choose their instructor.
3. Ensure that coursework includes practical applications and that course goals meet the students' goals.
4. Encourage students to become socially integrated, involved and engaged with the institution.
5. Provide counseling centers to help with the wide spectrum of issues adult students face.
6. Be pro-active in assessing the needs of adult learners and then adapt accordingly and creatively.

This review of literature has presented definitions and prior scholarly findings and information about theoretical bases pertinent to adult learners. An arena that needs further explanation is whether specific differences exist between the needs of DEM in nursing and MSN students. Next, the sample and methodology that will be used to conduct this investigatory study is explained.

EXAMPLE 2 (REPRINTED WITH PERMISSION OF KIM HUBER)

LITERATURE REVIEW

CHANGES IN READING MOTIVATION

Motivating students to read has been a troubling issue for numerous teachers. Much research has been conducted showing the change in students' motivation to read as they attain progress in school resulting in significant numbers of middle school students who are little motivated to read at all (Greenburg, Gilbert, & Fredrick, 2006; Sainsbury & Schagen, 2004; Unrau & Schlackman, 2006; Wigfield & Guthrie, 1997b). McKenna, Kear, & Ellsworth (1995) state in their research that first graders felt very positive about reading. These feelings, however, decline to "relative indifference by Grade 6" (p. 952). Researchers have found that motivational differences can be seen in different gender and ethnic groups; girls seem to value reading more than boys (Greenburg et al., 2006; Pitcher, Albright, & Delaney, 2007; Sainsbury & Schagen, 2004; Wigfield & Guthrie, 1997b) and the research by McKenna, et al. (1995) shows that though the motivation gap between girls and boys is relatively small in first grade, it widens with age suggesting that boys' motivation to read changes more drastically than girls' motivation. McKenna et al.'s research further suggests that Hispanic and African American children begin school with higher motivation to read than Whites, but by sixth grade, Hispanic and White children are almost equally low in their motivation to read and African American children are only slightly higher. This research suggests even more significant negative changes in reading attitude for Hispanic and African American children as they mature. Clearly there is no lack of evidence that the problem of declining motivation exists and certain subgroups, boys, Hispanics, and African Americans especially, are more highly impacted by this decline of motivation. These groups need more specific focus to encourage them to maintain motivation to read. Clearly the negative attitudes toward reading are not isolated to my classroom.

Why Motivation Changes

Many educators speculate why this change in motivation occurs and some research has been conducted to find answers. One theory suggests that students with low ability are less motivated to read and the cycle of difficulty with reading perpetuates the lack of motivation. McKool (2007) found that fifth graders who had difficulty learning to read and did not see themselves as good readers were the least likely to want to read. Though McKenna et al. (1995) confirmed that increasingly negative attitudes toward reading is related to ability and the trend is most rapid for students with the lowest abilities, all students, regardless of ability, experienced similar negative trends. They further found, however, that for girls, reading ability does not explain attitudes toward reading and therefore motivation to read. Gender differences also seem unrelated to overall reading ability. This research suggests that the problem of low motivation transcends reading ability.

Other issues that affect reading attitude and motivation have been documented in a variety of studies. McKool (2007) found a correlation between out of school voluntary reading, time spent watching television, and organized activities – the more time students spent watching television or participating in activities, the less time they spent reading. Additionally, low-income students often reported that chores and taking care of siblings often interfered with their ability to read at home. The lack of time negatively impacting reading makes sense; the limited amount of time available would require students to set priorities. Students who place a lower priority on reading would be less likely to choose this activity when other more engaging activities are available. Though consideration and possibly systemic issues involving income affects the amount of time students have to read after school, McKool did find that busy schedules often were used as an excuse rather than a reason to not read as avid readers often participated in other activities and still found time to read. Perhaps if students are required to read at home instead of participating in other activities, they will be more likely to read.

What May Work

Silent reading during school is a strategy that has received mixed results. McKool (2007) found that time to read was highly motivating and found that avid student readers shared that they appreciated and felt others would be motivated to read by uninterrupted reading time in school. Greenburg et al. (2006) further supports the use of in school reading time as it emphasizes the importance of reading. On the other hand, Wigfield and Guthrie (1997a) found that in their study of fourth and fifth graders that frequent readers do not become more motivated to read with increasing classroom opportunity; rather motivated readers are simply more likely to participate in reading activities. Additionally, Kelley and Clausen-Grace (2006) and McKool (2007) warn that silent reading alone will not motivate students to read, and the in school reading time is often poorly implemented so that it does not achieve the desired results including that of motivating students to read. Though some studies have shown positive results of giving kids time to read, other studies suggest that simply providing time to read will not necessarily motivate students; other strategies need to be incorporated as well.

Access and option to read choice materials seems to be important in motivating students. Edmunds and Bauserman (2006), and Guthrie, Hoa, and Wigfield (2006) found that elementary students were more likely to want to read texts that were of personal interest to them. Greenberg et al. (2006), Moss and Henershot (2002), and Pitcher et al., (2007) confirm that adolescents prefer to read and would benefit from materials that they feel a personal connection to or that focus on areas of their interests. These studies would suggest that if students are given a choice of reading materials, or materials tailored to their personal interests, they may be more motivated to read. Preferred reading materials include high-interest options such as magazines (McKool, 2007; Pitcher et al., 2007; Worthy, Moorman, & Turner, 1999), series books (Cavazos-Kottke, 2006) which often act as a gateway to more advanced literature (McKool 2007), scary stories, car and truck books, and drawing books (Worthy et al., 1999). Knowing what students like to read and giving them access to those materials may provide for more motivated reading.

Access to materials which Edmunds and Bauserman (2006) and McKool (2007) found to be motivating for students, however, is problematic for different groups. The most common ways for students to obtain books are through borrowing school, classroom, and public libraries, and through private purchases. School libraries, however, were found by Worthy, et al. (1999) to be the most likely for 6th graders to use with a small portion of students using the public or classroom library. McKool (2007) shared that the 5th graders surveyed were least likely to use the public library. These two studies suggest that a well stocked school library that students can visit frequently can be a motivating source of students to read. Besides borrowing books, many students choose to read personally purchased materials. Edmunds and Bauserman (2006) reported that among elementary students, the single greatest reported factor in their reading motivation was if books were purchased for or given to them. Worthy et al. (1999) and McKool (2007) provide interesting information based on economic status, finding that low income students were more likely to borrow materials, especially from the school library, than to purchase them. The opposite was true for higher income students who were more likely to purchase books from books stores or other places than borrow them. This suggests that issues of income need to be addressed when looking to motivate students by assuring they have access to preferred reading materials.

Extrinsic motivation to read was the subject of some studies and provided a variety of results. In general, extrinsic motivation generally did motivate students to read more (McKool, 2007; Wigfield & Guthrie, 1997a); however, McKool found that though extrinsic motivators may cause students to read more, the many students continued to have negative attitudes toward reading. Additionally, students who initially felt positively about reading, felt negative reading during many reward programs because they felt forced to choose from books that they did not want to read. Guthrie, et al. (2006) found that getting a reward actually had a negative effect on third grade students, though making the teacher happy had a small positive effect. Unrau and Schlackman's (2006) study of urban middle school students, showed that extrinsic motivation such as grades and social compliance most affected girls and the extrinsic motivator of competition most motivated boys. However, they found that extrinsic motivation had a negative effect on reading motivation and achievement among Asian students and no significant effect on Hispanic students. Given these results, if the goal is simply to have students read more, extrinsic motivation may help. However, extrinsic programs should be designed and used with caution so as not to turn students away from reading.

Making reading a social activity seems to have a positive effect on reading motivation. Recommendations by various people, most especially peers, but also family members and teachers have been found to be a motivating factor in student's reading (Edmunds & Bauserman, 2006; Kelley & Clausen-Grace, 2006; McKool, 2007; Moss & Hendershot, 2002) Besides just recommending books, students were found to be motivated by opportunities to talk about what they were reading. Talking about books with friends seems to be one of the most powerfully motivating factors on student reading (Guthrie, et al., 2006; McKool, 2007). The changing social condition of adolescents suggests that incorporating social interaction into reading activities can have positive effects on their motivation to read.

Though there is a plethora of research on the subject of reading, it is difficult if not impossible to pinpoint what will motivate individual students. As Wigfield and Guthrie (1997a) state, "children are motivated to read by different but interrelated constructs" (p. 429). While the majority of research has been conducted on elementary students, adolescents experience significant decline in motivation from when they first learned to read. Because this decline exists, and students are motivated by a variety of strategies, looking into how my students are motivated provides data for programmatic maintenance or change as needed.

CHAPTER 4

COLLECTING DATA

An Overview of Qualitative Techniques

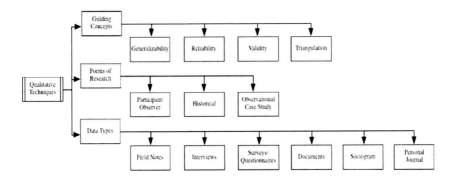

CHAPTER OVERVIEW

Chapter Four begins the discussion on methodology, focusing on qualitative data collection techniques. The chapter will address some general concerns about quailtative methodologies, and discuss a variety of data collection tools for qualitative studies.

INTRODUCTION

A student had shared the following with us a number of years ago:

> The kindergarten class had settled down to its coloring books. Bobby came up to the teacher's desk and said, "Miss Francis, I ain't got no crayons."
>
> "Bobby," Miss Francis said, "you mean 'I don't have any crayons.' You don't have any crayons. We don't have any crayons. They don't have any crayons. Do you see what I'm getting at?"
>
> "Not really," Bobby said. "What happened to all them crayons?"

What does this have to do with qualitative research? Recall that a qualitative researcher looks at things from the eyes of those being studied. The teacher now needs to see things the way Bobby is seeing them—which certainly has nothing to do with grammar!

75

If your problem statement requires that you use qualitative methodologies, there are two important things to know: you will be both the primary data gathering and analysis tools and you will be using your powers of inductive reasoning. Because data gathering and analysis rely so heavily on the person conducting the study, questions concerning the validity and reliability of the work need to be addressed throughout the study.

GUIDING CONCEPTS

This section will help you with the issues of **generalizability, validity** and **reliability** in qualitative work; and provide you with a variety of ways you might wish to collect data.

GENERALIZABILITY

In research, generalizability means whether your results will hold true for subjects and settings beyond those in your study. If a researcher finds that student writing scores increase significantly after using a particular language arts curriculum, can any teacher using that curriculum safely assume his/her students' scores should likewise increase? Typically, qualitative studies do not presume to be generalizable. Because qualitative studies examine specific subjects in specific contexts, the results are not necessarily applicable beyond that group, nor is that the intent of the research. Recall that qualitative research is hypothesis generating, not hypothesis testing. As Borko, Liston and Whitcomb (2007) so aptly describe, this type of research study

> seeks to describe, analyze, and interpret features of a specific situation, preserving its complexity and communicating the perspectives of participants. Interpretive researchers attempt to capture local variation through fine-grained descriptions of settings and actions, and through interpretation of how actors make sense of their sociocultural contexts and activities. (p. 4)

Bogdan and Biklen (2006) suggest that generalizability in qualitative work may be a quality of those working in grounded theory. Since most of us will probably be working on action research projects or studies other than grounded theory, it is important for us to remember that we are not suggesting what we find in our particular context is necessarily what others will find in theirs. As Bogdan and Biklen (2006) state "if (researchers) carefully document a given setting or group of subjects, it is then someone else's job to see how it fits into the general scheme of things" (p. 36).

RELIABILITY

Reliability has a slightly different meaning for qualitative and quantitative research methodologies. In quantitative studies, reliability has to do with a level of internal consistency. Can you trust that the tool measures correctly? You might be familiar with this concept from assessment classes. If the test is reliable, it means the results are what you would get if you could go back in a time machine and have the students retake the test. The findings are stable. There are statistical measures that can be applied to tests, attitude instruments, and the like to determine the reliability of the instrument. These will be discussed in the chapter on quantitative methodologies.

Since qualitative studies use a human as the instrument, it is not possible to apply statistical methods to the tool! So, we need to reframe what we mean by reliability. If qualitative data are reliable then what is observed by the researcher matches what actually occurred in the field. How can a reader determine the reliability of a qualitative study's findings? The reader must be convinced that what the researcher reports is unbiased and not subjective. Is that possible? Not completely. Whatever we observe is naturally tainted by our own past experiences. There are ways to help overcome this. Qualitative researchers often use video recordings, tape recordings, and multiple observers when collecting data. Also, it is important that the researchers address their **observer bias**.These will all be addressed in more detail later in the text.

VALIDITY

Validity is a term that typically goes hand-in-hand with reliability. If an instrument is not reliable, it cannot be valid. Validity tells us if a tool actually measures what it is purported to measure. Again, you may be familiar with this term from an assessment context. In that case we are looking at **content validity.** Do the tests measure the content that was taught? We have all taken tests, probably in college classes, where there were questions neither the professor nor the text had ever addressed. If the test was to examine what you had learned from the class presentations and materials, then those questions would not be valid. There are types other than content validity, and for research purposes are often grouped as internal and external validity. What these different types are and how to measure and deal with them will be explained in the quantitative chapters. Again, since the tools for qualitative studies are different, how is validity addressed?

Validity becomes more a matter of fit. A broader definition of validity is applied: it is a judgment of whether the data collected is appropriate for the decisions/ conclusions that are being made. Does the method of data collection fit the problem? Does the sample fit the problem? How was the data analysis performed? Is it appropriate? Is there sufficient evidence for any claims?

TRIANGULATION

To help with addressing the validity and reliability of findings of a qualitative study, a process called **triangulation** is frequently used (Schwandt, 2001). Triangulation involves using multiple data sources to help ensure that the data collected are accurate and a true representation of what you are studying. The term is used in trigonometry and geometry, and it is the process of using two reference points to locate a third position, hence a triangle. What this means in research is that many data sources are better than one. This can be achieved by using a combination of any of the following:

- Multiple researchers – more than one observer can add validity to the findings if there is agreement between/among the observers (usually not an option for most of our students for their first study)
- Multiple forms of data – collecting a variety of data, for example, interviews and observations and written documentation
- Multiple subjects – collecting multiple viewpoints about the same topic (talking with various age level students; interviewing principals, teachers, and staff; talking to respondents who represent different points of view).

For a concrete example, in a study of reform teaching practices used by student teachers (Morrell, Wainwright, & Flick, 2004), we used three different methods to gather data. We performed classroom observations of their teaching; we used a scoring instrument to record levels of use of specific reform practices; and we interviewed each student teacher. This gave us the means to compare what the subjects said, to what we observed in our field notes, and to what we recorded as incidences of reform. As another example, think of a fight between two students in the hallway. Do you just speak to one of the students to find out what happened, or do you speak to both and to onlookers? The more data you have to work with, the more likely you will be able to reconstruct a fuller, more complete account of the incident. These data sources can be both qualitative and quantitative in a mixed methods study.

Now that we have covered a bit more background on qualitative research, let's move onto the "nitty gritty." The sample you select and the method(s) you choose will largely be determined by your problem statement. But at this stage, you can easily revise your question if after examining the methods you decide this is a need. Recall that qualitative questions/problem statements tend to be a bit fluid and often evolve as data collection progresses.

COMMON FORMS OF QUALITATIVE RESEARCH

There are several main ways that data are typically collected when doing a qualitative study. In any particular study, you may need to use several of these methods to get a complete picture of what you are examining. Because different types of studies require different collections of tools and techniques, it might be useful to provide an overview of the types of tools/techniques with different types of qualitative studies before going into the specifics in more detail. The most common forms of qualitative research are **participant/observer studies, historical studies,** and **case studies.** By providing you with an introduction to these, you will be in a better position to decide which might be best suited to your particular study and help prepare you to design your methods section.

Participant/Observer

Many qualitative studies by their nature require that the researcher is a part of the study context. The degree of involvement varies along a continuum from complete observer to full participant. For example, a researcher may just be sitting in on lessons, observing other teachers and students. This passive researcher would be a complete observer, or what some call a non-participant observer. There is no interaction with the teacher or the students. If the researcher mostly observes, but sometimes interacts with the subjects, the role shifts to a participant/observer. An example of this that you may be familiar with would be when a cooperating teacher is observing a student teacher giving a lesson. For the most part, the mentor teacher observes the student teacher, but on occasion, she might help with student questions during seat time or lab work. Because she is not just passively observing, but does occasionally get involved with the class, there is movement from observer to participant. At the other end of the spectrum, the researchers may be observing students in their own class. Because they are teaching and interacting with the students as well as observing their behaviors, the researchers in those instances would be participants. Frequently during any one study, where a researcher lies on the participant/observer continuum may shift.

There are a number of things to consider when you are a participant/observer in a research setting. You must be able to overcome any bias or preconceptions you might have before making observations. Let's say that you are researching how teachers enhance their teaching with the use of open-ended questions. You might, at the onset, think that the science teacher would be better at this type of instructional methodology than the language arts teacher. You would need to be sure that you are judging the questions used by the two teachers according to the same standards. What makes an open-ended question should be held constant. Since this is often a judgment call on the part of the observer, you must try to not let your judgment be tainted by what you expect to see. A phenomenon related to this is dubbed the **halo effect.** This is where the researcher's initial opinion or impressions of a subject color subsequent observations. For instance, if you know a teacher has won awards you may view his teaching as more superior than it actually is; or, conversely, if you have seen a teacher interact negatively with students during recess, your observations of his teaching may be more critical than would occur otherwise.

Another concern is an **observer effect.** Even if you are truly a complete observer, your mere presence in the room might be affecting what you observe. Think about how your students behave when a principal, for example, is observing a lesson. Do they act the way they would if the principal were not in the room? Typically, if the researcher spends enough time in the setting, the "novelty" of his presence will wane and the behaviors will be "normal." If you are examining questioning strategies of teachers, and they know you are looking at their teaching (even if they do not know specifically what you are looking for), consider whether you are being invited in to view a lesson or if you can visit anytime that suits your schedule. If you are being asked to come to observe a specific lesson, does that lesson typify how the teacher generally teaches or is the teacher "performing" something special for you?

A problem with being the data collection tool is a human's limited ability to see all things at once. If you have ever watched someone teach and you wanted to really get a feel for the "whole picture" you know how difficult it is to see the teacher, the students, the interactions, the body language, and the myriad of other things going on in the classroom simultaneously. Also, a researcher has to be alert to subtle clues. Does body language change? Does word choice change during a formal observation? Is this in response to being observed or a change in context?

A researcher also has to decide what might be needed in terms of data in addition to observations. For example, back to the example about questioning strategies—besides looking at what teachers do, would it be helpful to speak with the teachers and learn about how they plan? Do they feel open-ended questions are essential to student learning? Are they aware they use or do not use them? Do they write formal lessons? Would you like to have a copy? Do the lessons plans include planned questions? By supporting your observations with written lessons and interviews, you can easily triangulate the data.

Being a participant/observer raises validity issues. Is the researcher reporting what is truly being observed and is what is being observed true/typical behavior? How can issues of observer bias and subjectivity be overcome? There are several things researchers can do to strengthen the validity of their work (see Figure 4-1). First, they need to be honest about their preconceptions and their role in the context. For example, if you are trying to advocate that the district provide inservice training for all faculty on incorporating open-ended questioning into their teaching, you need to let the reader know this. While it may make the reader suspect of your findings (especially if they are in strong support of this professional development), it also lets the reader know that you are aware of your bias and that you may have kept this in mind while collecting your data. As noted earlier, multiple observers will strengthen the validity of the data collection. On occasion researchers use **member checking** (Creswell, 2008). This is where you let the subjects read your interpretation of what occurred (during an observation or interview) so they can corroborate the findings. Multiple observations will help reduce the effect of the observer's presence on the sample. Full, detailed descriptions also help the reader to get a truer sense of what you observed. Video and audio taping are additional tools that assist in helping to validate what you observed.

In participant/observation studies, the research relies most heavily on observational notes, but the researcher can also collect interview data and documentary evidence to help support the observations.

You can strengthen the validity of participant/observation studies by:

- Making known any biases you have as the researcher
- Using multiple observers if possible
- Taking advantage of member checking
- Making multiple observations
- Providing full, detailed descriptions
- Employing video and audio taping tools
- Using a variety of data sources to help triangulate the observation data

Figure 4-1. Strengthening validity.

HISTORICAL STUDY

If you are doing a historical study, you are looking at an organization over time, either retrospectively or as it emerges. Things that would fall under this category would be examining the development of a charter school or the adoption or adaptation of a new curriculum. Data for this type of study may come from: pictures, interviews, observations, minutes of meetings, newspaper clippings, letters, and other documents. Concerns would be similar to those of other types of qualitative studies. Do you have access to sufficient documentation (does it even exist) when studying past events? In studying current events, again concerns about access and the research/subject relationship come into play.

OBSERVATIONAL CASE STUDY

In a case study, you focus on one organization or person or group or some aspect of an organization. You might be studying interactions of school counselors, effects of ability grouping on students' self-esteem or achievement, or how divorce affects student school behavior. Typically data would come from observations, interviews, photographs, and documents. If you choose to focus on one person and write a case study from that person's perspective, you must be particularly careful about your subject. For example, let's say you have a teacher that you feel is exemplary. You may want to delve into why that teacher is excellent according to that teacher. To be successful, that teacher must be articulate, willing to speak with you about themselves, and have a good memory. If the teacher is not comfortable sharing thoughts, needs to be prodded to elucidate on ideas, or finds it difficult to open up, it will be difficult to obtain rich data.

SPECIFICS ON DATA TYPES

Most qualitative studies rely on observations, interviews, and various forms of documentation. How do we go about collecting these types of data? What do we need to keep in mind when doing these? We will provide an overview and description of some different means of collecting data here so you can begin thinking about which of these make sense for your study. In the next chapter, we will delve into these more fully, including more pointers and helpful hints.

Field Notes

When we are making observations, what we need to do is take copious **field notes.** The field notes include a description of the setting as well as the "action." They will serve as an anecdotal record of the event and should include direct quotations (as pertinent—be sure to use quotation marks to indicate these are direct quotes as opposed to paraphrasing) as well as reflective notes. Personal comments are often denoted by the use of "OC" meaning observer's comments. For example, if a researcher was making observations of someone's teaching it might include comments like:

OC: The class seemed tense. The students seem to fear the teacher.

OC: Rapport between teacher and student was good.

The OCs go beyond a reporting of what was seen to provide a sense of interpretation, and captures in writing what the observer was sensing at the moment. It adds a dimension that cannot be as accurately filled in later, and humanizes any video or audiotaping that might be done. Please read through Appendix 4-A, which provides a sample of some field notes during an observation of a high school biology class (notes taken by Norman Lederman and used with permission). Note the use of quotation marks, what was recorded as observation, and what was noted as observer's comments. Can you see how all three work together to provide a rich description of the class, and how it will be easier for the researcher to analyze what occurred because of such rich observational data?

Interviews

Interviewing is another common data collecting technique used by qualitative researchers. There are three basic types of interviews, based on the "formality" of the interaction: **structured, semi-structured**, and **unstructured.** In a structured interview, questions are preplanned and followed like a script. You may be familiar with these from some job interviews or graduate school interviews. The interview guide is followed very closely, and no serious deviation is made. That is, no additional questions are added or no follow up questions to comments made by the interviewee are asked. This type of format is more frequently used when there are a number of interviewees being compared to ensure that the interviews were consistent throughout the data gathering. Beginning interviewers are often most comfortable using this type of format; the structure makes it easy to conduct.

During a semi-structured interview, guidelines are prepared and followed as closely as possible, but deviations from the script are permitted. Follow up questions can be asked, comments by the interviewee can be explored in more detail. While every interviewee will not necessarily be asked the exact same questions, this may allow for a fuller picture of what the interviewee has to offer on a topic. It is more conversational than a structured interview, though not exactly free-flowing. While the exact questions may vary, the intent of the questions is covered in all interviews. Of the three formats, this is the one most commonly used by our students. While it requires more skill than structured interviewing (to know what to follow up on at the current moment and not in hindsight), most find it more comfortable because it does allow for more give and take.

In an unstructured interview, there are no formal preplanned questions. It is very much like a conversation, with no artificial directionality cues. This type of interview format is not frequently (if ever) used by our students.

Besides deciding on how strictly to adhere to an interview script, there is another major decision to be made when planning interviews. If a researcher will

PROS OF FOCUS GROUPS

Requires less time on the part of the interviewer because there are fewer interviews to conduct
May be easier to schedule interview times
Encourages brainstorming of ideas among interviewees
Allows for natural groupings
Some interviewees may prefer this format (safety/comfort in numbers)

CONS OF FOCUS GROUPS

Depending on the group make up, some interviewees may feel restrained/constrained in offering ideas resulting in mimicking of comments rather than the offering of original or conflicting thoughts
Requires skill on the part of the interviewer to encourage all interviewees to contribute while not "shutting down" members who are tending to dominate the conversation

Figure 4-2. The pros and cons of focus group interviewing.

be interviewing a number of people, should the interviews be conducted with individuals or with **focus groups**? For example, if you are going to interview five teachers, five students, and five parents about looping, should you conduct 15 separate interviews by meeting with each individual separately; or conduct three interviews by meeting with all the teachers, and then with all the students, and then with all the parents? In a different scenario, let's pretend you are interviewing the teachers in your building about the newest writing curriculum. Did you want to interview each teacher separately, or by blocks of grade levels, or in one big gathering? There are pros and cons to each method. Please review Figure 4-2. The biggest considerations are generally the sample size (so you can determine if you have the time and are able to conduct separate interviews) and which type of set-up you feel would be better to maximize the information you can receive. Consider your specific sample in helping to make this decision.

Surveys/Questionnaires

While we tend to think of surveys and questionnaires as quantitative tools, open-ended questions allow for qualitative data gathering. If you have a sample size that is too large to be conducive to interviewing, providing a survey is often a viable alternative. It takes skill to be able to convert your interview questions into written questions. The questions need to be specific enough to gather the information you need without being so specific as to elicit a particular response.

Unlike interviewing, it is not possible to follow up a written response and ask for clarification or elucidation. What is possible, however, is to include a statement on the survey to solicit candidates for follow up interviews. Those who are willing to participate in an interview can be asked to provide contact information, which allows the researcher an opportunity to gather more information if the need arises.

DOCUMENTS

Qualitative researchers often use documents as data sources. These may include "personal" documents such as lesson plans, samples of student work, journals, essays, PowerPoint presentations, or other documents generated in teaching. This written documentation is particularly useful in case studies and participant/observation studies. Official documents, such as minutes of meetings, reports, and publications, are frequently used in historical studies. A third possible category of document-tation data is student records and personal files. These may provide insights on a situation, but they are typically one-sided. Teacher comments on report cards or in a student's file are not always substantiated in those venues.

Another type of data is visual and/or audio depictions. Because digital still and video cameras are often available in schools and homes, pictures, video clips, and recordings are becoming increasingly common data sources. You may want to consider if this type of evidence would be useful in researching your question: photographs of student projects, videos of student presentations or teacher lessons, recordings of songs, or other recorded visual information.

Sociogram

If your question involves understanding relationships in a classroom or within a group, a **sociogram** (Moreno, 1953) may be a good data collection tool. Basically, you ask the students or group members to respond to a question by using other students'/members' names. Typically, the respondent provides a first, second, and third choice. Students' names are then listed and connected to their choices using arrows or directional lines. By charting everyone's responses, it becomes easy to identify "stars" and "isolates" in a class and see group dynamics in a different way (Hubbard & Power, 2003).

As an example, the research question may be "How do whole-class share sessions influence student writing?" A sociogram question that could be used is "What classmates do you most like to have read their writing to the class?" The students would be directed to list a first, second and third choice. You could easily see if there are particular students whose writing stands out as preferred or less appreciated. Referring to the hypothetical sociogram in Figure 4-3 where, for simplicity, only the students' first choice was charted, we can see that girls' writings are preferred more often than boys'; that Rosa's writing is the most liked, followed by Lorraine's; and that there are a number of students whose writing was not chosen by anyone. Interestingly, Rosa's first choice was not the preferred choice of any other student. (Are they best friends or is there another reason?) How would the sociogram change if we had graphed all three choices for each student? Generally, a sociogram does not stand alone, but requires follow up data to help in answering a question. In our example, a question that begs to be asked is what is it about the preferred writings that make them appreciated?

What classmates do you like to have read their writings to the class?

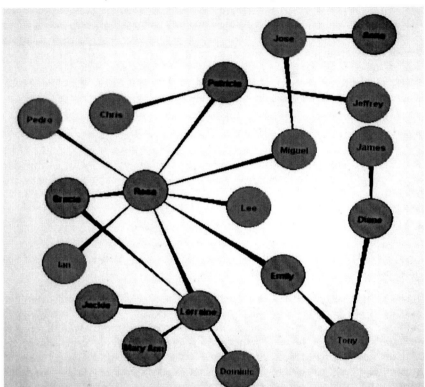

Figure 4-3. Sample sociogram.

Personal Journal

If you are studying your own students, a **personal journal** is a useful data source. Get in the habit of jotting down quick reflective notes at the end of each class session. If you jot down noteworthy happenings on post it notes soon after they occur, these can act as memory jogs. At the end of each day, set aside some time to write a more detailed description of the day's events using your quick notes or post its. If you are doing a case study, you may want your subject to keep a personal journal.

SUMMARY COMMENTS

Keep in mind that in qualitative research, it is up to the researcher to convince the reader that what is observed and reported is an accurate accounting of what occurred. The richer and more varied the data collected, the greater the likelihood the data will be considered valid and reliable. Here is an example to help put all this into perspective: In our university's teacher education program, we have our students do weekly reflections during their student teaching experience. We switched from an open format where the students wrote whatever was on their mind, to having the students respond to prescribed prompts for their weekly comments. We wanted to see if focusing our student teachers' thinking prompted the students to reflect more deeply about their practice (Morrell, Steinbock, & Casareno, 1999). That study will form the basis for examination.

Purpose

The purpose of this project was to examine the effectiveness of how we incorporate reflection into the professional year field experience for our undergraduates and MAT students.

Sample Data

Here are some excerpts from our students' reflective essays, along with the categories we felt best depicted the responses:

Students' Individual Needs: "I'm not quite sure of the factors I will use to determine whether or not I should move ahead or reteach a concept—I think it is all relative to the individual student and the class as a whole. In other words, what is keeping a student/s from understanding the material—is my instruction too formal, have I not allotted enough time to work on problems is the concept not congruent with the instruction, or is it because the student/s is repeatedly absent from class, makes no effort outside of class to work with me individually, or has no desire to achieve in class…"

Assessment: "I have become a huge fan of asking the students what they think I need to do to help them better understand the materials I am teaching or the different ways that they might want to show that they have learned the concepts…The feedback I got was great and gave me some guidance in planning my lesson for the work sample. For example, a lot of students said they would like to draw pictures to show their understanding, so I planned this interactive website activity where students found information about the leading polluters in the community – who, what chemicals, the effects, etc. They had the option of either writing me a two-page essay, or drawing a picture based on their findings and describing that piece with a paragraph."

Altering Preconceptions: "Over the summer the words (a particular high school) conjured up images of base animalism and wanton disrespect in the classroom. Today [5 weeks later] I laugh at the notions I had of [the school] over a month ago. I like the students I have, and as I've gotten to know them, I've rediscovered the fact that every student is a rational human being. They keep the classroom climate conducive to learning, and I have yet to see anyone act up during class...It might also be that they have always been this way, and it was my perception of the climate that has changed."

Relevancy: "...I asked the CT if I could lead a discussion of some sort. So, I had the class read the chapter and I asked them to get out a piece of paper and write down every conflict they have experienced in their life in two minutes (e.g., me versus parents). After they did that, we separated the conflicts into the four literary conflicts—person v. person, person v. society, person v. self, and person v. nature. The students gave me their conflicts and we listed them under a category. After that, we listed each conflict in the present novel under one of these categories. The students were very responsive and enjoyed this discussion. Each student had the opportunity to participate in the discussion as well as connect events in their life with the book. Each student learned more about the book through relevancy of their own life and the ability to discuss the book as a class."

CONCLUSION

Based on an analysis of the students' weekly reflection entries, we concluded that:

This attempt at reflective journaling during the students' field experiences was very successful in fostering the type of personal analysis and professional growth we want our students to engage in and develop as a matter of routine. Their focus switched from self to individual students.

QUESTION FOR THOUGHT

Based on the quotes we presented, do you believe our conclusion? Are the supporting data we provided sufficient evidence to determine our new reflection assignments were fostering professional growth in our students? Is it possible the students were just giving us lip service and providing what they thought we wanted to hear rather than truly reflecting on their personal experiences? If we relied solely on the reflective essays, we might not know if the students were just fabricating a response to an assignment. To help overcome this, we actually had several data sources. While the journal entries served as our primary data source, we had secondary data sources as well. These included oral reflective interviews with the students and a document analysis of the evidence of reflection in the student teachers' lesson plans and work samples. Because we did have multiple sources of data that supported the same ideas, the study had greater validity—the reflective journals seemed to match what the students were experiencing and thinking.

Moral of the Story
Consider what types of data you should and could collect to be sure that not only what you have is an accurate depiction of the situation, but that others will also believe that what you say is based in reality. It is far better to collect too much data and then decide you don't need it all, than to collect too little. It is like teaching—better to over plan and cut back than be left with dead time. While we may rely on

our experience to get us through a "lull" in a lesson, there is no way to get through gaps and holes in research data. It is not always possible to go back and recollect data we need.

Carefully decide on your data sources. When you write your research report, it is important that you state what you did and why, to convince your readers that the data are of quality and were carefully collected.

NEXT STEPS

Now that you have some idea of the types of qualitative data that can be collected to help you in answering your research question, you need to take some time to consider which types of data will work best for your problem statement. Is there a combination of tools that would work? Do you want a survey along with some follow up interviews? Would observations and lesson plans work? Will qualitative data be sufficient or do you need to also collect some quantitative data? The next chapter will go into each of the qualitative tools/methods in more details, to provide more specific guidelines, tips, and possible pitfalls to be wary of in conducting your qualitative data collection.

CHAPTER SELF-CHECK

Having completed this chapter, you should be comfortable discussing the following:
- generalizability, reliability, validity, triangulation
- how generalizability, reliability, and validity apply specifically to qualitative studies
- the participant/observer continuum
- types of data typically collected for participant/observer studies, historical research, and observational case studies
- taking field notes
- interviewing structures and formats
- data collection by means of surveys/questionnaires, other forms of document-tation, sociograms, personal journals

CHAPTER REVIEW QUESTIONS

1. Define the following terms: generalizability, reliability, validity, triangulation, sociogram.
2. How does a qualitative researcher address issues of generalizability, reliability, and validity?
3. Describe the participant/observer continuum.
4. What are some considerations when a researcher is involved in a participant/observer research setting?
5. What kinds/types of data are generally gathered in a qualitative research study?
6. What information is collected and noted when taking field notes?

7. Distinguish among the three basic structures of interviews.
8. What is a focus group interview? What are the pros and cons of using this type of interview format?

REFERENCES

Bodgan, R. C., & Biklen, S. K. (2006). *Qualitative research for education: An introduction to theory and methods* (5th ed.). Boston: Allyn & Bacon.

Borko, H., Liston, D., & Whitcomb, J. A. (2007). Genres of empirical research in teacher education. *Journal of Teacher Education, 58*(1), 3–11.

Creswell, J. W. (2008). *Educational research. Planning, conducting, and evaluating quantitative and qualitative research.* (3rd ed.). Upper Saddle River, NJ: Prentice Hall.

Hubbard, R. S., & Power, B. M. (2003). *The art of classroom inquiry: A handbook for teacher-researchers* (Rev. ed.). Portsmouth, NH: Heinemann.

Moreno, J. (1953). *Who shall survive? Foundations of sociometry, group psychotherapy and sociodrama.* New York: Beacon House.

Morrell, P. D., Steinbock, S., & Casareno, A. (1999, January). *Reflective journaling: A way to enhance preservice teachers' field experiences.* A paper presented at the Annual International Meeting of the Association for the Education of Teachers in Science, Austin, TX.

Morrell, P. D., Wainwright, C., & Flick, L. (2004). Reform teaching strategies used by student teachers. *School, Science, and Mathematics, 104*(5), 199–213.

Schwandt, T. A. (2001). *Dictionary of qualitative inquiry* (2nd ed.). Thousand Oaks, CA: Sage.

APPENDIX 4-A: EXCERPT OF FIELD NOTES. REPRINTED WITH PERMISSION OF NORMAN LEDERMAN

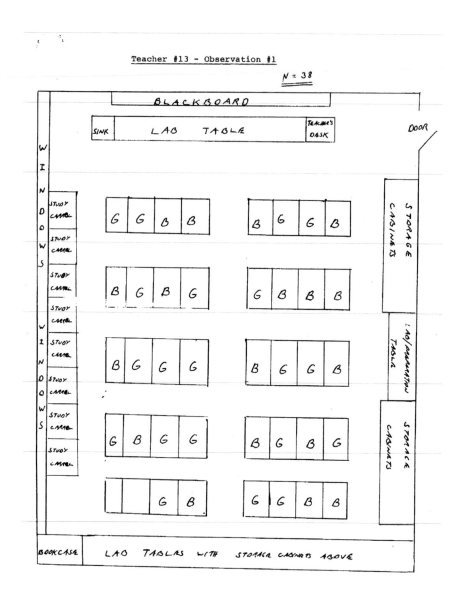

Teacher #13 - Observation #1

-2-

7:50:   As students enter the room they move immediately to their
        seats and open their notebooks. The teacher is not present.

        After notebooks are open students begin to converse about
        the world series and their weekend activities.

7:55:   The bell rings and the teacher enters from the hallway
        and closes the door behind him.

        The students quiet down upon the teacher's entrance and
        direct their attention forward. The room is extremely
        quiet eventhough this class has 38 students.

        The teacher stands in front of the lab table at the front
        of the room and says: "Did everybody read the article?"

(O.C. He has given them an article to read about cellular respiration
over the weekend.)

The class answers "yes" in unison.

Teacher: "The first thing I got hit with today was Mr. _____
          I'm confused."

The teacher says the latter portion of this sentence beginning with
"Mr. _____" in a high shrilled voice.

The class laughs and one student nearby turns to his neighbor and
says: "This guy's such a goof."

Teacher: "How many of you are confused by the supplementary readings?"

Approximately 20 students raise their hands to signify their confusion.

The teacher looks straight at the class without expression and says
"Good."

There is a momentary pause and the class realizing it is a joke
begins to laugh. At this response, the teacher laughs along with
them. Before the students stop laughing the teacher walks to the
blackboard and writes the word 'OXIDATION' in large capital letters.

Teacher: "Now take out that pretty colored handout I gave you on
          Friday about anaerobic respiration (see attached). That
          is, if any of you still have it. I'm sure that the janitors
          really appreciated the way you decorated the floor with
          them. They'll probably show their appreciation with a
          swift kick to your head."

          "Barlow and James over there would probably like that kind
          of treatment. Right?"

The class seems to appreciate his razzing of students and humor.

The teacher continues:
"Remember on Friday I burned a piece of paper up here?"

The class laughs lightly in a manner which indicates something humorous occurred during this particular demonstration. The teacher continues.

Teacher: "Yeah, the janitors sent me love notes for that also."

The previous laugh of the class had almost disappeared but this last comment elevates its volume again. The teacher appears to enjoy the class appreciation of his monologue. He continues.

Teacher: "Well, I noticed when I lit that paper up, some of you Pyros were chomping at the bit." (He makes a gruesome facial expression to go along with his words.)

Now the class is laughing quite loudly. However, they are not out of control. They are simply enjoying the teacher's humor. The students do not start joking amongst themselves. They continue to be attentive as they wait for the next joke to come.

(O.C. The teacher appears to joke a lot. It appears as if it is an integral part of his lecturing technique. It certainly keeps the class awake and interested.)

Teacher: "Now, what is oxidation?"

The teacher's tone is extremely serious. The transition from joke to specific content is very smooth.

A number of students raise their hands. The teacher picks a volunteer.

Student: "The loss of electrons."

Teacher: "Good, I see that we are getting something out of this reading."

Teacher: "If its the loss of electrons these electrons must be given to something. Right? So, something must be gaining electrons. We will call this gain of electrons reduction."

Another teacher enters the room to borrow some microscope slides. He jokes around with this teacher by giving her various materials that she has not asked for.

The students are quite humored by this as well. The other teacher finally leaves and he continues his presentation.

-4-

Teacher: "Now don't be confused by the term reduction being
           associated with a gain. There is some reducing going
           on. Can anybody tell me where?"

The students do not respond. He continues.

Teacher: "What are we gaining?"

Hands go up. He picks one volunteer.

Student: "Electrons."

Teacher: "And what is the charge on an electron?"

Same
Student: "Negative."

Teacher: "OKAY, now think back to your math days, what happens
           when you add negative numbers to positive numbers?"

Student
vol.:   "You have less."

Teacher: "Its subtraction right?"

           "So when we add electrons we are adding negative charges
           and so we are reducing the charge."

The students nod in approval.

(O.C. The teacher's questions are usually responded to by many
students raising their hands. He seems perfectly content to call on
those who volunteer. It is also important to note that students
do not call out answers in this classroom. They raise their hands
and wait to be called upon.)

Teacher: "But you know, oxidation and reduction do not have to be
           described in terms of gaining and losing electrons. How
           can we express these in another way?"

Student: "Anaerobic and aerobic."

Teacher: "No, not yet. We'll get to those later."

           He repeats:

           "If we refer to reduction as the gain of electrons and
           oxidation as the loss. How can we say either of these
           . . . just as meaningfully without electrons being involved
           in the definition?"

-5-

Student: "How about gain of oxygen and loss of oxygen."

Teacher: "Well, actually people used to believe that for a long
            time.   But, we can have oxidation take place without
            oxygen being present. Can't we have compounds gain and
            lose electrons without involving oxygen? What else can
            be involved in oxidation other than oxygen?"

Student: "Hydrogen."

Teacher: "Hey, where did you come up with that?"

Student: From the reading."

The student chuckles lightly as if he doesn't expect "From the
reading" to be an acceptable answer but the teacher simply replies:

            "Okay, fair enough."

Teacher: "Now, why don't we change our mind set a little and simply
            define oxidation as the loss of hydrogen and reduction as
            the gain of hydrogen. But can we do this?"

The teacher turns and draws a hydrogen atom on the board:

Teacher: "Okay, here's our hydrogen atom with its one electron and
            atomic weight of 1. Now will you all agree that this
            single electron is moving pretty fast and that it has
            a lot of energy?"

Students nod.

Teacher: "And would you agree that this electron is highly
            reactive? Will it tend to combine with other elements
            readily?"

There is no student response to this question. He continues WITH
another approach.

Teacher: "If something is energetic is it dynamic? Is it easily
            subject to change?"

Student: "Yes, it's changeable."

-6-

Teacher: "Okay, so if something is dynamic its likely to change.
           If its dynamic it is likely to react with other physcial
           objects easily."

           "Like, Bill reacted on Warren Street the other night?"

The class laughs loudly as Bill blushes.

Teacher: "You see Bill they know, they laughed."

The class continues to laugh as the teacher begins to smile.

Teacher: "Okay now, hydrogen atoms are extremely reactive. That
           is, they are easily given away by some compounds and taken
           up by others."

           "Now think on this carefully. Hydrogen only has a mass
           of 1. This is not large and therefore if we forgot
           about that one proton we wouldn't be forgetting much. Do
           you buy that? The mass of hydrogen is so small that it is
           insignificant in relation to other atoms."

           "So, I want you to consider a new mental picture. A new
           model o.k! We will equate electrons with hydrogens."

The teacher writes on the board:

                     ELECTRONS = HYDROGENS

TAACHER : "So now if we looked at oxidation as the loss of electrons
           do you see how we could lose a hydrogen and still qualify
           as oxidation. Hydrogen is really nothing more than an
           electron. "

The class is busily writing down notes as the teacher speaks.

Teacher: "Okay, so we will use the following mind set:

                     Electrons equal Hydrogens."

           "If we oxidize something it will lose hydrogens. If we
           reduce something it will gain hydrogens. Do you accept
           that?"

The teacher glances around the room and the students offer no
resistance. They are simply poised and ready to take notes.

Teacher: "Now then, if something is oxidized then something must
           be reduced as well."

           "Do you accept that? I mean must the two go hand-in-
           hand?"

Student: "Yes."

Teacher: "Why?"

Student: "Because the law of conservation of matter and energy says that nothing can be lost from the system."

The teacher pauses and says to the same student:

Teacher: "Keep talking."

Student: "If one compound loses electrons they must go somewhere, they cannot just be lost."

Teacher: "Okay, so if I remove hydrogens from one substance they are not totally lost from the system they must be picked up by something else."

          "Does everybody else agree with our reasoning? Be sure now because this is an important point."

The teacher pauses and walks around the room. At first no hands go up but then Helen raises hers.

Helen: "So in other words, hydrogens spend their time jumping from one molecule to another?"

Teacher: "Well, not all of them do. There is molecular hydrogen which doesn't jump around as readily. But, in oxidation - reduction reactions that is exactly what is happening."

          "It's just like if I dropped a $5.00 bill here on the floor. That would be my loss. But I'm sure that it wouldn't stay there very long. Carey over here (he points to Carey) would certainly snatch it up after I left and it would be his gain."

The class laughs.

Teacher: "Unless he had a sudden fit of honesty and turned it into the office lost and found."

Carey: "Not me, I could think of better things to use it for."

Teacher: "Okay, but the point here is that one compound loses and the other one gains. It's not as if those electrons try real hard to escape from the system and run around saying "Ah hah, Ah hah, I've escaped, I've escaped."" He says the latter part of the previous statement in a high pitched voice. He continues:

          "The electrons must go somewhere."

(O.C. The students appear to be amused with the teacher's explanation. However they appear to becoming passive toward the lesson. They just don't appear as involved as before.)

The teacher turns around and writes "Anaerobic Respiration" on the board. He turns around and pauses.

Teacher: "Katie, what does anaerobic mean? You've been pretty anaerobic this morning."

The class does not laugh at this remark. (O.C. The tone is one of disciplining. It gives the impression that Katie has been suspected of daydreaming.)

Katie: "Without oxygen or air."

The teacher smiles at her answer. (O.C. It appears as if he is surprised that she could give a correct answer.)

Teacher: "Okay, good."

"Now if I told you this anerobic reaction that I have on the handout (see attached) occurs in the middle of an environment which has plenty of oxygen how can I call it anaerobic?"

Student
vol.:   "Because the reaction doesn't require oxygen.

Teacher: "Not only doesn't it require oxygen, but it cannot use oxygen even if it wanted to."

"How come? Julie?"

Julie does not respond.

Teacher: "Julie doesn't know because she has been doodling. Haven't you Julie?"

"C'mon   class stay with me now. I know its Monday morning but this stuff is not easy to grasp. You have to give it a chance to sink in."

(O.C. For the first time the teacher's mood appears to be shifting away from the earlier "jovial" approach.)

Teacher: "What determines metabolic pathways?"

Many hands go up. Jeff is called upon.

Jeff: "Enzymes."

Teacher: "Good, enzymes. And what if the enzymes employed in the process are not the kind that can employ oxygen?"

COLLECTING DATA

A Closer Look at Qualitative Techniques

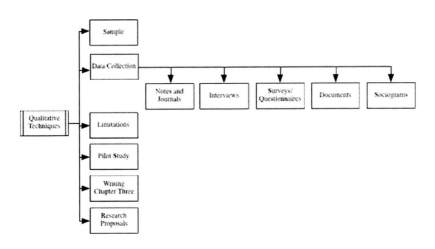

CHAPTER OVERVIEW

Chapter Five continues the coverage of qualitative data collection techniques. The chapter includes information on choosing a sample and ethical considerations. It will also provide details on collection, tips, and pitfalls to avoid when collecting data. The chapter will conclude with how to write a qualitative methods chapter and the research proposal.

INTRODUCTION

Knowing what types of data you can collect is not the same as knowing how to best collect them. This chapter will share some pointers on qualitative data collection, as well as help provide the missing pieces to complete your understanding of qualitative research methodology. Something to consider from the onset, especially with qualitative research, is that your methods for data collection may begin to evolve as you actually start to collect your data. New ideas form, possibilities you had not considered emerge, and both your research question and data needs may change and grow as you progress. While this does not always happen, know that it can and it is a natural part of qualitative research. Researching a question does not always follow a clear, predictable path!

SELECTING A SAMPLE

Often, the types of data you collect depend partly on your sample. Look at your research question. Who will you be studying? Who makes the most sense? While your question will generally suggest its own sample (your class, your colleagues, your school, yourself), you may need to consider if narrowing or broadening the question is more appropriate for your needs. For example, let's say you want to examine the district's newly adopted writing curriculum. What do you really want to know about the curriculum? The following are some possibilities:

- Is the professional development being provided sufficient to help the teachers implement the curriculum? In this case, the sample would probably be all teachers in the district.
- How do the teachers feel about the curriculum itself? Depending on what you really want to focus on will determine your sample (is it general impact—look at all teachers; is it how it fits the needs of the students in your building—limit yourself to the teachers in your school; is it how it meets the developmental needs of young children—you would be interested in a fraction of the teachers in the district, say 1st-3rd grade teachers).
- Is the new curriculum changing how students feel about writing? (Would this be all students; just the students in your classroom; just the reluctant writers with whom you work?)

The specifics of a question will determine not only the best sample but also the best methods of data collection. Let's go back to the first suggested question about professional development. Many questions are likely to emerge about collecting data. Is your question sufficiently narrow? Do you want to know if the teachers *feel* the professional development is adequate? Are you able to interview everyone? Could you use focus groups to help expedite the collection process? Would an open-ended questionnaire be more appropriate? Are you more interested in actually *seeing* if the professional development training is sufficient to implement the new curriculum rather than just whether teachers feel it is? Do you want to view teachers implementing the curriculum in their classes? Would field notes and lesson plans be appropriate? Would you like to interview the teachers as well? Should you narrow your observations to teachers in your building? How many? You may start by observing five teachers, but find one person is fully embracing the new curriculum while another is quite reluctant to give up the old. You may be more interested in why some teachers are early adopters and others are not—so your research question may actually change as you begin data collection. Remember, interest in your topic is what will keep you sustained and motivated throughout this process. Being realistic, if you are doing your research project as part of an educational program, do keep in mind that you will have deadlines and you do not want to switch your focus too often or you may not meet those time constraints.

As noted above, your question will suggest both a sample and its size. In our research classes, our students generally choose what is termed a **sample of**

convenience. Rather than a large, random sample so often equated with research, our students tend to focus on the pupils in their classroom, the teachers they work with on a daily basis, or other individuals close at hand who may have information they need. They choose these because they are truly convenient: the researcher has ready access to this sample, already has a bond established with them, sees them frequently during the course of a work week, and the like. Depending on the specific research question, our students might use a **purposeful sample.** Unlike a sample of convenience, here the researcher hand- selects certain people to study because of specific reasons pertaining to the problem statement. The researchers might be looking at students who are reluctant writers, or the reading habits of students identified as talented and gifted, or colleagues who are using inquiry-type lessons in their daily teaching.

If you choose not to use a sample of convenience (perhaps you feel you are too close to them to remain unbiased or the research question you find most interesting does not lend itself to such a sample), do remember that you will need access at a time that is mutually convenient. If you are being an observer, be sure you can frequent the setting often enough to not be "disruptive" or cause the observed behaviors to change because of your presence. You will also have to arrange for the observations or interviews.

Some researchers use a type of sampling called **snowball sampling.** In this method, you identify some of your sample and ask them to identify others who can participate. Think of a chain letter: you send a notice to ten people and ask them to send it to ten others. Now instead of a sample of 10, you have a sample of 100. The main disadvantage with this method is you have no control over who is in your sample so your sample may not be representative; the main advantage is it can lead (snowball) to large sample sizes. This is a useful technique for sociology studies. In educational studies, giving up control of who is in your sample may be too high a price to pay for a larger sample size.

Regardless of your method of sampling, before meeting with potential subjects to discuss participating in your study, decide what you will tell the sample about your project. Be specific enough to get access to the information you need without biasing their responses or behaviors. For example, if you want to observe whether teachers exhibit gender bias in their instruction, you would not want to be that specific when discussing your research problem. Saying something more vague, like you are interested in observing the teacher/student interactions, would be more appropriate. That way you can better insure that when you observe them, they are treating both sexes the way they typically would; that their behaviors are not being modified because they know you are looking at their interactions through a "gender lens."

In all cases, in your write up, it is important to describe the sample as fully as possible *and* to state why and how the sample was chosen. For examples of the latter, see Figure 5-1. Always keep in mind the rights of those participating in your study, and get informed consent as needed. Review the guidelines in Chapter 2 of this text if you need to refresh your memory about confidentiality, risks, and other human subjects study issues.

CHAPTER 5

EXAMPLE 1. (REPRINTED WITH PERMISSION OF TOM KUNTZ)

This study will investigate the effects on problem solving ability of middle school science students when lesson presentation alternates between visual demonstration and oral/written information to initiate a lesson. The sample group for this study will be two seventh grade physical science classes in a rural southern Oregon community of about 7,000 people. The study groups are a sample of convenience. They represent two randomly selected groups from six classes of seventh grade science students taught by the researcher.

EXAMPLE 2. (REPRINTED WITH PERMISSION OF SHERILYN MOONEY)

A purposive sample will be used, including only those students who receive their writing instruction in my special education classroom. The sample will be made up of 14 students in a multi-categorical resource room at the middle school level. Two of these students qualify for services as students with mental retardation, two as students with other health impairments, one as a student with a speech/language disorder, and the remaining seven as students with learning disabilities.

EXAMPLE 3. (REPRINTED WITH PERMISSION OF DEBBIE BALE)

The teachers of this school were chosen for this study because I am a member of the teaching staff as well as the Instructional Leadership Team. I want to find out how teachers are collaborating in XXX School. The data collected will be used to help teachers in the school identify ways in which they are effectively collaborating and ways in which the Instructional Leadership Team can help facilitate more collaborative opportunities.

EXAMPLE 4. (REPRINTED WITH PERMISSION OF CAROLYN CAMERON)

…This sample of teachers was selected because the individuals represent a range of professional experience and backgrounds. My sample includes teachers at every stage of their career and includes teachers with expertise in both elementary and junior high programs. The following chart gives an indication of the teachers' range of experience.

EXAMPLE 5. (REPRINTED WITH PERMISSION OF DAVID DEMPSEY)

The purpose of this study is to determine the extent to which participatory decision-making through a teacher leadership committee impacts teachers' implementation of yearly school goals. To determine this, an interview process as well as a survey will be undertaken with teachers from a school that utilizes participatory decision-making through a leadership committee. The leadership committee is made up of a sample of volunteer teachers, each representing a specific demographic in the school. There is representation from each of the five grade levels present at the school as well as representation from both school administration and special education. In conducting interviews, three lead teachers will be selected as teachers who will be open and forthright in their answers, and three teachers who are not members of the teacher leadership committee will also be invited to be interviewed. The purpose of selecting both groups is to determine if the goal setting in the school does not stop with simply the leadership committee but impacts the rest of the teaching staff as well.

Figure 5-1. Examples of student research papers showing different types of sample selection.

DATA COLLECTION TIPS

As noted in the previous chapter, there are many tools that are used to collect qualitative data. What follows are helpful tips to strengthen your use of those tools and avoid common pitfalls associated with data collection.

Field Notes/Personal Journals

When you take notes while you are a participant/observer, you need to be as descriptive and complete as possible so when you review them later, you can accurately "relive" the experience. With the popularity of laptops, many researchers type field notes directly into the computer. Others are more comfortable using paper and pencil. Use whichever method would be most efficient for you. You should begin with a description of the physical setting; include a sketch if you think that may help. Note the players (teachers, students, others who might be present), and describe them. Record your impressions (what do you sense, feel, what is the "mood" of the room). How involved are you in the observational session?

When you record your observational notes, be as exacting as possible. For example, do not say the teacher was interacting with students as they entered the room; rather, say the teacher was standing by the door and greeting each student as he or she entered by saying either "good morning" or "good to see you." Each student received a smile and/or an acknowledging nod upon entering the room. During the lesson, describe the activities. Was the teacher sitting or standing, stationary or pacing? Were the blackboard, overhead, or other instructional supports used? What was the interaction like between the teacher and students? Among the students? When you record dialogs, are you paraphrasing, using direct quotes, writing summaries? Be sure to state which you are doing, and do use quotation marks as needed. Also record the non-verbals occurrences: facial expressions, gestures, inflections, and the like. Remember to record observer comments when appropriate. What you choose to describe will be based on your problem statement but deciding to describe more rather than less is almost always a good choice.

If you hand-write your notes, it is best to transfer them to a computer as soon as possible after the completion of the observation. It will be easier to read quickly scrawled words and abbreviations when they are freshest in your mind. Whether you hand write or enter the notes directly onto a computer, reread the notes as soon after the observation as possible. If thoughts enter your mind as you review what you have observed, include those as observer comments (OC). When you (or any one else) reads your field notes at a later date, you should be able to reconstruct the experience as closely as possible in your mind based on what you have written. Note taking is a skill that develops with practice. If you have never tried to take observational notes before, it is risky to use an observation important to your study as your first experience. We recommend a few practice sessions in a benign setting to help you get used to the process.

If you are fully a participant, write your journal notes on the experiences as soon as possible after they occur. Keep a journal open on your desk or a stack of Post-it™ notes handy for entries or memory jogs and flesh these out as soon as you are able.

It may be quicker and more accurate to record your thoughts and recollections into an MP3 player or cassette player and transcribe the recording as time becomes available (the same day, preferably!). Remember to include the same rich descriptions, and note which are your comments, which are true observations, and which are direct quotes.

Interviews

There are three important steps in planning and conducting an interview (besides sample selection and consent): the first is the writing of the questions; the second is the actual interview; and the third is the post interview reflections.

Writing your questions. Your questions should be focused broadly on the topic; that is, you want to get information on a specific topic, but not in a way that solicits "what you want to hear." The questions need to be narrow enough to get useful information, but not so narrow that the interviewee feels compelled to respond in a certain way. I am reminded of a telemarketing survey I once took via telephone. I was asked what soap I used in the shower. (It was a deodorant soap.) Then I was asked what type of soap I keep in the shower for my face, because I *certainly* didn't use (the deodorant soap) on my face. Well, in all honesty, I don't keep two bars in the shower. But I "certainly" wouldn't admit to that after the phrasing of that follow up question! Think about ways that you can remove as much bias from your questions as possible.

In addition to the phrasing of the questions, you also need to be considerate of how many questions you can reasonably ask, being mindful of both attention spans and time constraints. If you are using a structured format, you have to be sure your questions are inclusive and will cover all the possible areas you want to follow. (If necessary, review interview formats in Chapter 4.) You may want to try out your questions on an appropriate subject (a colleague, a friend, a neighbor's child) to check that the questions you have written elicit the types of responses you desire and to practice asking the questions. This will also help you ensure that the subjects will understand your questions and that you are not using vocabulary or jargon that confounds the question. Have a clean copy of the typed questions (with a font that is comfortable to read) prepared for use at the interview.

Besides questions, determine if there is any demographic information you might need from your interviewee. Is it important to know, for example, how many years of teaching experience they might have? Is knowing their grade level, content area, gender, or other demographic information important to your study? Might it be? Again, remember, too much information is better than too little. Write down all the information you will want to collect on the interview sheet so you will remember to gather this information during the interview.

Be sure to pay attention to what you found in review of the literature when writing your questions. Did other researchers use this technique? What questions did they use? Are there items/factors that seemed important in other studies? Be sure to ask about these in your interview. Keep a note of which researchers and what other influences impacted the questions you choose to use. You will include these when you write the methods chapter and describe the crafting of your questions.

The actual interview. Decide whether you want to have individual or focus group interviews. Review Figure 4-3 and consider your actual sample in helping you to make this determination. Prior to the interview when arranging a convenient time and place to meet, advise the interviewee of the general scheme of what you will be asking. Providing the actual questions before hand is not recommended as that may lead to the interviewee preparing a scripted response, which may or may not be what he actually feels. It also detracts from a conversational tone of an interview and tends to limit the flow of information. On some occasions, you might provide a list of questions at the time of the interview (when asked) because some of interviewees feel more comfortable with a visual in addition to the oral question.

It is helpful to record the interview. Many MP3 players have the capability to act as a recorder and can be less cumbersome than a cassette recorder (no need to worry about running out of audio-tape or having to flip it over in the middle of the interview!). Whether using an MP3 player or cassette recorder, be sure the battery life is more than sufficient and you have ample space or tape. Recording allows the interviewer to focus on the responses and not worry so much about getting everything down (especially verbatim quotes). Do ask verbally for permission to record before the interview and then verify at the start of the recording that the conversation is being recorded and that the interviewee is aware of and comfortable with that. If you do record an interview, transcribe the interview as soon as possible after the interview is concluded. It may be possible to fill in inaudible pieces when the conversation is fresh in your mind.

Start the interview with some small talk to get a comfort level established between the interviewer and the interviewee. It is often convenient to get some demographic information at the start (How long have you been teaching? How long have you been at this school?). Assure the interviewee of confidentiality. It is fine to take notes during the interview (even if you are recording); it helps to remind you of things to follow up on or just some impressions to be noted. During the interview, do not interrupt and do allow for pauses and wait time. Do not be judgmental of any response! Do not suggest a particular response or encourage or discourage answers. Be careful of your tone of voice, your non-verbal expressions, and your reaction and follow-up to an interviewee's comments. For instance, something as simple as beginning to take notes after a comment might be construed as a reaction to the comment. How you react to an interviewee's answer may greatly influence further answers. Do interact with the respondent as an equal; do not talk down to the interviewee. If you are following an unstructured or semi-structured format, do explore the interviewee's answers when needed. Ask for clarification, examples, or any follow-up that you think may help you better understand the issue under discussion. You may ask: what do you mean by, can you provide an example, how so. If you are unsure of what a person is saying, do paraphrase and ask if that interpretation is correct (what I'm hearing you say is…is that right?). If you are not using a structured interview format, follow any other lines of discussion or thoughts the interviewee may bring up that you feel is interesting and pertinent to your study. Remember, this is your time to collect these data. It is generally not possible to revisit an interview—even if you can reconnect with the interviewee, clarifications of tidbits of past conversations are not always doable.

You may want to provide the interviewee with a pad of paper and a writing utensil. Some interviewees like to jot down some ideas for themselves before they answer or to note a thought they want to share in a focus group format. It may also help to have some manipulatives handy, depending on the focus of your interview. If you are asking students to explain their understanding of a particular concept, for example, having things they can use to assist in their explanations is often useful.

Post interview reflections. While you may not usually think of field notes with an interview, it is really useful to record your perceptions of the interview. As soon as possible after the interview itself (for example, immediately after getting into

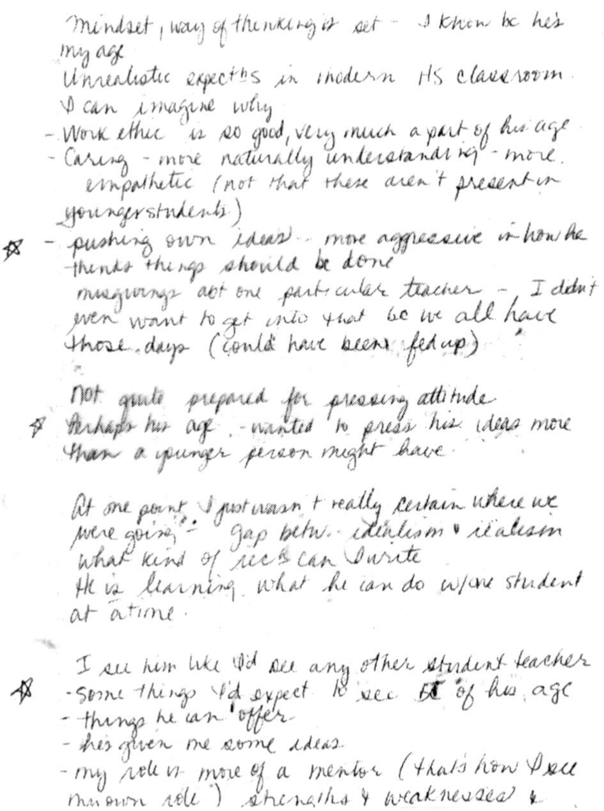

Figure 5-2. Sample post-interview field notes. (Reprinted with permission of Karen Eifler)

your car before leaving the site), write down (or audio record) your reflections on the conversation. Include your perceptions, descriptions, observations, and thoughts that are entering your mind concerning the interview or the problem statement. As an illustration, one of our colleagues was conducting research on non-traditional teacher candidates (Eifler & Potthoff, 1998). A portion of a post-interview field notes can be found in Figure 5-2. If you do decide to record your reflection, these too should be transcribed as soon as you are able. Add them to the end of the transcribed interview so you will have the interview transcript coupled with the interview reflection; this will help in organizing the data for analysis.

Surveys/Questionnaires

Remember that interviews almost always provide richer data than surveys but if your sample is too large or your access to the individuals is too limited to use interviews, an alternative is to use a questionnaire. To keep it qualitative, the survey would consist of open-ended questions rather than directed response type items. (Designing quantitative surveys is discussed in Chapter 10.) You will need to provide informed consent forms with the surveys.

At the start of the survey ask for important demographic information you may need (e.g., age, gender, number of years of teaching). Do not clutter the survey with requests for information you don't need, but this is a difficult call in qualitative research because data gathering often evolves as the study progresses. Remember confidentiality issues; names and other identifying items are generally not requested. At the end of the instrument, it is possible to ask the respondents to voluntarily provide their name and contact information if they are willing to allow you to follow up on their responses, if needed. For pre/post surveys, find a way to pair surveys while ensuring anonymity (as addressed in Chapter 4).

When writing the questions, there are a few things to consider. Since the instrument has to stand alone (you are usually not there to provide any clarification for any of the items), be sure the wording is unambiguous. Keep the questions short in length and be sure that each question only addresses one main idea at a time. Multipart questions generally are not answered completely. Respondents tend to answer one part and ignore or forget about the rest. The number of questions is a concern. If there are too many, respondents will be put off and may choose not to participate in the study. If there are too few, you may not get enough information to do your study justice. Be sure you keep a happy medium. Do not use jargon. As with interview questions, you want the questions to help the respondent focus on a particular area without leading them to a particular response. Do leave sufficient space immediately after the question for a written response.

Consider how you will distribute the surveys and collect them. Be sure both of these are done in a way that will encourage responses but not pose any kind of threat or coercion. For example, if you are doing a study on teacher morale, it may not be best to have the principal distribute the surveys at a faculty meeting and then collect them, if you think the principal might be a factor in causing low faculty morale. Faculty meetings and during a class are good places to have instruments distributed if time is provided for people to complete the survey. Surveys distributed for collection at a later time almost always generate lower response rates. If you cannot personally distribute and collect the tool, developing a relationship with a contact person at the site is always a plus. That person can administer the survey and collect and return the completed surveys to you. This puts a personal face on the request, even if that face is not yours. A central collection envelope that respondents can personally place their completed survey into is a good way to insure confidentiality in responding, too. The survey goes directly from the respondent to the reply envelope, without any middle person handling it. If it is not possible to get all the surveys completed simultaneously, having the envelope in a convenient location is an alternative (the school office by the faculty mailboxes or on the teacher's desk, for example.). Providing separate return envelopes pre-addressed with postage paid will encourage the timely receipt of the completed questionnaires, but can be costly.

There has been research done on the paper color of surveys. The findings are mixed, but some researchers found that certain colors may encourage a greater response rate than others, put the respondents in a more relaxed state of mind, or otherwise positively affect the process. If this is of interest to you, we suggest you do some follow up reading (e.g., Etter, Cucherat, & Perneger, 2002; LaGarce, & Washburn, 1995). If you are doing a pre/post survey, it is a good idea to use two different colors so you can quickly distinguish between the administrations.

There are tools available on the Internet if you are interested in distributing the survey and collecting responses on line. Survey Monkey (www.SurveyMonkey. com) is an example of these types of tools. A problem with this method of data collection is that it is easier to ignore an email request with a web link than a piece of paper with a pleading note.

Another question is whether respondents should be rewarded for completing the survey. Some teachers like to give pencils or some other nominal trinket to students for completing a survey. We have been asked to do surveys in return for coffee cards or gift cards to book stores. In most instances, students do not have funding for these kinds of rewards. And what about the student whose parents do not give permission for participation in the study? Should that student be penalized by not getting a pencil? Is saying "thanks" enough of a reward? Researchers might offer to share their findings with the participants. You can provide a request for contact information on a separate sheet so if the respondents are interested in the final results of the study they can receive them.

As with the interview, it is a good practice to find a mock sample to pilot, or try out, the questionnaire. By doing a trial run, you can get feedback on the quality of the questions, the length of the survey, and the quality of the responses so you can polish the tool before using it for actual data collection.

Imagine you are interested in studying why teachers leave the teaching profession. A few possible open-ended survey questions around this topic are included as Figure 5-3. Please look at the sample before continuing with your reading of this chapter. We will be exploring this tool further in the succeeding paragraphs.

Problem statement: The purpose of this study is investigate why teachers decide to leave the teaching profession.

A few possible survey questions might be:

1. Are there elements in your work with students that might affect your decision to remain a teacher? Please list these.
2. Are there elements in your work with school administrators that might affect your decision to remain a teacher? Please list these.
3. Are there elements in your work with parents that might affect your decision to remain a teacher? Please list these.
4. Are there factors other than those previously listed that might affect your decision to remain a teacher? Please list these.

Figure 5-3. Sample qualitative survey.

Although this survey is designed for teachers, can you think of ways this same survey might be redesigned for building administrators, or counselors? What demographic information might the researcher want from her respondents? Some possibilities include position, grade level, and number of years at that school and in the profession. What questions could be explored from the data collected beside teachers' feelings about the pressures of their work? Some we can think of are: are there differences in teachers by grade level or years of teaching, do more concerns appear around parents or administrators, does the number of recent retirements at each school seem to be related to teacher attitudes? Note that these follow up questions would require some quantitative analyses.

It would be very easy to change this open-ended survey into a closed, quantitative type survey. Revisit Figure 5-3 and see if you can rewrite this as a survey that could be administered and analyzed quantitatively. Compare your rewritten survey with that in Figure 5-4. Sometimes a qualitative survey is administered to a small but varied sample in order to be able to identify items that could/should be included on a quantitative survey. Although there are many ways that quantitative questions could be constructed, our example uses an index that counts the number and types of teacher concerns. The items for the list were developed from responses to the qualitative survey. (Quantitative surveys will be explored more fully in Chapter 10.)

Documents

If you are collecting documentation, be sure to note on the document what it is, when it was received, and how it was collected. Typically you will be working with photocopies rather than originals (teachers generally do not and should not part with original pieces of student work, lesson plans, or other records of their or their student's work.). Recall issues of confidentiality, and be sure you have permission or consent to use what you have collected. If you are using your own students' work and what they are submitting is something that you would regularly collect as a teacher, generally no permission is needed as long as confidentiality is maintained. Identifying references on any and all documents are removed (blacked-out). (Refer to Chapter 2 to review ethical considerations when conducting a study.)

Based on responses that we might get from the qualitative survey (Figure 5.3) a quantitative data gathering tool might look like this:

1. Select each item related to your work with students that might affect your decision to continue to teach:

    _____Discipline problems in the classroom

    _____Student attitudes

    _____Poor quality student work

    _____Poor preparation from earlier grades

    _____Class size

2. Select each item related to your work with school administrators that might affect your decision to continue to teach:

    _____Support with student discipline

    _____Development of school vision

    _____Quality of management decision making

    _____Top-down decision making

3. Select each item related to your work with parents that might affect your decision to continue to teach:

    _____Levels of parental involvement

    _____Interactions with parents

    _____Degree to which parents respond to requests

4. Select each item related to the teaching profession in general that might affect your decision to continue to teach:

    _____Availability of curricular resources

    _____State standards for student achievement

    _____Salary

    _____Time spent outside of regular hours preparing for class

    _____Lack of respect for the profession

    _____Emotional toll of teaching

Figure 5-4. Sample of a quantitative questionnaire made from a qualitative survey.

Sociograms

Sociograms can be used to help you understand relationships among your sample. As described in Chapter 4, you pose a question that is responded to with ranked names of colleagues. You then chart the responses to examine existing relationships. Information for the sociogram is typically collected in one of two ways. You could informally interview individuals, asking the question and getting names, or you could also pass out a response sheet that has the question written and instructs the students to provide their choices. Once you are armed with the data, you can draw the resulting sociogram. You can do this by hand or by the computer using any number of graphing programs. Start with any respondent. Write the name (or enclose it in a shape like in a concept map) and draw arrows to that respondent's three choices. You would use different types of lines to indicate first, second and third choice connections between the names. For example, use a bold or heavy line for first choice, a light line for second, and a dotted for third. There are also free concept map drawing programs available online (e.g., http://www.phenotyping.com/ sociogram/ Lewejohann, 2005).

Overall Considerations

As you plan your study, you need to decide what you think you should collect as data sources. Remember, it is better to collect too much than too little. You can always choose not to examine all that you have, but it is often difficult to add to what you have at a later date. As you collect data, you may find that you need to alter your methods. This is fine. For instance, you may decide that you need observations in addition to the interviews or that you want to see written lesson plans. Collect what you think you need and then revise your methods section accordingly. If themes and trends become identifiable as you collect data, make notes on these and focus on those you feel are most useful as you continue to collect data. For instance, if you are observing gender bias in instruction, you may find that males get different levels of questions than females. While this will cause you to pay greater attention to teacher generated questions and take more copious notes on questioning strategies, do not focus solely on this aspect of instruction too quickly. Remember that the purpose of qualitative research is to generate a hypothesis. Do not narrow your observations or exclude something you feel may be a bit off topic too early in the study.

When collecting data, ensure that you have sufficient evidence to support whatever claims you will make. Be sure to collect a variety of types of evidence (recall triangulation from Chapter 4). Do not rush through interviews or observations. Do not unnecessarily limit the time you spend with your sample. The more time you spend observing and/or interacting with the sample, the more data you can collect, and the richer that data typically will be; and the more trustworthy (valid and reliable) your findings will be. As you collect data and come up with possible assertions, see if future data confirms or disconfirms these assertions. Finally, do not be afraid to adjust your methods or your question if you feel either or both are needed.

LIMITATIONS

All studies have **limitations.** Limitations are conditions that make the outcomes of the study less than perfect; that is, factors that might either have biased or otherwise affected the results and/or generalizability of the study. We have already discussed that qualitative studies tend not to be generalizable. Limitations of qualitative research always include that the sample size is small, and it is not a random sample. By fully describing the sample selection and the rationale for choosing the study sample, we address some of these limitations inherent in this type of research. Our findings may be similar for similar samples, but not the population at large. Another common limitation in qualitative studies is the use of **self-report data.** If surveys and interviews make up the bulk of data for a study, for example, the findings are based almost solely on what the participants say. What is said (that is, self-reported) may not be the same as what actually is. A person's perceptions do not always match the reality. A teacher may think they do a great job of using follow up questions to probe a student's understanding while an observer may record that the teacher may use one or two very directing questions before supplying a response. This is another reason triangulation becomes important in qualitative research. There may be limitations specific to your study. Perhaps you did not receive permission to interview your number one choices and had to settle for "second best" interviewees as your sample. Maybe schedule changes limited the number of observations you were able to make. Perhaps there was a fire drill during your focus interview and the flow of the conversation was hard to resume. As you prepare your methods section, think about what limitations may be inherent in your study, how you might be able to avoid them, and definitely keep track of them, so you can report the limitations. In general, the reason to focus on the limitations of your study at this point is to overcome as many of those limitations as you can. Even though there will be necessary limitations to your study, it will not improve the case you make in the report of your research to say that one of your limitations was one that was "self-inflicted" and could have been avoided with a little forethought. We will address limitations again with quantitative data and in the writing of Chapter 5 of our research report.

PILOT STUDY

A useful tool in research is the use of a **pilot study.** This is like a mini pre-study. It is a great way to try out interview questions, surveys, practice observational skills, and the like. In a pilot study, a researcher chooses a small sample similar to the one they plan to use in their actual study. For example, if a researcher plans to distribute a survey to third grade students in their school, they may find a third grade class in a neighboring district to act as "guinea pigs." These third graders would take the survey and a handful could be asked if they had any trouble reading and/or understanding any of the questions. The survey responses could be examined to see if the answers address the intent of the questions. Based on this trial, the survey could be adjusted to address any problems or confusion. Piloting is a way to provide hindsight before the fact! Remember not to use respondents who may be in your final study in the pilot.

Pilot studies are used with both qualitative and quantitative (and mixed) research designs. It is also a way to add to the validity and reliability of data collection tools. And, as noted above, pilot studies can be used as a way to establish questions you might want to ask in a different form later. In that case, the pilot study acts as a small qualitative study that serves the purpose of helping you in the survey design of a quantitative study (as with Figures 5-3 and 5-4).

WRITING A METHODS CHAPTER

Chapter Three is the Methods Chapter of a research report. It provides the reader with a description of the research sample, data collection techniques, and proposed data analysis plans. You now have the tools to write most of your Chapter Three.

While this may seem repetitive, Chapter Three generally starts with a verbatim restatement of your problem statement. It is followed by a description of the project setting. The reader should have a clear understanding of the context of the research, especially for qualitative studies. Beginning writers often try to describe everything they know about the context. Focus on the elements of the context of the study that are truly relevant to your study. Be careful, though, that you have not omitted important characteristics that your reader is likely to want to understand. Remember that in qualitative research the focus of the study may change somewhat as you are gathering data. That means that describing the important characteristics of the context may have to wait until you are quite well along with your data collection and analysis.

Whom are you studying? The sample, as well as the method of sample selection, needs to be fully described. This portion of the chapter should not only familiarize the reader with the sample, but convince the reader that your sample is appropriate for the research question. Demographic information needs to be presented. Explain and describe any other elements of the context of your study that were not described already that will help the reader understand how the sample was selected. In addition, your role and responsibilities in relation to the sample and in conducting the research also need to be clearly explained. Are you a participant, an observer, both? What is your relationship to the sample? Are you the classroom teacher, a colleague, a teacher in the building, a stranger? If you are a stranger how did you get access to the sample? Do you have preconceptions about the outcome and/or a reason for conducting the study that may influence you as you conduct the research? Too much detail and rich description is better than too little or too scant. (Your advisor can always help you revise the draft if you are overly descriptive.)

The methods you plan to use for conducting the research must be described and explained. Will you be observing? When, how many times, and for how long? How will you take notes? If you are interviewing, are your interviews semi-structured, audio-taped, individual or focus group? How were your interview questions developed and what or who influenced your choice of questions? Any instruments or interview questions that you will use should to be included in the chapter or referenced and appended to the research report. Are you doing a pilot study? With whom? Why?

Any reader should be able to replicate your study by using the details you provide in this chapter. Several samples of students' work are in Appendix 5-1.

The only portion of the Methods Chapter that you are not yet ready to write is what you will do to make sense of your data. You will need to describe exactly how your data will be analyzed. You will be able to add this to your draft after reading the analysis chapters in this text.

YOUR RESEARCH PROPOSAL

If you have ever considered applying for a grant, agencies typically put out an RFP—a **request for proposals.** If at your institution you have a committee that will pass judgment on your research proposal, you typically provide all members with a copy of your proposal before proceeding with data collection. If your school district and/or university have an Institutional Review Board, they generally require a copy of your research proposal. So, what is a proposal?

A **proposal** is the first three chapters of your research report. It includes your introduction (what your problem statement/research question is and why it is important), literature review (an examination of what others have done in the area and "proof" that you have the theoretical understanding you need to be successful researching in this area), and the methods (what, specifically, you plan to do to answer your research question). If you have a faculty advisor, that person has probably been very involved from page one of your proposal. Other committee members generally will wait until you have a complete proposal drafted before commenting on your study. Be sure you get approval from your faculty advisor, committee, IRB, and/or building principal before proceeding on to data collection! Feedback on planning is more useful than a critique of a completed project. You can act on feedback received on a proposal.

NEXT STEPS

You are now equipped with a sound background in choosing a research problem and reviewing literature about your topic. You have been given information on what you would need to do to collect data for a qualitative study. Future chapters will provide information on how to conduct a quantitative research study. You may want to finish reading about data collection techniques before finalizing your research question. After learning about quantitative methodologies, you will be in a better position to decide if your research question could be addressed best with a qualitative, quantitative, or mixed methods study. If you decide to collect qualitative data, Chapter 6 provides instruction on how to analyze that type of data.

CHAPTER SELF-CHECK

Having completed this chapter, you should be comfortable discussing the following:
- selecting a sample
- tips when using field notes and personal journals as data sources
- designing and conducting an interview
- creating and administering surveys
- working with documents as data sources
- study limitations
- use of pilot studies
- organizing and writing Chapter Three
- research proposals

CHAPTER REVIEW QUESTIONS

1. What is a sample of convenience?
2. What is a purposeful sample?
3. What advice would you give to a new researcher who is conducting an interview for the first time?
4. Write four questions you might use if you were interviewing teachers to learn how they feel about state mandated annual testing for ESOL students using instruments not written in their primary language.
5. Why are post-interview reflections needed?
6. List several considerations when creating and administering a questionnaire.
7. What is meant by limitations of a study?
8. Why would a researcher conduct a pilot study?
9. What is generally included in a research proposal?

REFERENCES

Eifler K. E., & Potthoff, D. E. (1998). Non-traditional teacher candidates: A synthesis of the literature. *Journal of Teacher Education, 49*(3), 187–195.

Etter, J. F., Cucherat, M., & Perneger, T. V. (2002). Questionnaire color and response rates to mailed surveys: A randomized trial and a meta-analysis. *Evaluation & the Health Professions, 25*(2), 185–199.

LaGarce, R., & Washburn, J. (1995). An investigation into the effects of questionnaire format and color variation on mail survey response rates. *Journal of Technical Writing and Communication, 25*(1), 57–70.

Lewejohann, L. (2005). *Sociogram* (Version 1.0). [Computer software]. http://www.phenotyping.com/sociogram/

ANALYZING DATA

Qualitative Methodologies

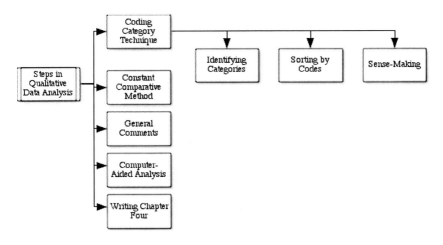

CHAPTER OVERVIEW

Chapter Six provides the instruction for analyzing qualitative data. It will deal with two basic qualitative analysis techniques: coding categories and constant comparisons. Additionally, it will provide instruction on both amending the methods section (to include method of analysis) and writing a results section for a quailtative study.

INTRODUCTION

Let's visit a Greek play. It tells the story of a young man, raised by royalty who learns that he may have been adopted. The young man goes on a personal quest to find himself. During his travels, he meets an ornery stranger. The stranger hits the young man and, in defense (and in accordance with the social norms at the time), the young man kills the stranger. Later in his journey, the young man successfully answers the riddle of a mythical creature that was threatening the city of Thebes. Because of his wit and bravery, the young man was offered the throne of Thebes and married the widowed queen.

How would you characterize the young man? Was he clever or just lucky? Was he courageous or impulsive? Does it sound like the story of a young lad who made out well?

The story takes on a different light if we know that the young man in the story is Sophocles' Oedipus. This would make the stranger his biological father and the King of Thebes. In killing him, Oedipus widowed the Queen of Thebes; and the Queen, who became his wife, was actually his mother. What are the implications of leaving out these details? Would this affect your characterization of the young man?

Making sense of your qualitative data is similar to interpreting the story line of the play. You will have in your possession compilations of interview transcripts and/or survey responses and/or field notes and/or other miscellaneous documents and pieces of information. You will need to try to make sense of them—and in a way that provides a true depiction of what actually occurred. And, you will need to support your assertions using evidence from your data set so your readers will accept your findings as valid.

Regardless of the type(s) of data you collect, qualitative analyses are typically done by reading and rereading the data and finding common themes that emerge from the data. Different names are sometimes applied to the specific qualitative methods depending on the type of data being analyzed (e.g., **discourse analysis** for interviews, **content analysis** for documents), but all qualitative analyses are inductive and involve the same primary steps. All methods texts recommend the use of coding and categorizing qualitative data (e.g., Bodgan & Biklen, 2006; Creswell, 2008; Gay, Mills, & Airasian, 2009). We prefer the terminology put forth by Bogdan and Biklen (2006), **coding categories**, to describe the analytical methodology because that is a true description of the actual process. You read the data and decide on categories in which to organize the data, and then code the data using those categories. Data analysis can be done once all the data have been collected or while data are being collected. We will first apply the methods to the situation where you have collected all the data. Then we will show how the steps can be modified for on-going analysis.

STEPS TO DATA ANALYSIS

Many biology teachers teach the classification system by having their students each place one of their shoes in a pile. The students then decide on a way to classify (organize) the shoe collection. Some may decide to first sort the shoes by how they close: laces, slip-ons, other (e.g., buckles, Velcro). Others may do it by material: cloth, leather, or synthetic. Perhaps the students might separate shoes by type: sandal, sneaker, casual, sports. Which classification is correct? Is one better than another? Analyzing your qualitative data is the same. There are probably multiple ways to categorize your data, and no one way is better than any other. What matters is that what you do makes sense to your study and you can share that "sense making" with others.

Qualitative data analysis can be outlined as followed:

1. organize the data;
2. read through the data and familiarize yourself with what you have collected;
3. generate a list of the main themes or codes;
4. go through the data again, assigning codes to data sections;

5. determine if you have overlapping codes, need additional codes, or have too many;
6. revise your coding categories, if needed, and reread/recode the data;
7. sort the data by codes;
8. make sense of your coded, separated data.

There are two preliminary steps to do *before* you begin any qualitative data analysis. When you are printing hard copies of your field notes, interview transcripts, or other data you have gathered, format the page so you have a wide margin on one side of the page. This will provide you with space to jot notes or identify sections for coding. Then, make at least one additional copy of your data set; place the originals in a folder in a safe place and work with the copy. (You may wish to make a few copies at the outset.) It is a good idea to have a "clean copy" so if you need to redo your categorizing or you prefer to do some actual cutting and pasting (we will explain this shortly), you will always have an untouched data set available as a template.

CODING CATEGORIES

Let's go through the steps one at a time. Sample data is provided in Figure 6-1 to help you to familiarize yourself with and practice this coding category methodology. The data are responses to the following open-ended question: "Think back on an undergraduate math course where you feel you really learned. What was it about this experience that worked so well for you?" The respondents were undergraduate seniors and Master of Arts in Teaching (5th year) students who were engaged in student teaching (Morrell, 2000).

Survey Question: Think back on an undergraduate math course where you feel you really learned. What was it about this experience that worked so well for you?

Responses:
– Environment-positive Prof., OK to ask questions.
– Hands-on experience, including manipulatives, and working in-groups.
– The teacher was so in tune with the students. She was excited about math and taught it in a simple way that everyone could understand. Manipulatives and candy still make math fun and interesting to adults.
– I took applied math so it worked well with my needs. I could use the math skills applied to my previous degree.
– More than one way of learning was taught.
– Group work, team work games and stories.
– Was using hands on objects.
– We worked with manipulatives with groups.
– Course that allowed me to have hands-on, based more on manipulative rather than lecture method.
– An atmosphere of acceptance.
– The instructor was wonderful and patient.

Figure 6-1. Portion of survey data for practice analysis.

119

- My instructor strongly encouraged and accepted any response we had to math. We worked in-groups and used manipulatives and my instructor had enthusiasm for the class of students to do well, personal interest in us.
- The teacher really valued the students and their questions, used lots of manipulatives and related and connected things to life.
- I didn't feel that I learned anything.
- I don't feel like I have expanded my math knowledge since high school.
- Professor was excited about material, wanted us to be excited about it and explained things simply, easy to understand.
- I learned from a lecture method because that was all that was offered. I would have liked more hands-on instruction.
- Very little cooperative learning.
- A teacher who was receptive to the needs of the student.
- Small class.
- It did not.
- Pure theory, all proofs, no arithmetic which was considered trivial.
- None stands out
- Not much of anything except where to look up formula.
- Gave me a good understanding of math that I use in everyday life.
- We broke up into small groups/ students were asked to actively participate.
- Good instructors.
- I have never learned anything in math.
- I do not feel I learned a great deal. It was kind of a review, but many concepts I did not understand.

Figure 6-1. Portion of survey data for practice analysis. (Continued)

Organize the Data

Before you begin to analyze data, it is usually helpful to organize your data first. You may want to organize it by type (interview transcripts, questionnaires, field notes). Or you may choose to do it by date. You may want to do it by groups or individuals. As an example of the latter, if you are doing observations of five classrooms and interviewing the teachers, you may want to group the lesson plans, field notes, and interview notes for each observation/session and then arrange those chronologically. Whatever makes the most sense to you is what you should do. Just note why you organized the data in that fashion. You will need to explain this reasoning in the methods section of your paper.

For our exemplar, the data were from a questionnaire that was distributed to a large number of elementary, middle, and secondary student teachers, which included both undergraduate and graduate level students. We targeted student teachers who would be teaching mathematics and/or science to their students. Because we had few middle level student teachers in the study, we grouped the middle and secondary students together. We organized them by college program and certification

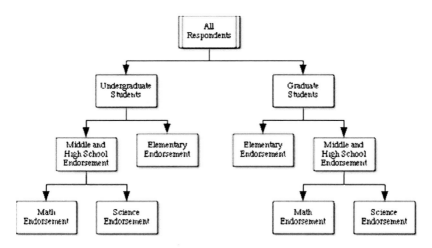

Figure 6-2. Concept map showing how data were divided.

level; that is, we grouped the undergraduates and graduate students separately and in those two sets, we subgrouped the elementary student teachers and the middle/high student teachers. In the middle/high sets, we further subdivided the data by content area (mathematics vs. science). This would allow us to determine if there were differences in the responses among those different segments of the population. (See Figure 6-2.)

Read through the Data

Once you have organized your data, you need to set aside a large block of time to familiarize yourself with what you collected. It is generally recommended that you give yourself enough time to read at least one set of the data that you have grouped. We concur that reading small bits of data at a time will not provide you with a sufficient grounding for the themes emerging from your data. It's like watching a feature length film in 15-minute segments. You don't follow the action as well as if you view it in one sitting. Your first time through the data is just to familiarize yourself with what you have.

After your first read through, read through the data again; but this time, start to "dissect" the data. Try to identify main themes. Write notes in the margins. Underline or highlight what you think may be important. Note your initial impressions. Do as many read-throughs as you need to feel comfortable with what you have collected. Please take some time now and familiarize yourself with the data in Figure 6-1.

Identify and List Categories

Make a list of the main themes or codes that emerge from your reading of the data. Look at your notes and impressions to help you in generating this list. You will soon be reading the data again, assigning codes to different sections. You may find it easier to do this if you abbreviate the codes.

Refer to the sample data. What categories do *you* see emerging from the sample data set? Some initial themes we saw were relevance, background knowledge, good modeling, poor modeling, active learning, passive learning, and characteristics of the professor. Did you see some of these? Did you have others?

Assign Codes

Read through the data again, this time assigning codes to the different sections. Write the codes in the margins where they apply. If you are into visuals, you may want to "color code" the data by using different colored highlighters for different categories. (Make sure you have a key of what color is what category.) Do the codes fit? Did you code everything you underlined as important in your earlier readings? Do you need to add codes? Are there pieces of data that fit more than one category? Do you have too many categories to handle? Do some of the codes seem to overlap?

Revise your coding categories, if needed. For example, we decided (based on our total data set rather than the excerpt provided) that we had a number of codes about specific personal characteristics of instructors. These were things like: patient, open to questions, enthusiastic, felt spoken down to, and created an atmosphere that intimidated students and made them uncomfortable asking questions. While there were many individual comments and the specifics varied, these all dealt with instructor characteristics. We felt we could combine these types of comments into one category. Other categories were fine as they were, e.g., relevance. It is easier to work with fewer codes; however, do not try to condense everything or you risk losing sight of subgroups and may lose some of the richness of your data.

It is possible that a piece of data may fit comfortably into more than one category. It is fine to "multi-code" it. Likewise, do not try to "force" data into a category. If you need a new one, go ahead and add it.

The number of themes you identify will be based on your research. Sometimes only three or four major themes will appear. Sometimes it will seem like data cannot be comfortably coded into fewer that seven or eight themes. When the latter happens you need to go back and focus on your problem statement. Are you finding themes that really don't relate to your problem? Is it possible that you have separated data into separate themes based on relatively minor distinctions? Can several of your coding categories be collapsed into a more general one? Usually, data even on larger qualitative studies settle into six or fewer major themes.

If you needed to adjust your original set of coding categories, you will need to go through the data again, and reassign codes. (Do you see now why you may need multiple sets of data, and having a "clean" set is necessary?) You may need to do this more than once until you feel comfortable that the codes you have decided on accurately organize and reflect what you are finding in your data sets. Figure 6-3 depicts part of a coded set.

prof
Clasoc ◆ The professor made time for question to be asked in the class and he made
every attempt to help everyone to understand the material.

none ◆ none stands out

◆ I took a math course where the teacher had us doing journal writing and
strat
man.p. explain not only our answers but how we got our answers. In this class we
relevance brought in articles from newspaper which contained some kind of math
problem for us to apply to real life. In this class we were encouraged to think
like our students would. We used blocks and other obj. to work through our
problems.

know ◆ Gave me a good understanding of math that I use in everyday life.

prof char. ◆ The instructor was very approachable and helpful.

strat. manip. ◆ Using manipulatives, small group discussions.
groups
strat. groups ◆ We broke up into small groups/ students were asked to actively participate.

prof char. ◆ The instructor was very approachable and helpful.

strat. ◆ The teacher gave direct instruction and explained our questions in simple
prof char terms and provided quick feedback so I could learn from my mistakes.

strat. manip. Hands on learning, repetition

strat. ◆ Teachers always had interesting activities for us to do.

pacing ◆ Allowed to work at own pace and individually, but at the same time support
was provided for any questions.

pacing ◆ I was able to work at my own pace.

none ◆ Did not have such an experience.

stud. ◆ I actually went to class.

none ◆ I don't feel I learned anything from any of my math classes-both instructors
were terrible.

none ◆ Nothing, I had a very strong math background from high school and took
very basic classes in college.

strat ◆ Working in groups and talking problems out.
groups,
disc?

Figure 6-3. Portion of a coded set of data. .

Sort the Data by Codes

When we report our findings, we tend to do it by sharing the major themes that we induced from our reading of the data. This is easier to do if we sort the categorized data by the codes we assigned to them. Some people are more comfortable doing this physically. They actually cut out the pieces of data that reflect the different codes and place examples of each code into a different folder. Others prefer to cut the pieces and paste them onto note cards, then bundle the note cards by category. If you choose to do either of these cut and paste methods, do note on each piece from where in the original data set the piece comes. Use abbreviations for ease, for example, I1p4 may mean interview one, page 4. (Be sure to write down your codes so you don't forget them later.) This will be extremely helpful if you need to view the excerpt in context later. Do the same even if you cut and paste using computer applications. Using color-coding for different categories makes it easy to sort while keeping the data sets intact. Do what you think you will be most comfortable doing. If you have a piece of data that is multi-coded, you will either need multiple copies of that piece of data to place in different folders or on different note cards. If you use highlighters, you can mark the margins with two colors.

We have tried to do this on computers by color-coding in Microsoft Word or by copying and pasting pieces of text from one place into a different place in the document that represents a theme. You may be comfortable doing this, but the iterative nature of this process makes doing this on the computer a bit confusing and you may be left with a more shallow analysis than you would have using colored markers or scissors. And, one more time, if you are doing this on a computer be sure that a saved original version exists because after numerous edits of your data set it will become impossible to go backwards.

Working with Multiple Data Sources

If you collected data from multiple sources, you need to examine each set of data separately and then collectively. Do the themes that emerge from one set match those from another? Do the findings support each other or are they contradictory? For example, let's say you are interested in what teaching strategies elementary teachers employ. You interviewed teachers about the strategies they use and also collected a random sample of weekly lesson plans. After coding the interview data and the lesson plans, match the findings. If teachers say they frequently use inquiry, do the plans support that? Do the teachers' verbal comments match their written plans or is there a disconnect? Triangulate your findings using the variety of data sources. Make note of when the multiple sources support an idea or asser- tion (confirming data) and when they do not (disconfirming data).

Working with Your Coded Data

Once you have your data coded and sorted, you will be able to write your discussion of your findings. In quantitative papers, this entire process is generally broken into two chapters: the results and the discussion/conclusion. The results chapter would show primarily the statistical findings. Making sense of them and discussing the findings would be in the last chapter. With qualitative research, the findings make no sense without a discussion. The "sense making" cannot be separated from the "findings." They are intertwined. Specifics on how to write the results/discussion section will be discussed after we talk about a slightly different analytical approach.

CONSTANT COMPARATIVE APPROACH

What if your data collection design allows you to begin to analyze the data while you are still in the process of collecting data? Let's say that rather than relying heavily on the administration of an open-ended questionnaire, you are doing a series of observations and interviews. Should you wait until all data are collected before you begin to try to make sense of what you are observing? The answer is an obvious no (since you probably cannot distance your mind from what you are seeing and you are mulling things over in your mind anyway!).

Your data analysis design would be similar to coding categories but since it is an on-going process, your analysis would more closely follow the **constant comparative method** (Glaser & Strauss, 1967). In this method, as you collect the data, you begin your coding and sense making. As you continue to collect data, you continually refine your coding system and sense making. Do the initial categories work? Do you need more? Less? Can you refine them? As you continue to collect data, you continue to modify your categories to best fit what is evolving with the new data. Are the preliminary hypotheses you were developing the same? Do they need to be reformulated? Do you need to gather additional information or different information to confirm or refute what hypotheses you are formulating? In this process, you are constantly comparing your preliminary findings and on-going analyses with your new data, hence the name of the method: constant comparative. While this is a cyclic process, if you would like steps to follow in this method of data analysis, the process might look like this:

1. Make your initial observations;
2. Develop preliminary coding categories that capture what you are observing;
3. Make additional observations, paying particular attention to see if your preliminary ideas are supported;
4. Are the coding categories still applicable? If not, refine the categories and hypotheses as needed;
5. Continue until you are satisfied that your hypotheses are fully refined and supported by the data.

Keep notes of what categories/hypotheses you discarded and modified and why. You can use that in your written analyses as you convey your interpretations of your findings to your readers. As a caution you can bias your observations by trying to *see* in terms of categories that you have established early in the process. Using consistent observational strategies may help avoid this.

As mentioned earlier in the text, often the way to know if you have gathered enough information in a qualitative study is to recognize that the information you are gathering starts to repeat itself. Your new data does not provide you with any new information. Constant comparative methods can help you see when this is happening.

For a fun example of the application of a constant comparative approach, read the excerpt from an article in *The Chronicle of Higher Education* in Figure 6-4 (Lang, 2004).

We have often noticed, as we stroll down the hallways of academic buildings, how the doors of the faculty beckon to us – with whispers and insinuations, exhortations and declamations, jeers and jests – via a motley collection of decorations: cartoons, articles, quotations, posters, advertisements, photographs, and artwork.

What motivates such postings by that increasingly threatened species, the North American professor? How do those office doors reflect upon the professors or the disciplines in which they study and teach? To whom are the collections of postings addressed?... we have undertaken to answer these questions with further research into the ways in which faculty offices and office behavior can help us classify the various members of this elusive species...

We began our new study with the hypothesis that office-door decorations would reflect the occupant's discipline: Education professors would offer study tips to students; philosophers would select thought-provoking quotes from Plato or Aristotle; art historians would showcase posters from local exhibits.

We found some initial confirmation of that hypothesis in the wing of a building that houses faculty members in the business school. A specialist in international business, for example, had photographs and postcards from nations around the globe, along with a photograph of Campbell's soup cans labeled in different languages.

A colleague of hers, who no doubt focuses his teaching and research on time management and negotiating skills, posted this announcement to all comers: "Mandatory Reading: Top Ten Reasons to Get Thrown Out of Prof. D's Office." The list included such verboten activities as "Ask if the exams are corrected yet" and "Ask to be signed into one of his closed courses."

But while this hypothesis held true in the business wing, it was not well-supported by our observations in other departments.

Surely the art and music departments – known for their creative expression – would feature the most varied, creative, and interesting doors.

Not so. With one minor exception, the doors of the art and music faculty members were bare.

"Too much pressure," one member of the species commented, by way of explanation. "Whatever they put on their doors, people will think they're showcasing it as great art. If it's not an original Picasso, they're not hanging it."

Despite the plausible explanation, we decided not to hang onto that hypothesis in the face of patchy evidence. We shifted instead to the more mundane possibility that office doors simply reflect the personalities of the faculty members...

Figure 6-4. Example of constand comparative method in action.

A professor in the English department who came to academic consciousness in the '60s, and who teaches courses in the literature of social responsibility and peace studies, uses her door to promote those causes. Postcards with rainbows and flowers, overarched by the word "Peace"; a sticker for Amnesty International; a sticker proclaiming her office a "Lesbian, Gay, and Bisexual Safe Zone"; and various quotes from religious and peace activists like Gandhi blossom across her door in varied and colorful patterns.

A theologian who wears a pious and serious demeanor around campus, but who will occasionally allow colleagues glimpses of a wicked sense of humor, features just two items on his door: a postcard memorializing the martyrs of his religious order, and a cartoon in which a man is ordering dinner for himself and his dining companion, a large fly, in a French restaurant. After he places an elaborate order of gourmet cuisine for himself, the man in the cartoon finishes with: "and bring some shit for my fly."

A senior philosophy professor who once purchased advertising space in the campus newspaper to publish abstruse musings on the nature of being, and who encourages his students to pursue such abstruse musings, decorates his door with newspaper articles on ... well, abstruse musings. "New Ideas on the Mystery of How Anesthetics Work," announces a headline on his door from a 1994 *New York Times* article, one sure to perplex any student who finds himself stuck with nothing to read while he awaits his appointed conference time.

The linguist down the hall plasters a wide array of cartoons, articles, and sayings about the nature of language on every inch of his door. Our favorite: "I just can't shake the feeling," says a parrot to his owner in a *Bizarro* cartoon by Dan Piraro, "that I don't really understand language as an abstract concept, but am merely imitating syllables as a trained response."

Some faculty members use their doors for more overtly political reasons – the very same professors, it will come as no surprise, who take an active role in political debates on campus...

Still, in the end, we discovered that personality type was also not a reliable predictor of office-door type. The most gregarious member of our department, who can buttonhole colleagues for 40-minute conversations on the way to the photocopier, has nothing on her door but her name, classes, and schedule of office hours.

Our final hypothesis suggested that what determines the nature of office-door decoration is the faculty member's conception of audience: How they decorate their door, in other words, depends upon the reader or viewer to whom they believe their office door is addressed: students, colleagues, administrators, the promotion and tenure committee, and/or visitors.

Figure 6-4. Example of constand comparative method in action. (Continued)

Most faculty members seem to use their doors to send messages to their students: The philosopher wants them to reflect on philosophical questions. The linguist wants them to see how wordplay and humor can be enriched by the study of linguistics. The theologian and the historian – at opposite ends of the political spectrum – are hoping to raise the consciousness of their students about current issues, and persuade them to think politically in a certain way.

Many faculty members use their doors to promote coming events for students, such as conferences or off-campus trips and activities.

A corollary decoration, in this category, consists of the photographs of the faculty member with students on such off-campus trips, inspiring student-observers to wonder and dream whether they, too, might one day earn a spot in an office-door photograph.

But while this loose conception of the student as audience can catch the majority of door-decoration styles – and hence may be too imprecise to be useful – it does not account for them all. Some professors, for example, clearly use their doors to send messages to their colleagues or to the administration about their productivity.

Witness, in this vein, the political scientist whose three postings all concern events at which he served as one of the keynote speakers. Or consider one of the decorations on the door of this very researcher, who has a postcard of his most recent book tucked just above the handle...

In the end, while the audience hypothesis seems the most potentially fruitful of the ones we have considered, the categories remain too broad. Further research and study might indicate specific types of students, for example, that professors imagine their doors to address.

One final door we encountered will prove challenging to the most astute researcher in this field, and to any hypothesis that proposes the audience as a category. In addition to the photographs of students, the *Far Side* cartoons, the quotes from great literary works, the promotion of local literary events and course offerings, the conference sign-up sheet, and the list of his class times and office hours, this peculiar specimen had taped, just above his nameplate, a dog biscuit...

"Come in," this door seemed to proclaim joyously to all passersby, both human and canine: "I have something for everyone in here!"

Hence although none of our hypotheses has been able to account fully for the door-decorating strategies of the North American professor, we have laid some basic groundwork for future research, and welcome the contributions of other readers in the field...

Figure 6-4. Example of constand comparative method in action. (Continued)

(*Source*: Lang, J.M. (June 11, 2004). Flamboyant features of the academic habitat. *The Chronicle of Higher Education*. C1, C3. Reprinted with permission.)

BACK TO THE METHODS CHAPTER/PROPOSAL

You may recall that when we talked about how to write a research proposal and how to write your Chapter 3: Methods, we said you were almost done with that last piece. What was missing was the section on how you were going to analyze your data. If you are doing a qualitative or mixed methods study, you can now finish or add to your methods section. For your qualitative data, you will probably be analyzing your data either by using a coding category procedure or using a constant comparative methodology. State which method you will be using and a brief (one to several sentences) description of the method. See Figure 6-5 for examples of how this might be written.

EXAMPLE 1 (REPRINTED WITH PERMISSION OF SHERILYN MOONEY)

Initial and final survey data will be examined for emergent patterns and analyzed using coding categories as described in Hubbard and Power (2003). On-going analysis of observed student reactions to journaling and archived copies of journal entries will also occur following the constant comparative method outlined in Hubbard and Power (2003). Conclusions will be based on triangulation of these various data sources (survey responses, teacher observational notes, and journal entries).

EXAMPLE 2 (REPRINTED WITH PERMISSION OF APRIL CRYSLER)

As well as the analysis planned for these data, I hope this journaling process allows me to get to know my students better and faster than in previous semesters and, as a result, allows me to adapt anything in my class to help students or an individual student. Once the data are collected, I will be using the coding category technique described in Bogdan and Biklen (2006) to make sense of the data.

EXAMPLE 3 (REPRINTED WITH PERMISSION OF KEN SZOPA)

The data collection techniques will include journaling my perceptions of the Wellness Center, what people in the building are saying about the Center, and what if anything has changed about the teachers (e.g. their energy level, enthusiasm, attendance, zest for teaching as a result of participating in the Wellness Center). In addition, all teachers will be asked to complete an open ended questionnaire at the end of October and again at the end of March. Data from the two questionnaires will be compared to note any changes over time. In addition, volunteers will participate in a semi-structured interview in late March. Interview questions will focus on the benefits of an on-site Wellness Center, the impact it has had on the individual, and why he/she uses the center. Interview data will be used to augment and add validity to my observational data. The interview data will be analyzed using the emergent category methodology outlined in Hubbard and Power (2003).

Figure 6-5. Examples of methods sections showing analysis plan.

GENERAL COMMENTS ABOUT DATA ANALYSIS AND COLLECTION

It is important to remember that in qualitative research, you are often the main data collection tool. As you are interviewing, you may find the initial list of questions you generated is not wholly adequate to capture the information you want. Feel free to change the interview protocol. Maybe you feel you need to collect artifacts you had not considered. Collect them. Make notes about what changes you made and why and include that in your final paper.

As you collect data, you may find that there is a sub-question arising that you really are more interested in exploring fully than your original proposal question. If you have the time, feel free to change the focus of your paper. Remember, we said qualitative research is evolutionary. As we collect information and start making sense of what we are finding, we often see the question differently. It is fine to modify our research methods as we go. Go back and modify the methods section of your final research report accordingly to reflect what you are actually doing.

If your original plan seems to be working, that's great. Don't feel things need to change. Just remember it is ok to modify plans as you go or keep them the same if they are working. You may also not be in a position to change your data collection tools. If you used an open ended questionnaire, for example, you generally cannot send out a revised version. As you analyze what you collected, think about what you would do differently if you could do it again. These will be included in the final chapter of your research report.

As you analyze your data, think back to your conceptual framework. Use that framework to help you as a lens through which to view your data. Always keep your research question in mind. How is what you are examining helping you to address that problem statement?

COMPUTER-AIDED DATA ANALYSIS TECHNIQUES

As you may have come to realize, qualitative data analysis is a very time consuming process. We would be remiss if we did not tell you that computer software programs exist to assist the qualitative researcher with data analysis. Two of the more common pieces of software are NUDIST and ATLAS TI. Before you think about running out and purchasing a copy, there are several things to consider. The first is you need time to learn how to use a program. And speaking from experience, it is not as easy as learning a new word processing tool! Another consideration is it is only a tool. While having the right tools makes the job easier, having the right tools does not automatically make you a master craftsman. Likewise, you need a firm understanding of qualitative data analysis before being able to maximize the use of the program. Consider how often you will use the program. Will it be worth your monetary and time investment (qualitative analysis software is generally not cheap)? In addition, much of the power these programs provide can be duplicated, admittedly with more effort involved, by using traditional word processing or spreadsheet software.

Finally, you should not deprive yourself of the experience of mulling over your data, coding, recoding, and interpreting your findings. Human eyes and what you bring to the data analysis having been the research tool cannot be replicated by software. These electronic tools can be wonderful aids once you learn to use them, but we recommend you have the actual experiences of data coding and analysis first before looking for the efficiency these tools may provide.

MAKING SENSE OF YOUR CODED DATA

What do you do now that you have "digested" your data and have stacks or folders or piles of coded data bits? You need to make sense of this so you can interpret the findings for both yourself and others. Gay et al. (2009) provide three guiding questions that we find most helpful:

1. "What is important in the data?
2. Why is it important?
3. What can be gained by it?" (p. 245)

Not every piece of data you collected is important to share. Look for the general patterns and themes that emerge from your data. Are there linkages or threads among the categories of responses? What are the commonalities? What is the big picture that is emerging? What light has been shed on your research question? What hypotheses can you generate?

Refer to our sample question concerning students' beliefs about their college classes (Figure 6-1). We received a large number of comments that we felt represented different types of teaching strategies and classroom activities; e.g., note taking, lecturing, group work, demonstrations, laboratory activities. The theme that emerges from these collectively is that the instructional methodologies used by instructors were important in influencing these students. Using instructional methodologies as an over-arching theme and revisiting the data, we see that students preferred active to passive learning. Our data coded as "relevant" could also fit with this pattern if we broaden the heading to something like instructor's pedagogy. Faculty members who actively engaged students and showed the relevancy in the course content were perceived as having a positive impact on their students.

In the interpretation of your data, think back to your proposal question. Into what were you trying to gain insight? What insights did your research highlight for you? Focus on the main ideas. If some minor questions/hypotheses/findings arise that you think might have merit, you can present these after discussing the salient ideas.

WRITING A QUALITATIVE CHAPTER 4: RESULTS AND DISCUSSION

In writing your Chapter 4, remember that when doing qualitative research, the structure of the chapter is a bit different from a purely quantitative paper. In a quantitative paper (as you will discover in Chapter 10), typically the results section includes only the statistical findings and whether these findings are statistically significant. It is a brief chapter. In a qualitative paper, because you need to lay out your findings with an explanation, Chapter 4 of the research paper can be quite lengthy. The results and the discussion go hand in hand as they are intertwined.

There is no set style that must be used with a qualitative results section. Typically, it is written as a narrative that describes what you found. It can be written in first or third person. Some journals and instructors prefer first person as data collection and interpretation is so personal, that using "I" and "me" seem most natural. Other journals and instructors prefer third person be used –as in "the researcher found"– because they feel it is more professional.

Begin writing your Chapter 4—that's right—with a recap of the research question. Next, briefly describe what you actually did. Who was ultimately involved? If you were using an open-ended questionnaire, how many completed copies did you receive, for example. You would also explain any modifications that may have been made to your planned procedures during actual data collection. For example, you may have stated in your methods section that you were interviewing five teachers on three separate occasions. Well, as you proceeded with data collection, perhaps one of the teachers decided to drop out of the study. Chapter 4 is where you say you started with five but after the first observation, one teacher decided not to continue with the study. If you know why, state the reason. Maybe, while you planned to do three classroom observations, the district decided at the last minute to require some additional testing, so you were only able to schedule two observations. If there are any modifications that need to be made to your methods *because of changes that occurred during data collection*, here is where those are described and explained. If you decide to change your procedures as you just begin to collect data—for example, you realize an interview question is unclear and you adjust it—you would just adjust your methods chapter.

Next, you need to present the interpretation of your findings. It is generally easiest to do this by presenting an introductory paragraph that lays out the major assertions/themes into which you grouped the data. You can then present your findings for each of these main ideas. Discuss your interpretation of these findings. Why are these ideas important and relevant to your study question? What insights into the issue do they provide?

As you present and discuss the generalizations, you must provide supporting evidence from your data. Use excerpts from the field notes, quotes from interviews and questionnaires, or other pieces of data that you may have to support interpretation. Three to five pieces of supporting evidence are generally considered sufficient. You can choose to present your generalization or assertion and then provide evidence or weave your evidence into the narrative. You can choose a combination of these approaches, as well. However, do not allow a quote to stand alone; always comment on what you present. Likewise, do not allow a generalization to stand alone; always provide documentary support. See Figure 6-6 for examples of both these types of writing. As you discuss each of your major themes, if alternative explanations could exist, state what they may be and why you chose the one you did. If there is any disparity in the responses of your participants for a particular theme, discuss this as well.

WEAVING QUOTES INTO THE NARRATIVE:
EXAMPLE 1 (REPRINTED WITH PERMISSION OF WILLIAM BURNS)

Further in the interview the same student states about his ability to do math (relates to self-concept and ability): "Well, this year I've...class has taught me to like breakdown sentences and learn what the math terms mean without going to a dictionary." He infers his math anxiety is reduced due to the socialization component built into the group activity. "You're socializing in a way but also learning at the same time...kinda like building bridges, that's what my grandparents say."

EXAMPLE 2 (REPRINTED WITH PERMISSION OF SHERILYN MOONEY)

These initial survey results suggested that over half of the students in my middle school special education program considered themselves poor writers. Nearly one-third of those who indicated why they considered themselves poor writers attributed their perceived deficits to poor penmanship. As one student wrote, "I am a horable writer my hand writing is horid."

EXAMPLE 3 (REPRINTED WITH PERMISSION OF OF SHERILYN MOONEY)

...Relative to maintaining communication with me through the use of their journal, however, only one student remained neutral, one gave no response, and the remaining students enjoyed this form of communication. The reasons they gave focused primarily on the idea of having an outlet for self-expression in a private, non-threatening arena and on the social-emotional aspects of the dialogue-journaling experience. One particular student wrote, "...I can talk without everyone hereing what I'm saying," while another wrote "...it gave me a way to communicate."

QUOTES FOLLOWING NARRATIVE:
EXAMPLE 4 (REPRINTED WITH PERMISSION OF DAVID DEMPSEY)

Those teachers who could identify some of the goals stated that this was mostly due to the fact that they had planned on addressing these goals for a time before the goals setting and they were guiding players in putting forth these ideas in the first place. One teacher had this to say:

> The reason that I know that writing was a goal was because I helped to set it. I've been working a great deal with the 6+1 Writing Traits program and I know how valuable it has been for my kids. I really think that the other teachers would be interested if they saw the great affects it has on student writing.

COMBINATION OF THE TWO:
EXAMPLE 5 (REPRINTED WITH PERMISSION OF GREGORY A. PROBERT)

I believe seeing a snapshot of demographic data is important. However, I was surprised to see the number of years a teacher has "put in" appears to have nothing

Figure 6-6. Examples of assertions in different formats.

133

to do with whether a person feels stronger in terms of a more negative or positive response to closure; everyone appeared affected equally. One newer teacher (two years out of a closure situation) mentions "I know how stressed I was, I can't imagine how others felt/feel that were there longer than me." An experienced teacher (eight years out of the closure situation) states "By far the most positive experience in my teaching career. Teachers and administrators become less complacent. Educators must realize they do not have a monopoly on knowing what is best for kids." In short, demographics (in terms of "number of years teaching" and "number of years since closure") of individual experiences did not have a huge variance of effect on respondents. Twelve of the 17 respondents still had a far more negative tone about their current attitudes as opposed to positives. Respondents also gave a more negative spin on their remarks regarding their mental and physical state:

> Even for the past 8 years, the possibility of the school completely closing is always in the back of my mind. Also, when the school first closed, I refused to send my children to the same school district in the new town. I, along with many other parents, still send our children to the other district. It still bothers me.

I feel people had judged me with the closure of the school. When a school closes you can't help but feel you failed. I feel staff at the new school formed opinions of me as if I was damaged goods.

Figure 6-6. Examples of assertions in different formats. (Continued)

Remember that how you present the data and what you choose to present as evidence will help the reader determine the validity and reliability of your findings. Be sure to use a variety of sources whenever possible to support your claims. Provide evidence from all sources that what you are asserting is a true representation of your findings. Discuss any contradictory findings. Make your triangulation explicit.

After discussing each of your major themes, if you had any other interesting findings that you would like to share, this would be the time. Perhaps out of 30 responses, there were a handful that were **outliers** and did not fit the general pattern. If you feel those comments had merit, you may now wish to discuss those comments and why you think they may deserve attention.

Close your results chapter with a summary paragraph. This could be a simple restatement of your major themes.

NEXT STEPS

If you were employing a qualitative research design, the hard work would now be done and you would only have one chapter left to your research paper! You would have designed your project, collected data, made sense of what you found, and communicated those findings to your readers. All that would be left are concluding remarks, limitations, and implications—the "so what" of your project. Before we move on to learning how to put on these finishing touches, we will discuss quantitative research methodologies.

CHAPTER SELF-CHECK

Having completed this chapter, you should be comfortable discussing the following:
- outline of steps to follow in analyzing qualitative data
- analyzing data using the coding category technique
- applying a constant comparative approach
- overview of computer-aided analysis techniques
- organizing and writing Chapter Four

CHAPTER REVIEW QUESTIONS

1. What are the recommended steps to follow in analyzing qualitative data?
2. Why are multiple copies of data sets generally required?
3. What is meant by "coding categories?"
4. How do you determine which and how many codes to assign to your data?
5. What is the constant comparative approach?
6. When is the constant comparative approach most appropriate?
7. Compare and contrast coding category and constant comparative methodologies.

REFERENCES

Bodgan, R. C., & Biklen, S. K. (2006). *Qualitative research for education: An introduction to theory and methods* (5th ed.). Boston: Allyn & Bacon.

Creswell, J. W. (2008). *Educational research: Planning, conducting, and evaluating quantitative and qualitative research* (3rd ed.). Upper Saddle River, NJ: Prentice Hall.

Gay, L. R., Mills, G. E., & Airasian, P. (2009). *Educational research: Competencies for analysis and applications* (9th ed.). Upper Saddle River, NJ: Prentice Hall.

Glaser, B., & Strauss, A. L. (1967). *The discovery of grounded theory: Strategies for qualitative research.* New York: Aldine De Gruyter.

Lang, J. M. (2004, June 11). Flamboyant features of the academic habit. *The Chronicle of Higher Education*, p. C1, C3.

Morrell, P. D. (2000, January). *What we know about our future math and science teachers.* A paper presented at the Annual International Meeting of the Association for the Education of Teachers in Science, Akron, OH.

CHAPTER 7

DESCRIPTIVE STATISTICS

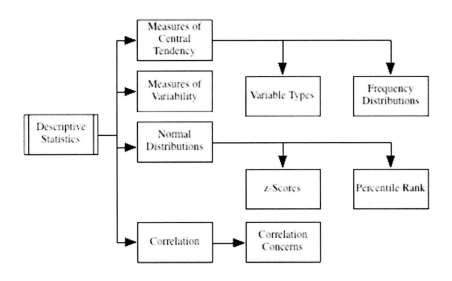

CHAPTER OVERVIEW

Chapter 7 provides an introduction to basic strategies for describing groups statistically. Statistical concepts around normal distributions are discussed. The statistical procedures of z-scores and correlation are presented.

INTRODUCTION

Although qualitative studies often include numerical information, that information is meant to provide more meaning to what you have been collecting to better understand the groups or individuals you are studying. It is another way to traingulate data gathered in qualitative research. Like all qualitative data gathering, the validity of numerical data is based on the degree to which it informs your research question. What if you are not doing a qualitative study, but have a question that requires quantitative methods and analyses?

As we discussed in Chapter 2, the usual form of a quantitative study is to gather and analyze numerical data in order to show if something you did or observed impacted one or more groups in a predictable way. Did a new curriculum raise test scores? Does age make any difference in teacher attitudes? Do intrinsic rewards

137

decrease disruptive behavior? Once you have a quantitative research question in mind your job as a researcher is to plan a strategy for gathering and analyzing data to answer the question.

This leads to one of the biggest differences between qualitative and quantitative research. Qualitative research questions are answered by using iterative and dynamic methods. You gather data, review what has been gathered and then gather more data until you have a sufficient understanding of your topic. What data are gathered and how it is gathered may change as the study progresses. In quantitative studies this is not the case. In quantitative studies once you have designed a strategy for gathering and analyzing data you will carry out the design. The methods of your study do not change as the study progresses. You need to have planned carefully before data collection begins. The next few chapters of this book are intended to give the tools necessary to plan well and to be able to complete insightful quantitative research.

DESCRIPTIVE STATISTICS

To begin, we need to approach numerical understanding of groups in a more formal way. This will eventually lead to analysis tools designed to describe differences among groups using a kind of formal mathematical logic. The first step is to get used to the ideas around using numbers (rather than words) to describe groups.

Think about talking to a friend and describing a party you recently attended. It is likely you would be talking about others who were there. John is now in graduate school. Mary has taken a job as a graphic designer. Bob has lost a lot of weight. Carol and Steve got married. To describe the group, you describe characteristics of the individuals. We do the same thing in quantitative research. If we want to know how tall a group of seventh graders is we would measure each child's height. The resulting list would be like the description of the party. William is 52 inches tall. Sally is 47 inches tall. Juan is 50 inches tall. When you look at all of the heights you would be able to get a sense of the general height of the members of the group.

The best way to analyze a group is to know each member of the group and be able to compare some characteristic among them. The problem is that our brains are not very good at keeping lots of detailed items separate and available for use. At some point there would be so many heights to remember that you would have trouble generalizing about the group. When this happens you have to figure out a way to summarize all of the numbers. In statistics, summarizing the characteristics of a group is called **descriptive statistics.**

Descriptive statistics are a kind of shorthand to make it easier to talk about a group as a whole instead of talking about groups by describing each individual. For example, it would not make sense to say the average age of children is 26.4 months old if there are only two of them, since you would get much more information if you were just given each of their ages. However, if you were given each child's height in a class this would get confusing. The summary numbers are much more useful when there are many members of the group.

MEASURES OF CENTRAL TENDENCY

Now it is time to begin to review those things that most of us already know about statistics. When describing groups quantitatively, we usually try to come up with some number that represents as many members of the group as possible. These "summary" numbers representing where most of the members of the group appear are called **measures of central tendency**. There are three of these. The **mode** is the number that appears most often in a list. If 6 of our seventh graders turned out to be 47 inches tall and no other specific height occurred that many times in the group, then the mode of the group would be 47. The **median** is the number where half of the group measures lower and half is higher—it is the middle, like the median of a road. If there were 23 students in the class and all of the heights were sorted into increasing order, then the 12th height—the one right in the middle of the list—would be the median height of the class. If you had 24 students, the median would be the average of the 12th and 13th heights (since there is no one middle number). The **mean** is the arithmetic average. If you take all of the measured heights, add them all together and divide by the number of students measured, that would be the mean height of the class.

Variable Types

The problem is figuring out which of these three measures of central tendency will give you the group summary which is the best description of the group. In order to do that we first need some background about how group data are collected.

When you start to research a group you will pick specific characteristics, or **variables**, of the individuals in the group that are of interest to you. These are things that you would not expect to be the same for everyone in the group. You might be interested, as in our example above, in the height of each student. More likely you might be interested in their grade point average or how many books they each read last week. There is an infinite number of possible variables in a group and it is your job as a researcher to choose just those variables that you need to help you answer your research question.

Generally, there are three types of variables. You need to know about these so that you can choose the best measure of central tendency to describe the variable for the group. Imagine wanting to know the pet preference for the children in your class. Some would like cats most and some dogs; maybe some have snakes as a favorite pet. When you are looking at how each child answered this question you could sort the responses into dogs, cats, snakes, birds and probably not more than a few other categories—7 children like dogs best, 9 like cats most, and so on. The responses have been sorted into containers but the containers do not have a logical order. It would not make any difference if cats were put before dogs or even snakes came first. You would not get any useful information from the order of the response categories as you were examining the results. Variables like this— responses that can only be sorted into containers that have no logical order—are called **nominal variables**. The most important thing about the response categories for these variables is the category's name, hence nominal variable.

Going back to the measures of central tendency, imagine trying to average pet preference. The question does not make any sense because the response categories do not have a fixed order. If we ask what the median pet preference is the same problem occurs. There is no way to order the responses so that you can figure out the middle point. So, with nominal variables the only measure of central tendency that is available is the mode. Which response category has the most responses in it? A statement describing a group with a mode would be something like: more students said cats were their favorite pet than any other pet type.

Most of the time we gather data from groups in ways that the response categories do have a logical order. Imagine asking your class how often they read at home. It might be very difficult for students to put an exact number to the answer of that question but they probably would be able to select from these categories: hardly ever, once a month, once a week, more than once a week. Responses to variables designed this way are called **ordinal variables**. The responses categories have a logical order, but the categories are not necessarily equivalent—a month includes a lot more possible reading days than a week. The most important characteristic of this type of variable is the relative order of the response categories.

When you got the data back from the students you would be able to sort the responses into the categories just like with nominal variables. If you wanted you could report the mode of the responses (i.e., more students said that they read once a week than students in any other category), but there is more information available to summarize the group because the response categories are in order. It is still not possible to average the responses because, as noted above, the response categories are not of equivalent size. Take all of the responses and put them in order—putting all of the "almost never" responses first, then the once a month responses, then the once a week responses followed by the more than once a week responses. Now count through the responses until you find the one in the middle of the list. This is the median response. It describes the point in the responses where half of the students responded below this point and half responded above. Since the purpose of descriptive statistics is to provide the best description of the group possible, the median gives more information about how the responses from the group are distributed than the mode does. That usually makes it the best measure of central tendency to use with ordinal variables. A sentence describing a group with a median would be something like: Reading at home once a week was the median response for the class.

Finally, whenever possible, researchers try to use variables where the response categories are ordered *and* they are of equivalent size. These are called **interval variables**. In our example of asking the students how tall they were, students responded with their height in inches. Certainly inch measurements have a natural order but it is important that each category—each inch measurement—is the same size. An inch is an inch whether it is at the 2 inch point on the ruler or the 40 inch mark. With interval variables the most important characteristic is that each response category represents an equivalent interval.

Interval variables are the only variable type where determining the mean (averaging) is possible. When the data are gathered, the responses can be averaged and the mean becomes a much more descriptive statistic than the median or the mode. The median and mode could still be computed for interval data, but those numbers would generally not tell as much about the group as the mean would. In our case a statement describing a group with a mean might read: The mean height of the students in this class was 48.6 inches. Read another way the mean represents a point around which we would expect most of the responses from the group to cluster.

There is a special case of interval variables called **ratio variables**. Ratio variable scales always start at zero. If you are talking about height you can say that someone is twice as tall as someone else. Or, you could say that a car got one third the gas mileage as another. These are ratio statements. Think about saying that someone is twice as smart as someone else—it does not make sense because intelligence scales or standardized assessments scales do not start at zero. In most cases, the way ratio and interval variables are used in statistics is the same but it is important to remember the difference between these types of variables.

We will describe in the next chapter how to do statistical analysis with these measures of central tendency. Right now you should keep in mind that whenever possible (and it will not always be possible—how would you gather interval data on gender?) you should gather data with interval variables because they not only provide the summary description of the group with the most information, but they also allow for the most sophisticated analyses of the data once they are gathered.

Frequency Distributions

When you are reporting descriptive statistics in a research paper you will almost always put the important numbers into a table. Sometimes it is valuable to look at your data in graphic forms other than tables to better understand what they mean. Start by determining how many responses from your group on a given variable there are for each response category—how many responded almost never, how many once a month, how many once a week and how many more than once a week. This is called a **frequency distribution**. When you make a bar chart from the frequency distribution it is called a **histogram**. Although histograms can be made for all three variable types, remember that the order of the bars in a chart for a nominal variable has no meaning. Regardless, charting frequency distributions is a good way to see how your data are spread out.

Here is an example using an interval variable. Imagine recording these scores from a 30 point test: 27, 28, 28, 27, 27, 24, 27, 26, 20, 30, 23, 23, 24. A frequency distribution and measures of central tendency of these scores would look like this.

```
20 — 1
21 — 0
22 — 0
23 — 2        mode = 27
24 — 2        median = 27
25 — 0        mean = 25.69
26 — 1
27 — 4
28 — 2
29 — 0
30 — 1
```

The histogram for the data is depicted in Figure 7-1. Review this figure to see how the scores are spread out. Can you make some generalizations about the class just from looking at the chart? The information in the frequency distribution and the histogram are the same; however, it is usually easier to get a sense of the group from the chart rather than the table of numbers.

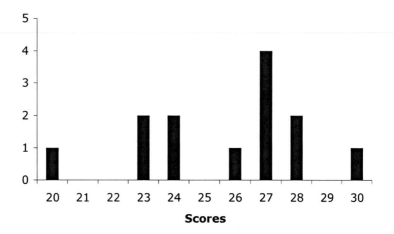

Figure 7-1. Histogram A.

Stop and try this yourself. Here are scores for a second 30 point test: 22, 22, 23, 23, 25, 26, 27, 27, 27, 27, 28, 28, 29. Compute a frequency distribution, draw a histogram and then determine the values of the measures of central tendency for these scores. Does your histogram look like the one in Figure 7-2? What generalizations about the class can you make from this histogram?

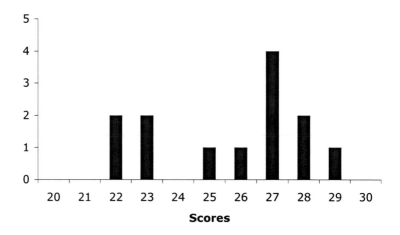

Figure 7-2. Histogram B.

MEASURES OF VARIABILITY

The two previous examples (tests one and two) pose an interesting problem. They represent two different frequency distributions but the measures of central tendency are identical. Since the purpose of descriptive statistics is to give the best possible summary description of the group, it appears that measures of central tendency may not always provide enough information by themselves for differentiating among different sets of data. Something else is needed to summarize differences in groups.

With interval variables (remember, the intervals between response categories are equal) the histogram represents not only how many responses are in each category but also how far apart the response categories are. Because the possible response categories are equidistant we can get a reasonable representation of whether the data are spread out across the histogram or whether the data seem to be clustered more closely together. Look at the two previous examples to get a sense of this. Another form of descriptive statistics, then, represents how far the responses are spread apart in a distribution. These are called **measures of variability**.

There are two measures of variability that are generally used. The **range** represents the difference between the highest and lowest responses in the data. Sometimes the range is listed as the actual highest and lowest scores and sometimes it is listed as the difference between those two numbers. In the first of the cases previously discussed, the range runs from a low score of 20 to a high of 30 or a difference of 10. In the second of the cases, the range would show responses as low as 22 and as high as 29 or a distance between those two points of 7. The range shows the responses being clustered into a smaller space on the response scale than the first set of data.

The second measure of variability is the **standard deviation**. In general terms this is the average distance the responses are from the mean score. To figure out what the standard deviation is you would find the difference of each score from the mean and then average all of those differences. In reality the calculation is a bit more complicated. To statisticians it looks like this:

$$s = \sqrt{\frac{\sum (X - \overline{X})^2}{N - 1}}$$

In this book we will leave that calculation to the computer. For a given set of data, higher standard deviations would mean that the responses are more spread out (greater average distance from the mean). Lower standard deviations would mean that the responses are more closely clustered around the mean (smaller average distance from the mean).

With the standard deviations computed it is possible to differentiate between our two example groups. See Table 7-1.

Table 7-1. Mean and standard deviation for two example tests

	Test 1 N = 13	Test 2 N = 13
Mean	25.69	25.69
Standard Deviation (S.D.)	2.72	2.43

The standard deviation for the second group is a lower number indicating a smaller average distance that the scores are from the mean. We would expect the histogram to show the responses clustered more closely around the mean than they would be in the first group. Go back to the two charts (Figures 7-1 and 7-2) and see if you can identify this difference.

As a teacher looking at test scores, a smaller standard deviation would generally mean that students all performed similarly regardless of the group's overall performance. A larger standard deviation would show that the scores on the test were more spread out. Some students scored particularly high or low compared to the rest of the group. To inform how to best improve student learning, it might be worth figuring out why that was so.

Since a standard deviation is a measure relative to a mean score, it is only available with interval data. The range is the measure of variability reported for ordinal data. Together, the measures of central tendency and the measures of variability give a powerful way to describe groups and eventually you will see that they form the foundation from which groups can be statistically compared.

You may feel that this introduction to statistical calculation inspires you to learn how to let the computer do much of this calculation for you.

NORMAL DISTRIBUTIONS

If we were able to measure the height of all middle-school aged boys, we would be able to determine the mean height. And then if we plotted a histogram of the heights we would find that most of the boys' heights would be clustered around the mean height, and that a few would be considerably taller and some would be considerably shorter. We would not expect every boy to be the same height, but we would expect most of them to be relatively the same, with only a few particularly tall or short. This characteristic distribution of lots of responses being close to the mean and fewer responses appearing as you move above and below the mean is typical of many variables measured in living systems: the size of apples from a tree, the weight of sea turtles, or the cognitive ability of 14- year- olds.

Keeping the histogram of this kind of distribution in your mind, imagine connecting the tops of each bar with a line. The bar in the middle with the most responses would be very close to the mean of the group. Then a line connecting the top of each bar would begin to fall in each direction as the bars got shorter (fewer people in those response categories). Now, with a bit of mental gymnastics, imagine smoothing out the line connecting the tops of all of the bars and you would be left with a smooth curve that is high in the middle and drops down on both sides.

If the group is large enough from which you were gathering data, this curve would be likely to take on a very even and symmetrical appearance (Figure 7-3). Because the curve represents "normally distributed" data (data that acts the way we expect) it is called a **normal curve**. Sometimes you will see it referred to as a characteristic curve or a standard curve.

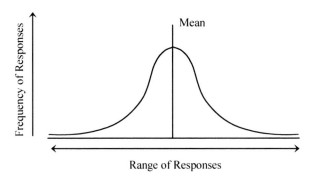

Figure 7-3. Normal curve.

This curve has certain characteristics. The mean is in the middle with data evenly distributed on both sides. The curve in its ideal form is symmetrical. The category that has the most responses (the highest bar, the mode) is also in the middle and because it is symmetrical half of the responses are on each side of the highest bar (the median). Consequently, the mean, median and mode are the same number in a normally distributed group of data. And, the curve represents this characteristic of normally distributed data in that most of the responses are close to the mean and there are fewer responses as the response category is farther from the mean.

Looking at this from the point of view of measures of central tendency and variability, the mean is in the center of the curve and the standard deviation controls how wide the curve is—with larger standard deviations the responses will be spread farther apart, with smaller standard deviations the responses would be more closely clustered around the mean.

There is one more characteristic of normal curves that is very important (see Figure 7-4). Look at the point on the curve that is one standard deviation beyond the mean. (Remember, the standard deviation is the average of the differences of the individual data points from the mean.) Having just said that the standard deviation determines the width of the curve, imagine what happens as the standard deviation gets bigger and smaller. As the standard deviation moves, the curve gets stretched out or compacted together. It is beyond the scope of this book to show you exactly why this is the case, but the area under the curve between the mean and one standard deviation (the responses on the histogram between those two points) represents the exact same percentage of the responses from the group regardless of what the mean and standard deviation of the responses are. Let's put this in mathematical terms. The percentage of the responses in a normal distribution between the mean and one standard deviation is a constant—it never changes. It turns out that 34.1 percent of the responses are in that area.

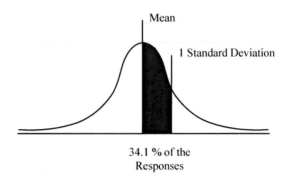

Figure 7-4. Area between the mean and one standard deviation in a normal curve.

Well, if the area between the mean and one standard deviation is constant then it is not a surprise that the area between one and two standard deviations is also constant. It is 13.6 percent of the responses. And, the area between two and three standard deviations represents 2.1 percent of the responses. If you add those up you will see we are getting very close to 50 percent (all those responses above the mean). In fact, in a normal distribution there will only be 0.1 percent of the responses beyond three standard deviations. Naturally, these relationships hold true if you look at standard deviations below the mean as well (see Figure 7-5). If a group mean is 24.7 and one standard deviation is 6.2 that would mean that 34.1 percent of the responses from this group would be between 24.7 and 30.9 (24.7 + 6.2). Similarly 34.1 percent of the responses would be between 24.7 and 18.5 (24.7 – 6.2).

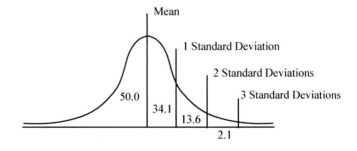

Figure 7-5. Standard deviation and percent of the normal curve.

Z-Scores

In general, statistics are used to describe groups and relationships among groups. Seldom are they used to describe individuals. In the examples of test scores, we were looking at the class data. For heights, we were describing the entire class. There is one notable exception to this in which statistics help to compare an individual to the group. In an earlier section of this chapter, we described the relationship of standard deviation to a normal curve. It is easiest to make that description by looking at the points that are whole number standard deviations above or below the mean. Actually, we could compute the area under the normal curve between the mean and any given standard deviation above or below the mean. For instance the area under the curve (recall, the area under the curve represents the percent of responses) between the mean and 1.23 standard deviations above the mean is about 39 percent of the total responses.

Since the normal curve is a simplified graph that really represents the frequency distribution of the group, we can look at any specific response (be it a particular test score, a certain number of books read, a specific height of child—whatever you are measuring) and figure out how many standard deviations above or below the mean that specific response is. The calculation to do this is very simple. Figure out the distance between the mean of the group and the specific response in which you are interested (subtract the mean from the specific response) and divide by the standard deviation. Using our example numbers of a mean of 24.7 and a standard deviation of 6.2, we can do this calculation for a specific individual's score of 32.

(Score-Mean)/Std. Dev. = Number of Standard Deviations Away from the Mean

or

$(32–24.7)/6.2 = 1.18$

If the specific response in which you are interested is to the left of the mean the result will be negative (Score-Mean will be negative) and if it is to the right it will be positive. Because ours is to the right of the mean it is a positive value. What you would have done through this computation is determine the distance from the mean to your score of interest in units of standard deviation. This number is called a **z score**.

Rarely are specific z scores reported as a way to compare an individual's response to the larger group. Instead, what is reported is the *z* score converted into the area under the curve (the percentage of responses) that the z score represents. Since the areas between the mean and any given standard deviation are all constants, this last process is really easy. Look up the z score on a table prepared for this purpose. This table is called a z table and you can find one in Appendix D.

The number that you get from the z table needs a little explanation. What we really want to know is how to compare a person's response to the larger group. To do this the comparison that is made is to determine the percentage of the responses from the whole group that are lower than the individual's that you are examining. If the z score is positive (the score of interest is above the mean) that would mean that the percentage of responses lower than that score is the area between the mean and the score of interest plus 50 percent. The 50 percent is the area below the mean.

In our example of a z score of 1.18 the area between the mean and 1.18 standard deviations is 38 percent. Add the 50 percent of the area below the mean and that shows that 88 percent of the scores of this group are below a score with a z score of 1.18. Figure 7-6 depicts this in graphic form.

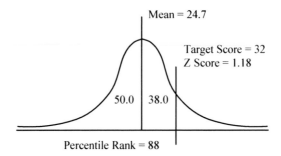

Figure 7-6. Positive Z-score.

If the z score is negative (it is below the mean) then you would subtract the area under the curve between the mean and score of interest from 50 percent. For instance if the z score is -1.18 you would subtract 38 (the percent of responses calculated from the z-table) from 50 with a result of 12 percent of the responses being lower than the score represented by 1.18 standard deviations lower than the mean. This is shown in Figure 7-7.

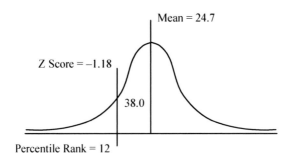

Figure 7-7. Negative Z-score.

Percentile Rank

You have probably run into this number before with a slightly different name. A response which has a z score of 1.18 has a **percentile rank** of 88. This trail through z scores has led to that magic number that is on students' standardized test results.

A student has a percentile rank in which his or her score on the test is compared to some group. It could be a comparison to everyone who has taken the test or it could be a comparison to some subset (i.e., school, district, gender) of the larger group. Percentile rank does not represent the percentage of the scores that a student got right or wrong on the test. It does represent the percentage of students who scored lower on the test than a specific student. Not only is the concept of computing the areas of a normal curve important for more complex statistical analysis but also, as a teacher, you may find yourself explaining percentile rank to parents.

CORRELATION

There is one more important way that you can describe a group. With percentile rank we are describing the relationship of individuals to the larger group. With a **correlation** you can describe the relationship of one characteristic of a group to another characteristic. If data were gathered from a group of teachers about their age and number of years they had been teaching we would expect that in general younger teachers would have taught fewer years and older teachers would have taught more years. This probably would not be true for every teacher you surveyed, but in general we would expect to see a propensity for this to appear over the whole group. The point of computing correlations is to see how strong that relationship is (how likely it is to be true in every case) and the direction of the relationship; that is, does one go up as the other goes up or does one go down as the other goes up.

All statistical computer applications, including Microsoft Excel, make computing correlations simple. When the responses from two variables are compared in this way, the numerical correlation, or the correlation coefficient, is a number between 1 and -1. If the relationship between two variables is absolutely predictable (in every case if you knew the score on one variable you could predict the score on another) the correlation would be +1 or -1. If the two variables change in the same way (as one is larger the other will be larger), the correlation is +1. It would be -1 if the variables behave in opposite directions (as one is larger the other gets smaller). As the measure of the relationship of two variables is less predictable, the number approaches 0 from the two extremes of 1 and -1. The closer a computed correlation is to zero the less likely that you would be able to predict one from another. In general if a correlation appears between 1 and 0.7 or -0.7 and -1 then it would be called a strong correlation. Those between 0.3 and 0.7 or -0.3 and -0.7 are considered moderate correlations, and those between 0.3 and -0.3 are weak (Figure 7-8). These are subjective terms but they serve to help to know when to pay attention to correlations and when to assume that there really is not much of a relationship between variables.

Many studies are designed so that examining the relationship among many variables in the study at the same time is important. Statistical programs will allow you to make all of the necessary computations simultaneously. If there are ten variables that you wish to check against each other, what results is a correlation table in which the correlation of each variable with every other variable of interest

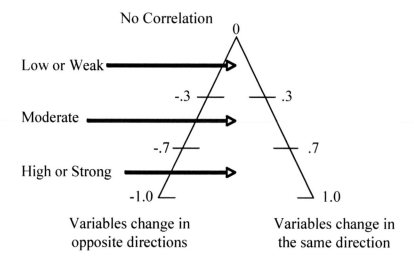

Figure 7-8. Levels of correlation strength.

is listed. In these tables the variables are listed on both the horizontal and vertical axis. At the intersection of any two variables, the correlation is listed. These tables have a characteristic diagonal appearance because the results are symmetrical. Comparing variable 1 on the horizontal axis with variable 2 on the vertical is the same as variable 2 on the horizontal with variable 1 on the vertical. Consequently, those redundant comparisons are not left in the chart.

Table 7-2 shows an example **correlation matrix** from student evaluations of a course. We wanted to know how strongly correlated the responses to each question were from the students. Note that the "q" represents question.

Table 7-2. Question response correlations from a course evaluation (N = 65)

	q1	q2	q3	Q4	q5
q1	1				
q2	.79	1			
q3	.62	.59	1		
q4	.73	.72	.77	1	
q5	.78	.73	.68	.71	1

Sometimes researchers will include the 1 in the results table at each of the points where something is correlated with itself (the diagonal row of 1s in the table) to make the table easier to read. In Table 7-2, the highest correlation is between q1 and q2 (.79, a *strong* correlation) and the lowest is between q2 and q3 (.59, a *moderate* correlation).

Correlations are a powerful descriptive tool because they can demonstrate the degree to which two variables are measuring similar things. In the course evaluation example described earlier, we designed the survey to ask students about the quality of teaching in the course. If the questions were designed well we would expect the questions to show strong correlations. If there were some that did not show strong correlations, we might want to look more closely to see if some of the questions were really measuring something other than perceptions of teaching.

Strong positive correlation (0.83)

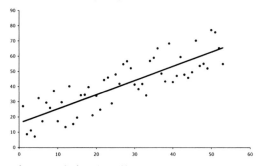

Strong negative correlation (-0.73)

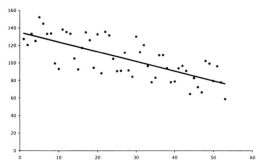

Almost no correlation (-0.02)

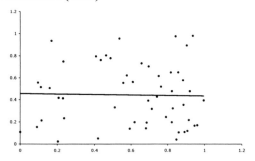

Figure 7-9. Correlation scatter plots.

151

There are a few other things that you should pay attention to as you are using correlations in your studies. First, it is a good idea to do a graphic representation of the relationship of the variables. By doing a scatter plot (one variable represented on the x axis of a graph and the other variable on the y axis) the resulting points on the graph would ideally cluster around a line called a regression line or a best fit line that runs through the plotted data points (Figure 7-9). In Microsoft Excel this line can be generated by adding a linear trend line to a scatter plot. The closer all of the points are to this line, the closer the correlation will be to 1 or -1. If the points do not seem to cluster around the line the correlation is more likely to be closer to 0. After making a scatter plot, you also need to make sure that the data appear as a single cluster no matter how tightly the cluster is around the best fit line. In some cases your responses will gather into two or more clusters. When this happens it is probable that something else is affecting these variables making the computed correlation a false representation of the relationship among the variables.

Notice in the examples in Figure 7-9 that with a positive correlation the regression line goes from lower on the left to higher on the right. As one variable increases so does the other. With a negative correlation the opposite is true. The regression line goes from higher on the left to lower on the right. As one variable increases the other decreases. As the correlation approaches 0.00 the regression line becomes horizontal.

Concerns when Using Correlations

In Chapter 8 we will discuss the probability that statistical relationships you observe happened by chance. Without going into detail about that right now, statistical programs will compute, along with the correlation, the probability that the observed correlation is something that might have appeared randomly. The determination of whether the correlation is likely to have happened by chance is related to the strength of the correlation along with the size of the group from which you have gathered the responses. Since it is possible to compute correlations without determining this probability they would appear by chance (for instance Excel does not provide probability numbers), you must be careful that you are not reporting on a relationship that is meaningless because chance is a better explanation of the relationship than any other meaning you might attribute to it. This is particularly important if you are discussing moderate correlations with group sizes of less than twenty. Use the table included in Appendix E to determine when a computed correlation is not likely to have occurred by chance.

Two other problems appear in using correlations. First, you will occasionally read reports on studies (usually but not always in non-peer reviewed sources) where the author suggests that a high correlation indicates that one variable causes the results on the other. In our example above this would be like saying that years of teaching causes age. As easy as it would be to humorously suggest that relationship, it clearly makes no sense. It may be that a causal relationship between variables exists but a correlation cannot be used to demonstrate that.

The other difficulty is that correlations need to make sense. Statistically it may be possible to demonstrate correlations between variables that don't seem to be logically connected. You might find a relationship between height and reading scores but it would be difficult to make the case of why these two should be related. Usually, there should be something in the literature that you can reference to support any curious findings. Otherwise be clear when you are reporting on unanticipated relationships that further investigation is warranted to better understand them.

There are two common ways that most correlations are computed. One is called a **Pearson's r**. It is used when both variables being compared are interval variables. When one of the variables is ordinal then a more conservative calculation is used called **Spearman's rho.** If the statistical program you are using doesn't differentiate between the two types of correlation (i.e., Excel) then you should assume it is using the Pearson calculation. Whenever possible you should try to set up correlation studies to compare interval variables.

NEXT STEPS

Descriptive statistics are often part of qualitative research studies. They can serve as important triangulation data for your results. When descriptive statistics are used in quantitative studies, they usually are the foundation for statistical analysis. Quantitative studies require substantially different designs from qualitative studies to accommodate statistical analysis. In the next chapter we will take a closer look at those analysis tools. Regardless of which type of research you are thinking of doing, understanding these basics of measures of central tendency, normal curves, and correlation will be important not only for gathering and analyzing data for you own study, but for reading and evaluating others' research as well.

CHAPTER SUMMARY

Having completed this chapter, you should be comfortable discussing the following:
- measures of central tendency: mean, mode, median
- variable types (nominal, ordinal, interval)
- frequency distributions, including histograms
- measures of variability: range and standard deviation
- description of a normal distribution
- z-scores and percentile rankings
- correlations

CHAPTER REVIEW QUESTIONS

1. How will you know which measure of central tendency will be best for your study?
2. What are the differences among the three variable types? Why are those differences important?

3. What is a normal distribution? What does it represent?
4. What is percentile rank and how is determined?
5. When would you use a correlation in a study?

ANALYZING DATA

Inferential Statistics

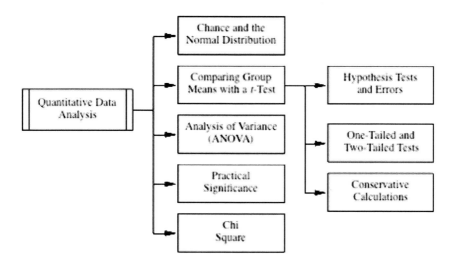

CHAPTER OVERVIEW

Chapter 8 is the quantitative counterpart to Chapter 6. This chapter provides instruction on statistical data analyses, focusing on those most commonly used by classroom teachers in their research. We will not include multiple regression, analysis of covariance, or factorial analysis as most beginning researchers do not design a study that requires these types of statistical analyses.

INTRODUCTION

We like to believe that the things we do have some positive impact. Sometimes this is an illusion. As an example, not long ago I wanted to see if I could get better gas mileage in my car. Because I have a long commute from home to work, I drive mostly in the left lane. I wondered if the slower pace of the right lane would make a difference in my gas mileage. I switched to the right lane and carefully computed the gas mileage for a week. To my joy the mileage was a bit better. But, alas, over the next few weeks it turned out that right lane driving was actually worse. All the stop and go caused the vehicle to consume more gas. The first week's mpg was simply an example of normal random variation in my mileage and switching had not really made a difference. The illusion is that often we believe we have affected something in our lives but the reality is that differences may appear for other reasons.

Statistics can help us sort out the normal variation in the things we are trying to do and help us see when we really have had an important impact. The tools to do this fall in the category of **inferential statistics**.

Studies that use inferential statistics (studies that look to see if chance is a good explanation for a result appearing) are designed in a lot of different ways. We will talk about some of the designs that are likely to be most useful to you in the next chapter. Right now you need to know that the way to organize the variables in your study, regardless of its design, is to identify **dependent** and **independent variables**. A dependent variable is the thing you are measuring. If you want to know if students learned more, then test grades might be the dependent variable. If you want to know if boys were taller than girls in your class then height would be the dependent variable. If you want to know if one group of teachers had been teaching longer than another then years of teaching would be the dependent variable.

Independent variables are called the grouping variable. In inferential studies you will be comparing one group to another or comparing the same people before and after something happened to them (an intervention). So, the independent variable is the variable that identifies which comparative group someone is in. In the case of where the dependent variable was learning the independent might be when the scores were gathered (before the intervention or afterward). In the case of comparing the heights of girls and boys the independent variable would be gender. In the case of looking at years of teaching the independent variable might be whether the teachers were elementary or secondary teachers. You get the idea. Generally, you will gather independent and dependent data for everyone in your study. Independent variable data tell you who is in what group that will be compared and dependent data gathered will be the same for everyone so that you can compare the groups.

CHANCE AND THE NORMAL DISTRIBUTION

As educational researchers we spend a lot of time trying to figure out if something happened by chance (i.e., it is likely to have occurred randomly) or if it happened because of something that affected what we were measuring. Did a curriculum really improve student learning? Did a new conflict management program really reduce student referrals? Did an exercise program for 3rd graders really increase time on task? We want to know, like the gas mileage reduction example discussed earlier, that change we see after we have done something cannot easily be explained as something that is likely to have occurred by chance. If it is unlikely to have occurred by chance then we can have confidence that what we did actually had a predictable effect.

In Chapter 7 we figured out how to compute percentile ranks. Percentile ranks were the percentage of scores that appeared lower than a given score in a normal distribution. A percentile rank of 90 meant that 90 percent of the comparison group scored lower than the score that represents the 90th percentile. Conversely that would mean that 10 percent scored at that point or higher. If we were interested in any given student before they took the test we could ask how likely is it that that student would score in the 90th percentile or higher. Since 10 percent of the students score at those levels you could say the student had a one in ten chance (10 percent) of scoring that high even if we knew nothing else about that student.

Instead of looking an individual student's score, how could we determine the probability that a mean score for a group would appear? We said earlier that statistics is almost never about looking at individuals but rather about under-standing groups. So, we need to understand how to look at what would seem to be the percentile rank of a group. The procedure for doing this looks similar to what we did to determine percentile rank for an individual, but it is a bit more complicated. The 20 students in Mrs. Johnson's math class take a standardized math exam. The mean score for the class is 81.47. How does Mrs. Johnson's class compare to other classes taking this test? Trying to figure out the percentile rank of 81.47 has a problem. The normal distribution for the test is based on individual scores, and our mean score is based on averaging the scores from a group of 20. Those two are not the same. To overcome this problem a new normal distribution is built based on the mean scores of comparable sized groups; in this case, a group of 20. If the mean score of every possible combination of 20 students was determined and then plotted to show a new normal distribution it would look very similar to the original distribution based on individual scores. If random groups of 20 students were selected, some averages for these groups would be higher than the mean for the whole group and some would be less. After enough randomly selected groups of 20 the mean scores will begin to cluster around the whole group mean with fewer considerably higher and lower than the whole group mean. What happens is the new distribution of means of groups of 20 ends up having the same mean as the whole group, but because it is based on means of 20 students, fewer means appear as you move farther above and below the mean than would be the case with the distribution based on individual scores. This new distribution has a name—**sampling distribution of the mean**—and the new standard deviation that appears also has a name—**standard error**. In other words, the same parameters we examined for individual scores have a counterpart when we examine group or population scores: the mean becomes the mean of the sampling distribution and the standard deviation is replaced by standard error (see Figure 8-1).

With this new distribution we could figure out how likely it was that Mrs. Johnson's class mean score would have appeared by chance. This might be nice to know because if it was really unlikely to appear by chance, we might begin to believe that there was something unique about the students in her class or her teaching.

Unfortunately, when we are doing our own research it is rare that our study collects scores on standardized assessments. Most of the time we are looking at some assessment to which there is no larger group to compare; that is we use criterion referenced vs. norm referenced assessments. If Mr. Smith teaches a unit on dinosaurs to his second graders, it would be common for him to use an assessment he designed himself. So how could we know if Mr. Smith's students' scores

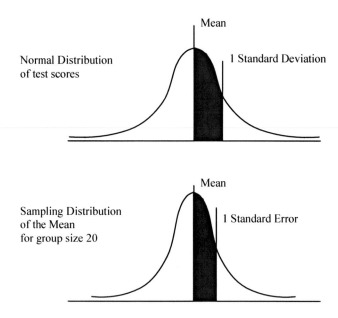

Figure 8-1. Comparison of normal distribution formed with individuals and a distribution formed from group sizes of 20 (sampling distribution of the mean).

on the test could be explained as likely to occur by chance or, as we would hope, more likely to have occurred because of Mr. Smith's instruction on dinosaurs? Since there is no population to which to compare Mr. Smith's class, some other group needs to stand in as the comparison group. In this case the group that took the pretest on the dinosaur curriculum will be the comparison group; that is, his class at the start of the unit. Is the group that took the pretest somehow now a different group after having experienced the curriculum?

The last bit of statistical maneuvering that is needed to accomplish this task is called **estimating parameters**. If we do not know the mean of the sampling distribution or the standard error, then they have to be estimated. From Mr. Smith's students' pre-test scores we could easily compute the mean and standard deviation and we know the group size. We need the group size to estimate the sampling distribution of the mean, the standard deviation to estimate the standard error and the mean of the group to estimate the mean of the sampling distribution of the mean. At this point you may be beginning to glaze over. Think back to percentile ranks. What we want to know (in theory) is the percentile rank of Mr. Smith's class in some theoretical distribution of a number of other classes of 20 students. If Mr. Smith's post-test scores were unlikely to occur by chance in this distribution that would be an indication that Mr. Smith probably taught the unit well (or poorly if the scores went down). Fortunately, you will never have to do all of these theoretical calculations. The computer will do them for you.

Take a look at Figure 8-2. The idea is to find the position of the post-test score in relationship to the theoretical distribution generated by estimating the parameters from the pre-test score. This works whenever you are comparing two group means even if they are not pre-test/post-test; for instance when you would compare two classes in which you used different instructional strategies.

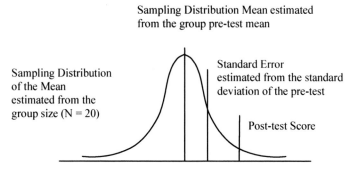

Figure 8-2. Mr. Smith's curriculum (estimating parameters).

COMPARING GROUP MEANS WITH A *T*-TEST

In the case of percentile rank, an individual score is being compared to the larger group. From the last chapter, you will recall that the calculation to do that is called a z-score (the distance a score is from the mean in units of standard deviation). When we are looking at a group mean in comparison to another group the idea is the same—how far is a group's score from the mean of a distribution of scores of groups of the same size in units of standard error? The calculation to do this is similar to the z-score, but because it involves estimating parameters, it is not the same. It is called a *t*-score or more familiarly, after all the calculations are done, a **t-test**. Just as a reminder, because we are dealing with mean scores, we are talking about analyzing interval data.

Here is an example. Mrs. Greene gives her students a pre-test on earthquake facts. She then teaches a unit on earthquakes followed by the test again. She puts all of the scores into a spreadsheet and then tells the computer to compare the two sets of scores, the pre-test and the post-test, using a *t*-test. What the computer returns is a **probability** (a *p* value) that the two sets of scores were likely to have occurred from the same group by chance. If the probability is high that they could have appeared by chance, there is no evidence that Mrs. Greene's teaching had any impact. If the probability was low that the group means could have occurred randomly, then we would assume that the second set of scores came from a different group or, in our case, from a group that had been changed by something. The most likely reason for the difference is the teaching. Good thing.

This sounds easy but we have a subjective judgment to make here. At what point could we say that a difference in mean scores is so unlikely to have occurred by chance that it did not occur by chance; that is, a **significant difference** occurred? Researchers make different decisions on when groups are significantly different based on the importance of being wrong about that decision. In other words, how sure do we have to be that the difference is the result of something we did and not have occurred purely by chance? If a researcher is testing a drug to see if it has critical side effects, that researcher is going to want to be really sure that the results did not occur by chance. In that case, she might set the significant difference level at one in ten thousand. She would want to be as sure as possible that the drug did no harm.

With social science research we are seldom this exacting. Generally, we set our probability level at .05 or 5%. When studying the behavior and opinions of people, we assume that if there is less than 5% chance (1 in 20 chance) that group differences could have appeared randomly, then they did not appear randomly. They appeared because there was an actual difference between the two groups. In statistics, probabilities are always expressed as a decimal rather than a percent so a probability of random occurrence 5 percent of the time would be .05. To say this slightly differently, when comparing groups, we want to know that the probability that the group mean differences could have occurred by chance is less than .05. If we can show that the group mean differences are likely to occur by chance less than 5 percent of the time ($p < .05$) then we can say that the group differences are **statistically significant**. (As a habit when you are writing reports on quantitative research you should not use the word "significant" except when referring to statistical significance.)

Think back to Mrs. Greene and her earthquake test. Here is what is conceptually going on when she tests for group mean differences (does a t-test). She gives a pretest. Using estimated parameters the computer generates a theoretical distribution of group mean scores from groups the same size as her class. Then when she gives the posttest the computer figures out how likely it is that the second group mean score could have appeared randomly in the theoretical distribution of group mean scores on the pretest. If it is highly probable (more than a 5 percent chance) that the second score could have appeared randomly, she would conclude that there is no difference in the two groups. In other words, the children had not changed in a statistically significant way in their ability to answer questions on the test after instruction. If the probability that the group mean difference could have appeared by chance is really low (less than 5 percent), then she can conclude that her students are not the same as the group that took the pretest. There is a statistically significant difference, presumably due to her instruction. She knows this instantly after the computer does the t-test because the computer generates a p value. If p is less than 5 percent (written $p < .05$), there is a statistically significant difference.

When you are doing research in which you are comparing group mean scores what you care about is whether the group mean differences are significant (unlikely to have occurred by chance). When the computer calculates the p value it will be a precise value, like .035. What is important is whether the p value is smaller than the level you as a researcher have set to test for significance. How much smaller the number is doesn't really make that much difference. Even so, in the 6th edition of the APA manual APA is suggesting that the actual values generated by the calculation are put into the tables in the results portion of your study report. You and your research mentor need to agree on what style of presentation makes the most sense.

Hypothesis Testing and Errors

When you read quantitative research in which group comparisons are reported, often the reports will be constructed by reporting whether group differences are significant, much the way that it was described above. We feel quite confident making conclusions based on statistically significant differences, but those conclusions may not be correct 100 percent of the time. The truth is that we can never know things absolutely. What we find is the best explanation for the moment but leaving open the possibility that a disconfirming fact may still be discovered. So, researchers end up doing something that always sounds way more complicated than it needs to be. They do studies in which they try to reject the explanation that what they want to find is not true.

Here is what that looks like: I think that implementing a new discipline strategy wherein students are taught conflict management will reduce referrals in my school. My *hypothesis* is that if I compare a group that was taught the new strategy to a group that was not, I will see significantly fewer referrals in the group that received the instruction. In order to show my hypothesis is probably true I am going to start by stating the hypothesis in a form that says it is not true: the new discipline strategy will have no effect on student referral numbers. This is called a **null hypothesis** (null as in none or no difference). After I have gathered the data and run the *t*-test, I find that the probability that there is no difference in the groups (my null-hypothesis) is really small ($p < .05$). I can now reject the null hypothesis that there is no difference because it is so unlikely there is no difference. This means there probably is a difference. And, the best explanation that I have (although it is possible that there are others) is that the difference in the two groups came from implementing the new discipline strategy.

Trying to keep all of the negatives straight when you are reasoning out hypothesis testing is a daunting task, which is why research reports often omit the statement of the null hypothesis. Procedurally, it makes little difference whether you include the statement of the null hypothesis in your report because readers assume that it exists whether or not you state it. Technically, the null hypothesis has to exist if we are doing good research because we always have to be cautious about the existence of alternative explanations to what we have found. We can never prove that something is true in all cases because we would have to test every possible case—hence, the approach of the null-hypothesis. Practically, you will read many research reports where the null hypothesis is never mentioned. You and your research mentor will have to make decisions about the report style that is best for your work.

Thinking in terms of hypotheses does help us pay attention to an important problem in social science research. Earlier we said that establishing significance levels in research, called **alpha levels**, is based on the importance of not being wrong. If the alpha level is .05 that would mean that you would reject the null hypothesis and believe that the alternative (what you are interested in finding) was likely to be true if the probability that the null hypothesis was true was less than 5 percent. Put another way you could be wrong to reject the null hypothesis 5 percent of the time. We just assume that 5 percent is so small that it is worth the risk of being wrong.

When the null hypothesis is rejected but should not have been (group differences did just appear randomly) that is called a **Type I error** or a false positive. That is, you thought the two groups were significantly different, but they were not. The opposite can be true also. It is possible that the null hypothesis was not rejected but that there really were differences in the groups. If the t-test says that the probability that the groups were the same (null hypothesis) was .25 we would say that was a pretty high probability and we would not reject the null. But, it is possible that there really were differences and we just lacked the evidence to be confident that we had seen them. Not rejecting a null hypothesis when there really were differences is called a **Type II error** or a false negative. That is, you thought there was no difference between the two groups when there really was.

Generally, for social scientists, the best way to reduce both Type I and Type II errors (that is, to be truly sure your results are not due to random error) is to have larger groups from which you gather data and to randomly select participants from the populations to which you wish to generalize. Often in our work neither of these are possibilities. Educational researchers are often using intact groups of students or other school personnel in which group sizes are limited and random selection is not a possibility. This is the point at which to remind yourself to be very humble about your findings. We need to work hard in designing research (especially quantitative research) to reduce alternative explanations to our findings, but alternative explanations are almost always possible. Reflecting on what those alternative explanations might be is part of what you will need to write in the conclusions section of your report.

One- Tailed and Two-Tailed Tests

When Mrs. Greene teaches about earthquakes, if the assessment of her students' learning is aligned with the curriculum, it is hard to imagine that the group mean score from pretest to posttest would do anything but go up. In most other cases of doing social science research we cannot be so confident. For instance, using our example of teaching a conflict management strategy, it could be that our efforts had exactly the opposite effect that we had hoped or some other mitigating factor intervened and referrals actually go up in the treatment group. When comparing group mean scores it makes an important difference if we know ahead of time which set of scores will likely be higher than the other. This is easiest to visualize by looking at a normal curve (see Figure 8-3).

As researchers, we have set the alpha level for our study at .05. What does this really mean? In most instances, when doing t-tests we want to know if the second group mean is so unlikely to occur that it appears in the area representing 5 percent

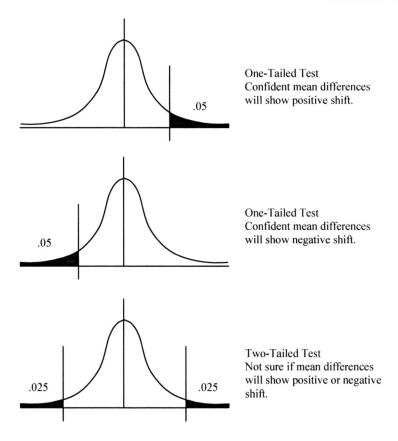

One-Tailed Test
Confident mean differences
will show positive shift.

One-Tailed Test
Confident mean differences
will show negative shift.

Two-Tailed Test
Not sure if mean differences
will show positive or negative
shift.

Figure 8-3. Differences between one-tailed and two-tailed tests with p set at .05.

of the mean scores at the far end of the sampling distribution of the mean. If the score does reside in this area then we say it is so unlikely to occur by chance that it did not appear by chance; rather, it occurred for some other reason, which we hope is our intervention. That 5 percent area could be at either end of the distribution. In the case of the dinosaur curriculum we hope to see the class mean on the posttest at the right end of the distribution because we expect student test scores to increase after instruction. In the case of the conflict management strategy we would hope to see the group mean for referrals at the left end of the distribution (significantly fewer referrals), as teaching conflict management should reduce behavioral referrals.

What if we do not know ahead of time which direction the second group mean will be from the first? What if we are unsure whether the treatment will cause an increase or decrease in the second group mean? Are you absolutely sure using cooperative learning as an instructional strategy will help students learn math facts better or is it possible they may actually do worse? We still have to abide by having the second score appear in the distribution less than 5 percent of the time. If we do not know which end of the curve to look toward, then the 5 percent has to be split between both ends of the curve. The score for the second group mean would have to appear in the area that represents 2.5 percent of curve on either end. If you did not split the 5 percent area and allowed the possibility of 5 percent at each end of the curve, then you would actually have 10 percent of the area available to demonstrate significance—double what you had set for your study.

When you know ahead of time what the direction of change is likely to be for your study, you can establish that the 5 percent area to show significance is in fact all at one end of the distribution. This is called a **one-tailed test**. When you can not anticipate the direction of change, you must split the 5 percent of the area to show significance to both ends of the distribution. This is called a **two-tailed test**. This makes a big difference in your study. Practically it becomes twice as difficult to show significance if you are using a two-tailed test.

As a researcher you have to decide which test to use. Establishing that you can anticipate the direction of change is not always that easy. In cases where it may not be obvious, you should support your claim for using a one-tailed test with other research related to yours. As you read research papers you will find many examples where researchers inappropriately used a one-tailed test. It is surprisingly difficult in almost all social science research to be absolutely confident of the effect of an intervention. We do research because we are not sure of the answers. Therefore, almost by definition we should be cautious about anticipating the results of our work. When in doubt, use a two-tailed test.

Most statistical programs will give both the one and two-tailed results automatically so you, the researcher, must choose the correct value to report. If the statistical program you are using only provides the one-tailed result, it is very easy to compute the two-tailed result. The p value for a two-tailed test is exactly double that of the value generated for a one-tailed.

Conservative Calculations

Part of the art of quantitative research is to design studies that eliminate all possible explanations of changes that are observed except those changes that occurred because of the intervention that you are studying. We want to know that what we did (or what we watched happen) made a difference. The problem is that studying people is really messy. And to make it worse we are usually studying them in natural environments where we have little control over all of the other things that might be affecting behavior other than our intervention. For example, we generally do not test on Mondays or during spirit week or during other times when students' minds might not be totally focused on their work. As another example, we have little control over whether a student studies at home, or how much parental help or encouragement students receive.

To a certain degree, statisticians compensate for this lack of control by making the ability to show significance mathematically more difficult in situations where variation in the groups is more pronounced (one of the things that is hard to control).

The calculations are designed to reduce Type I errors (where we have shown an important difference in groups and probably shouldn't have). If we feel the two groups we are comparing were different from the start (e.g., college bound and non-college bound seniors), we choose to do our statistical analyses using **unequal variance**. If we feel the two groups we are comparing are similar (e.g., a control and treatment group for two different seventh grade science curriculum on the same topic), we choose to do our statistical analyses using **equal variance**. A special kind of analysis is done if the two groups being compared are composed of exactly the same individuals (e.g., a pre/post test design); in that instance we can use a **paired** *t*-test.

Here are more detailed examples of these comparisons. Let's say we are interested in knowing if participation in after school sports affects GPA in high school students. A common way to do this would be to look at the students in a given high school and split them into two groups: those that participate in after school sports during the year and those that do not. Gather all of the GPAs for a given semester and run a *t*-test to see if the groups are significantly different. The problem with this study is that there are so many possible things that could be affecting these students' choices about participating in sports that our "test" may not be measuring the relationship between GPA and sports at all. The two groups are probably enormously different on a number of characteristics to begin with: after school responsibilities, interests, hobbies, etc. We would say that the two groups have unequal variance to mean that the groups are not very much alike. Caution would be warranted in this case to not get too excited about the results of the *t*-test before beginning to eliminate some of the other possible influencing factors. Since we cannot control for all these variables between the groups, we rely on mathematics to help us. With your statistical program you would automatically make a more conservative estimate of possible significance by choosing a *t*-test of groups with unequal variance.

On the other end of the scale is a case like Mrs. Greene and the earthquake test. The students who took the pretest are exactly the same as the students who took the posttest. In cases where exactly the same people are in the two compared groups we would use a paired *t*-test. For this situation the differences in the two groups are dramatically reduced and we do not have to worry as much about other differences in the groups accounting for what we thought we saw as a significant difference based on our intervention. The calculation of significance can be less conservative because the groups are so similar.

Depending on the statistical software you are using there is a third choice. Imagine you are comparing two 7th grade classes in the same school. You have every reason to believe that these children are similar in most ways and (this is important) the size of the two classes is essentially the same. In this case we still need to be worried about unaccounted for differences in the two groups, but less so than in the case of GPA and sports participation. This third category is when you would use a *t*-test for groups with equal variance.

Here again the researcher needs to make some subjective judgment. If the two comparison groups have absolutely the same members in both groups (you can not do this if one student was gone on the day of the posttest) then use a paired *t*-test.

If you believe the groups to be similar in most important ways and the two groups are almost the same size then use a *t*-test for groups with equal variance. All other cases, especially when comparing groups of different sizes, use a *t*-test for groups with unequal variance.

ANALYSIS OF VARIANCE (ANOVA)

It is very common that researchers design studies in which more than two groups need to be compared at once. For instance, in a study of strategies for improving reading comprehension you might want to have Group A read the stories only, Group B read the stories and draw pictures to illustrate what they read, and Group C complete a worksheet after reading the stories. After these interventions all of the students would receive the same comprehension test. To find out whether group mean differences were significant, it would seem that three comparisons would need to be made: A with B, A with C, and B with C. Doing three *t*-tests to make the comparisons would violate statistical logic. Statisticians would worry about all of the comparisons being independent of each other. The correct procedure is to use an **Analysis of Variance (ANOVA)** whenever more than two group means are being compared at the same time. An example of how this might look in a results section is shown in Chapter 9 (refer to Figure 9-4).

An ANOVA generates a *p* value interpreted the same way it would be for a *t*-test. It tells whether group mean differences are likely to have occurred by chance. Some-where in the comparisons of group means one or more of the comparisons is statistically significant if $p < .05$. An ANOVA does the multiple comparisons (in our example, A and B, B and C, and A and C), but just tells you whether a signi-ficant difference exists—not which groups are statistically different. To determine which of the comparisons are significantly different, a further test must be done. These are called **post hoc tests**. Although there are a number of procedures available the two most common are Tukey's and Scheffe's. Generally, Tukey's is used when group sizes are equivalent and Scheffe's when they are not. (Scheffe's is a more conservative calculation under the same reasoning as more conservative *t*-tests above.) Most statistical software will allow you to choose which post hoc analysis to use. Unfortunately, as of the writing of this text, Microsoft Excel does not provide that calculation although there are some third party "add-ins" which do.

When the post hoc analysis is run, the results will give another *p* value for the specific two group comparisons which are subsumed under the larger ANOVA analysis. As a caution, it is possible for a post hoc analysis to show a significant comparison even when the *p* value for the ANOVA is not significant. Always look at the results of the ANOVA before determining if post hoc analysis is warranted. Reporting on significance can be done from the post hoc *p* values, but the results of the ANOVA should also be shown.

Although different statistical programs display results differently, the example shown in Figure 8-4 is typical. Each group mean and standard deviation is calculated. Then the calculations for the ANOVA are presented in an ANOVA Table. In this table, one block is marked as "*p*". This the result of the significance test for the overall ANOVA. In this case it is .002. Then, depending on which post hoc analysis is chosen, a table will display the specific group comparisons. In this case there is no significant difference between groups 1 and 2 (p = .382). There are significant differences between groups 1 and 3 (p = .001) and 2 and 3 (p = .025). In most of the papers, you will read the significant difference between groups 1 and 3 would be reported as $p < .01$ (you would have to assume that the .001 was rounded from a larger number) and between groups 2 and 3 as $p < .05$. Again, the newer APA guidelines suggest putting the actual p values into the table. With ANOVA tables this presents more challenges than with t-test results tables. We provide an example of how this may be done but you need to discuss the style for your report with your research mentor.

In most cases when you are using statistical software, calculations will be reported that are more sophisticated than what you need. If you look at Figure 8-4, you will see many numbers returned in the read-out that you do not need to deal with at this point in time. We want you to be cautious, informed users of statistical analysis, but descriptions of all of the terms reported are beyond the design of this book and the number of terms displayed may vary depending on which statistical program you are using. On the other hand, we hope that this introduction will make you curious enough to investigate further on your own.

| Grand Mean | 111.60 |
| N | 93 |

Group(group)	N	Group Mean	Std Deviation
1	31	95.35	29.62
2	30	104.43	48.88
3	32	134.06	52.57

ANOVA Table

Source of Variance	SS	DF	MS	F
Between Groups	25867.941	2.000	12933.971	6.422
Within Groups	181262.338	90.000	2014.026	
Total	207130.280			

| P | .002 |
| Eta Squared | .125 |

Post Hoc tests	Comparison	Mean Difference	T-Value	P - Unadjusted
Group_1				
	1 and 2	9.078	.881	.382
	1 and 3	38.708	3.585	**.001**
Group_2				
	2 and 3	29.629	2.294	**.025**

Figure 8-4. Example ANOVA results.

PRACTICAL SIGNIFICANCE

In a study of the differences of test scores between boys and girls on a standardized mathematics test in a school district, it might be discovered that boys scored significantly higher than girls. On closer examination of this study we would see that 423 boys and 412 girls took the test and that the mean score for the boys was 67.7 and the mean score for the girls was 66.2. Statistically the differences were unlikely to have happened by chance ($p < .05$) so we would conclude that boys on average scored significantly better on the test than girls. But, is a 1.5 point difference really meaningful? When group sizes grow very large, statistical significance appears with smaller and smaller numerical differences between the groups. In our example the significant difference is real, but it represents a very small difference in the actual mean scores of the girls and boys. From this study it would be difficult to rationalize changing the mathematics curriculum to assist girls because practically they are already doing as well as the boys. A difference of 1.5 points out of 100 is not of true concern. So, while the difference is statistically significant, it is really of little **practical significance**. Practical significance refers to how useful a statistically significant finding is in real life.

How can you tell how much weight to give to statistical findings? First it is important to discover if statistical differences appear. The probability that differences we see could happen by chance needs to be very low to start with. Once that has been established then we need to figure out how to determine if these differences are big enough to justify further action. Some tool needs to be used that can look at any study to determine the size of the impact of an intervention. This standardized computation of the amount of a difference between groups is called **effect size**.

Determining effect size looks similar to determining z scores. The idea is to figure out the number of standard deviations between the two group mean scores (instead of between the mean and a given score as we do with z scores) in terms of standard deviations. Start by determining the mean of both groups and then subtracting one from the other to compute a "distance" between the two mean scores. Then we need to figure out this distance in terms of standard deviations. The question is which standard deviation should be used for the division. (Recall, there are two groups, so two means and two standard deviations.) Generally, averaging the two standard deviations and dividing that number into the mean differences will solve the problem. Statisticians do something a bit more complicated even though it seldom gives a solution much different from the suggestion above. They use something called a "pooled" standard deviation. This is computed by averaging the square of both standard deviations and then finding the square root (see Table 8-1).

Table 8-1. Computing effect size

Effect Size = mean^1 – mean^2 / ((std dev^1 + std dev^2)/2)

Once you have the effect size of a group mean difference, you can report practical significance in your study. In general if you have an effect size around 0.2 (that is, 0.2 standard deviations difference) the effect size is considered small. Effect sizes around 0.5 are labeled medium and around 0.8 or larger are considered large. This is another of those subjective judgments we make as researchers. When reporting effect sizes, try to provide a rationale for why you believe in your case they represent small, medium or large effects in addition to the computed number.

Here is an example. In a section of a biology class (section A) you teach a unit on mammals and administer a unit test at the end. In another section (section B) of the class you teach the same unit but this time you allow the students to examine some web sites that reinforce what you have been teaching. That group gets the same unit test at the end. Group A has a mean of 45.2 on the test and a standard deviation of 14.3. Group B has a mean of 52.7 and a standard deviation of 12.4. You run a t-test and the group mean differences turn out to be significant. Group B scored, on average 7.2 points higher on the test. The average of the standard deviations is 13.35. The mean score difference divided by the average standard deviation equals 0.56. Since this is a distance between the two mean scores it makes no difference if the computation comes out positive or negative. Just use the absolute value of the result. You can report a moderate practical significance in this case.

Effect Size $= 52.7 - 45.2 / ((14.3 + 12.4) / 2) = .56$

CHI SQUARE

So far we have been talking about looking for statistically significant differences in groups by comparing group means. Sometimes you will have gathered data from groups that are not interval data and consequently no mean will be available. When data are in the form of nominal (using categories, e.g., gender, ethnicity) or ordinal variables (things can be ordered, but not uniformly measured, such as scales like once a month, once a week, once a day), it is still possible to use chance as way to determine if differences are likely to have appeared randomly or if something else important is going on. The statistical procedure for doing this is called **Chi Square**. As you will see, the richness of interpretation from this procedure is considerably less than comparisons of group means. Nonetheless, Chi Square can be a useful tool for group analysis. Unfortunately, Chi Square can also take more work to calculate than comparisons of group means.

For Chi Square, the number of responses in each response category is listed in a table when two variables are compared (one on the x axis and one on the y axis of the table). The resulting table is called a **contingency table** or a **cross tabs**.

Imagine that a reading teacher wants to know if students have preferences for the kind of stories they read. She asks each student if they would rather read stories about people, animals or travel. But, she is worried that boys might have a different preference than girls so she keeps track of whether each response comes from a girl or a boy. The question is, can she just ask for reading preference or will gender make a difference in the responses. She wants to know if the variables of reading preference and gender are *independent* or if she must know one to understand the other. The Chi Square test in this case is called a **test of independence**.

With a test of independence the observed data are from two variables at the same time. To calculate whether boys and girls have statistically different reading preferences, start by placing the observed frequencies into a contingency table. In this case, we would have gender as the rows and types of stories as the columns. Refer to Figure 8-5, which compares reading topic preference for boys and girls.

	Reading Preference		
	People	**Animals**	**Travel**
Boys	5	8	13
Girls	19	6	10

Figure 8-5. Cross tabs example.

Generally, the logic of Chi Square is to look at the distribution of the responses in the cells of the contingency table and to use a calculation to compare those responses to what you would have expected to find in the cells. The calculation produces a probability that the differences between the observed responses and the expected responses could be explained by random variation. If the probability is really low ($p < .05$) then random variation is not a good explanation for the differences and something else is. The two variables are not independent. Onto to the calculations!

Once you have the observed frequencies in the table, most statistical software will be able to calculate what the expected frequencies ought to be in each cell. If you are using Excel, however, you will need to determine the expected frequencies by hand. Calculate the number of responses in each column of the table. Then calculate the total number of responses in each row of the table. Select one cell in the contingency table. Multiply the row total for that cell by the column total for that cell and divide by the total number of responses. The resulting number will be the expected value for that cell. Refer again to Figure 8-5. In the case of the cell that lists the number of times boys picked people stories (upper left cell), multiply 26 (the row total) by 24 (the column total) and divide that by 61 (the total number of responses in the whole table). The expected frequency is 10.230. See the expected frequencies in Figure 8-6 calculated using this method.

If you have gotten this far, even Excel can do the rest of the Chi Square calculation for you. As noted above, if you are using a more sophisticated statistical program, calculating expected frequencies will not be necessary because the software will do it for you. In either case, you will want to have the expected frequencies when you report your findings. Whatever statistical program you use, it will provide you with a number appropriately called theChi Square (in this case it turns out to be 7.68). You will also be given a *p* value (in this case it turns out that it is .021) that

Gender		**People**	**Animals**	**Travel**	**Row Total**
		Reading Preference			
	Boys	5	8	13	26
Expected		*10.230*	*5.967*	*9.803*	
	Girls	19	6	10	35
Expected		*13.770*	*8.033*	*13.197*	
Columns Total		**24**	**14**	**23**	**61**

Figure 8-6. Observed and expected frequencies in a chi square.

is interpreted like any other *p* value. In Excel you have to use a formula called a chitest, but in most programs when you build the contingency table if you want it simply lists the Chi Square and *p* value below the table.

Since the probability is low ($p < .05$) that the differences between the observed and expected frequencies could have occurred by chance, the teacher would conclude that the differences did not occur by chance. Preference for reading topic is dependent on gender. You have to know the gender to help predict reading preference. The two variables are not independent.

Unfortunately, the Chi Square does not tell you much more about what the differences in the preferences for the two groups are. It just tells you that the differences between the observed and expected differences were unlikely to occur by chance. It does not tell you which differences were unlikely to occur by chance. It is similar to the ANOVA in this aspect; however, there is no post-hoc test for the Chi Square. As a researcher you now have to make a case for what the Chi Square has told you. Often this is a subjective process. Go back through the table showing the observed and expected frequencies and look for inordinately large differences. In our example you might suggest boys seem to select books about people less often than was expected, where girls selected people more often than expected. Remember that this is not statistical proof. You only know that it is really unlikely that gender and reading preference are independent, and you are making informed suggestions of where that dependence has appeared.

A common use of the Chi Square is with questionnaire responses. Very often you will see response category sets like: never, seldom, sometimes, and frequently. We have no trouble seeing these as ordinal data. The categories are clearly ordered but it is a struggle to believe that the intervals between these responses are equal. Ask yourself the question: is the distance between never and seldom the same as the distance between sometimes and frequently? Just saying that out loud makes it clear that that is a question that makes no sense. So, these are ordinal categories and not interval. These data should not be coded with a cardinal number (never = 1 and so on) and analyzed with means, standard deviations, or group mean comparisons. The more appropriate analysis with ordinal data is Chi Square.

As an aside, while there are many statistical software programs available on most college campuses that students have access to, we have found that nearly all of our students have Microsoft Office on their home or school computers and are comfortable using Excel spreadsheets. As mentioned periodically throughout this and Chapter 7, Excel can be used to perform basic statistical analyses. Because Excel is a software program that most of our students will have ready access to both now and in the future, we have included a set of basic instructions to perform common statistical analyses using Excel in Appendix F.

NEXT STEPS

In this chapter we have looked at ways to show statistically that important differences are appearing between groups. When you design a study with the intent of testing the impact of some intervention, usually this is what you would want to find. Statistical analysis is very good at showing if differences in groups are due to random chance or more likely to be because of something we did. Unfortunately statistical analysis is not very good at revealing if the design of your study may have allowed something else to impact your results beyond the intended intervention. We need to take a careful look at how to make as sure as possible that the impact you think you see from your intervention really is responsible for the results you observed. Before we do that, however, let's look at some specific designs often used in quantitative research.

CHAPTER SELF-CHECK

Having completed this chapter, you should be comfortable discussing the following:
− normal distribution, including standard error and estimating parameters
− tests of significance: t-test, paired t-tests, ANOVA, Chi Square
− null hypothesis
− statistical vs. practical significance
− Type I and Type II errors
− one and two tailed tests
− setting significance levels

CHAPTER REVIEW QUESTIONS

1. Why is it important to see if mean score changes are statistically significant when you can clearly see that scores have improved?
2. Why is it so difficult to *prove* something in quantitative research?
3. How do you convince a reader of your research that it was appropriate to do a one-tailed test?
4. Under what circumstances can you use a paired t-test?
5. What are *post hoc* tests?
6. Why is practical significance important?
7. When do you need to use a Chi Square test?

The following references provide additional explanations of many of the concepts in this chapter:

REFERENCES

Creswell, J. (2009). *Research design: Quantitative and qualitative approaches* (3rd ed.). Thousand Oaks, CA: Sage Publications.

Gall, M. D., Gall, J. P., & Borg, W. R. (2007). *Educational research: An introduction* (8th ed.). Boston: Allyn & Bacon.

Gay, L. R., & Airasian, P. W. (2009). *Educational research: Competencies for analysis and application* (9th ed.). Upper Saddle River, NJ: Prentice Hall.

QUANTITATIVE STUDY DESIGNS

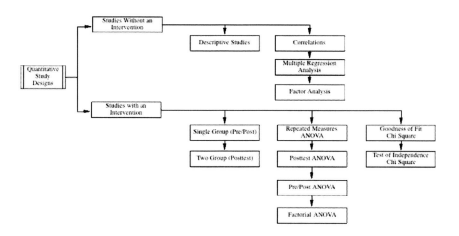

Chapter 9 examines the variety of designs available in quantitative research and why to choose one over another.

INTRODUCTION

As educational researchers, when we are doing quantitative studies, generally what we are trying to do is to gather and analyze data in such a manner that we can show that it is very likely that something we did (an intervention) caused a change in those to whom the intervention was applied. The problem is that we need to make the case that the intervention caused the change and not some other influence that was outside of our control. To minimize the impact of outside influences you need to do a lot of work before data are ever gathered. In this chapter we will examine quantitative study designs as a starting point. In subsequent chapters we will add survey design and validity and reliability to the list of things needed to improve your confidence that you really are measuring what you thought you were measuring.

QUANTITATIVE STUDY DESIGNS

Recall our discussion of quantitative research types in Chapter 1. Each of those types generally uses specific quantitative analysis tools. Experimental and causal-comparative studies use comparisons of group means; correlational studies, appropriately, use correlations; descriptive studies rely on descriptive statistics; and survey research may often use some combination of these strategies. Experimental and causal-comparative designs require a closer look.

In most of the examples in the previous two chapters, a single group was examined before and after an intervention to see if anything had changed. This is called a **pre/post design**.

$$\text{Pretest} \Rightarrow \quad \text{Intervention} \Rightarrow \quad \text{Posttest}$$

Data are gathered from the group (a pre-test) before the intervention occurs (a curriculum unit, perhaps) and then more data are gathered from the group after the intervention (a post-test). In many cases, this design works fine. In analysis you would probably use a *t*-test or paired *t*-test to compare the pre and post scores.

Frequently, though, you may have this nagging question as to whether your group would have changed anyway regardless of the intervention. Usually, the way to test for that is to have a second group, as similar as possible to the first but not having had the intervention, also take the pretest and posttest at the same time as the group you are studying. In other words, use a **control group**.

| Study Group | Pretest $\Rightarrow$ | Intervention $\Rightarrow$ | Posttest |
| Control Group | Pretest $\Rightarrow$ | | Posttest |

A word about control groups: as you can see above, the control group gets no intervention. For example, if a group is already receiving an intervention (a specific reading curriculum, say) and you want to see if a different group would do better with a different curriculum, it may seem like the first group that keeps getting the current curriculum can be a control group while your new curriculum group gets the intervention. Groups cannot necessarily be considered control groups if they are being *treated as usual*. Since the *usual* is in fact itself a treatment you would be cautious about calling this a control group. In a study like this you would be comparing two interventions—the original curriculum to the new curriculum. This can be done and is an acceptable research design; however, when describing your study, you would not use the word "control." In order to have a control group for the new reading curriculum, you would have to find a group that was not getting any specific reading instruction, including a reading curriculum that everyone *usually* received. The moral is to be careful about the use of the term *control group* when you are describing your study. You do not use it to compare something new to something already in practice. Using control groups would be more appropriate in a case where you were trying an intervention that was not part of the normal curriculum. As an example, you might implement Drug Awareness and Resistance Education (DARE) to one group of fifth graders and no anti-drug and alcohol curriculum to another to determine if the DARE curriculum had any impact on students' attitudes to the use of drugs and alcohol. In most of our content areas, however, a control group is not possible. We are generally altering a curriculum or means of instruction rather than introducing something completely new.

If we do use a control group, analysis of our pre/post control and intervention groups is a bit more complicated as well. It would seem that ideally what we would want to find is a significant increase in the study group's scores and no significant increase in the control group's scores. Unfortunately this procedure ignores other important possible comparisons. Were the two groups significantly different to begin with (comparison of pretest scores)? Were the groups significantly different after the intervention (comparison of posttest scores)? And, in some cases it might be valuable to know if the pretest of one group was significantly different than the posttest of the other. As a rule you should apply the same strategy whenever there are more than two sets of data that could be compared at the same time in a study—an analysis of variance or ANOVA. As detailed in Chapter 8, an ANOVA makes all of the possible comparisons to see if a significant difference appears anywhere in the study. This is followed by a post hoc analysis to show you exactly where the differences appeared. The problem with an ANOVA is that as the group sizes become smaller, the likelihood of being able to demonstrate significant differences decreases.

Being sure that you have sample group sizes that are large enough for statistical comparison is important. Technically, the computer can help you make the necessary statistical calculations even when sample group sizes are very small. Practically, however, as group sizes become smaller and smaller, the likelihood that significant differences can be demonstrated also becomes smaller. Whenever possible you should try to have groups that have at least 30 for statistical comparison. Often this is not possible because we are working with intact groups (our classes) with fewer than 30 students. This should not keep you from doing the study; however, it will necessitate that you have larger group differences before significance will appear than you would have had to with larger groups. That is; it is easier to find significant differences in large samples sizes than in small sample sizes.

Sometimes you will see researchers measure the gain that different groups have made and then statistically compare *gain scores*—pre/post differences for group A are compared to pre/post differences for group B. The result is two sets of data (gain scores for the two groups) so a *t*-test is used for analysis. This type of design is not the best one to use, although it may be unavoidable in some studies. Using gain score differences eliminates the other comparisons of the groups that are possible and potentially meaningful. The validity of your study may be put into question unless you attend to initial group differences as well as differences related to the intervention (see *differential selection* below).

There are other study designs that you might use. For instance, you may have a study in an environment where pre and post data gathering is not possible. It may be that the only thing available to you is to compare two or more groups with data on a single measure only (no pre-test is possible.)

Whatever study design you use, the question of whether your intervention caused changes or some other influence was responsible for differences always remains. The remainder of this chapter is intended to introduce you to the most common study designs used in educational research. Some of these designs are more sophisticated than you are likely to use, but they appear frequently in literature that you will be reading for your study. With the exception of multiple regression analysis and factor analysis, the statistical analysis for each of these can be handled in Excel. Some of these designs have been described in more detail earlier.

STUDY TYPES IN WHICH THERE IS USUALLY NO INTERVENTION
(DESCRIPTIVE AND CORRELATIONS)

Descriptive Study (Summary description of group characteristics)

Generally, descriptive studies are intended to provide statistical information that gives a detailed summary of a group. These studies describe *what is*. Information is gathered on characteristics of the group and summary reports are generated using descriptive statistics appropriate to the scales used for data gathering. Sometimes group comparisons in descriptive studies may incorporate inferential tools, that is, extend the data beyond just descriptions of the group at hand and infer what might be in larger groups. Although historical studies often use descriptive statistical methods they usually do not include information directly gathered from respondents. Since descriptive studies often incorporate surveys to gather data this is sometimes called *Survey Research*. Descriptive research is often used to triangulate data in qualitative studies.

Example: Most states now produce Report Cards of school progress on various characteristics related to No Child Left Behind. These are descriptive studies. (e.g., Oregon Report Cards: http://www.ode.state.or.us/data/reportcard/reports.aspx).

Correlational Studies (Describing relationships among group characteristics)

Characteristics of the participants are measured through observation or a survey. The strength of the relationship between pairs of characteristics is identified with a correlation. A Pearson's r is used if both characteristics have been measured on interval or ratio scales. A Spearman's Rho is used if either characteristic has been measured on an ordinal scale.

Example: You want to know if the number of years of teaching is related to interest in participating in inservice activities. You design an instrument that uses a Likert type scale to evaluate teachers' interest in participating in inservice activities. The correlation coefficient resulting from the comparison of years of teaching and the interest instrument results tells you the direction and strength of the relationship of these two variables.

Be aware that it is possible to measure correlations using multiple ordinal variables or nominal variables but that the study designs take a great deal of care. If you see one like this in a study don't be surprised but make sure the researchers seem to know what they are doing.

We have included an example of a correlation matrix (Figure 9-1) as it might appear in a study report. These tables vary considerably in published papers. Our approach is to closely follow APA guidelines but to not include superfluous information. This is another point to discuss with your research mentor.

Table 1

Correlation of Years Teaching, Years in Grade Level, and Number of Principals

	Years teaching	Years in grade level
Years in grade level	.25	
Number of principals	.69*	.40

* $p < .05$

Figure 9-1. Example correlation matrix.

Multiple Regression Analysis (Assessing the power of predictive variables)

Multiple regression studies are designed to identify the power of two or more variables to predict a third. Generally, data are gathered on a criterion variable (the thing you want to predict) and then combinations of variables are compared to the criterion variable to assess the degree to which they explain the variance in the group responses. Variable combinations that do a good job of explaining the variation in the group are good predictive variables.

Example: You want to know what issues will be the best predictors of students completing homework. You gather data on homework completion from all of your students (criterion variable). The literature tells you that nutrition, parent support and peer associations all influence homework completion. You design a survey instrument that asks multiple questions in each of these areas. An accumulated score in each area is then used in the multiple regression analysis to determine which is the best predictor of homework completion and how the prediction is strengthened as each predictor is added to the analysis.

In statistical language you are measuring the amount of variance that is explained by each variable or a combination of variables. After looking at the results you would be able to say how much these variables you chose to examine explain the variation (variance) in the criterion variable.

Multiple regression is normally done with interval variables but again it is possible to construction regression studies that use ordinal or nominal variables. The same rule applies with these, that if you see them in the literature you are reading, check to make sure the authors explain clearly how they have done this analysis. The variations of the presentation of multiple regression result are numerous based on how the regression was done. Look to published research or the internet for examples of how studies similar to yours can be presented in table form.

Factor Analysis (Identifying related variables)

A factor analysis is one of a group of analysis types that is used to identify patterns and relationships among multiple correlations. The analysis computes all of the possible correlations among all the variables in a data set and then groups the variables based on identifying those highly correlated with each other but not with other variables in the study.

Example: You are designing a course evaluation instrument and the criteria you wish to evaluate are quality of content of the course, the appropriateness of instructional strategies in the class and the quality of the student/teacher communication in the course. You design an instrument with multiple questions that address each of those criteria. When data are gathered with this instrument a factor analysis will show how the questions actually group together. If they match your criteria then your instrument is likely to be measuring what you thought it was measuring. If they don't match you may be measuring other criteria that you hadn't anticipated.

The reported results of a factor analysis hide the complexity of the logic and calculations behind them. Factor analysis is not for the faint of heart even though most commercial statistical packages will do the calculations relatively easily. Like regression analysis there are many variations of factor analysis. Look for examples in published studies or on the internet of how others have presented similar results to yours.

STUDY TYPES THAT MEASURE THE IMPACT OF AN INTERVENTION
(COMPARISON OF GROUP MEANS)

Single Group Pretest/Posttest (t-test)

As discussed above, a measure of the impact of an intervention (that is, an assessment tool) is selected. A sample group is assessed on that measure. The sample group experiences some intervention. The same or a similar measure is applied to the group after the intervention. Group mean scores from the pretest and posttest are compared using a *t*-test to look for statistically significant differences.

Example: You are teaching a new unit on American history. Students are given a test on their knowledge of American history. You then teach the unit. At the end of the unit students are given the same or an equivalent test of American history as the pretest. You use a *t*-test to see if there has been a statistically significant improvement of students' knowledge from one test to the other.

Below is an example of a table including *t*-tests (Figure 9-2)—a comparison of semesters on a unit posttest and then again on learning gain scores. In the newest edition of the APA manual researchers are being asked to include actual *p* values in tables.

Table 1

Comparison of Overall Means of Posttest Scores and Learning Gains for Fall and Spring Semester

	Semester						
	Fall			Spring			
	n	Mean	*SD*	*n*	Mean	*SD*	*p*
Posttest	1989	76.87	20.4	1901	74.85	21.7	.003
Learning Gain	1868	34.76	23.9	1872	37.53	24.7	.001

Figure 9-2. Example t-test table.

Two Groups Posttest only (t-test)

This type of design is often used with a treatment group and a control group. In this type of study design, an assessment tool for the intervention is selected. One group receives the intervention and the other does not. The assessment tool is applied to the groups after the intervention. Group mean scores from the two groups are compared using a *t*-test to look for statistically significant differences.

Group 1	Intervention $\Rightarrow$	Posttest
Group 2		Posttest

Example: You want to know if the teachers in your school actually got anything out of the inservice you led. At the end of instruction you give the teachers an assessment related to the training. You also give the same assessment to a group of teachers who did not participate in the inservice. You use a *t*-test to see if the two groups scored statistically significantly differently.

Repeated Measure Study (One-way ANOVA)

All participants in the study get the same treatments. The same assessment measure is used after every treatment. Significant differences between treatments are identified with an ANOVA. Post hoc tests are used to determine which group mean score comparisons are significant. The strength of this study design is increased if the treatments are repeated in a different order throughout the study.

Intervention 1 $\Rightarrow$	Posttest
Intervention 2 $\Rightarrow$	Posttest
Intervention 3 $\Rightarrow$	Posttest

A variation of a repeated measures study is called a *time series study* in which subjects experience a single intervention and are assessed on the same measure three or more times over selected time intervals. Typically this would be a pretest, posttest and a repeat of the posttest some time later.

Pretest $\Rightarrow$ Intervention $\Rightarrow$ Posttest $\Rightarrow$ Second Posttest

Example: You want to know if how students are assigned to cooperative groups makes a difference on how well they work together. You develop a measure of cooperation that you will use to judge students' ability to work together. On different projects you use different cooperative designs: students are randomly assigned to groups, students choose their own groups, or you group students by academic ability. Your measure of cooperation is used after each project and then an ANOVA tells you if significant differences appear based on group assignment strategy.

The following table example (Figure 9-3) represents the same assessment given to a series of groups. Note that the table lists the overall ANOVA *p* value and then lists the specific value for each pot hoc comparison.

Table 1

ANOVA Course Evaluation Comparisons for Five Iterations of Ed 558

Course	N	Mean	SD	ANOVA Comparisons[a][b]			
				1	2	3	4
1	10	1.45	.75				
2	15	1.55	.40	.67			
3	17	1.80	.64	.21	.20		
4	23	1.18	.36	.17	.01	< .001	
5	22	1.56	.81	.73	.98	.31	.05

[a] ANOVA significance $p = .034$.
[b] Post hoc comparisons computed using Tukey's HSD.

Figure 9-3. Example ANOVA table.

Two or More Groups Posttest only (One-way ANOVA)

This design is used when there are two or more interventions being compared. Each sample group experiences a different intervention. One group may be designed as a control group; that is, receives no intervention. The assessment tool is applied to the groups after the intervention. Group mean scores from all of the groups are compared using an ANOVA to look for significant differences. Post hoc tests are used to determine which group mean score comparisons are statistically significant.

Group 1	Intervention 1 $\Rightarrow$	Posttest
Group 2	Intervention 2 $\Rightarrow$	Posttest
Group 3	Intervention 3 $\Rightarrow$	Posttest

Example: You want to know if having science "kits" works better than teaching science without kits. In one class a textbook but no kits are used, in another kits are used in lieu of a textbook, and in a third class both kits and textbooks are used. You use the same unit test for all three classes. An ANOVA is used to see if the test scores were statistically significantly different. Post hoc tests are used to determine which group mean score comparisons are significant.

Two or More Groups Pretest/Posttest (One-way ANOVA)

An alternative to the two or more groups posttest design is to use pretest/posttest scores for each group. These two designs are essentially the same, except a pretest measure is used prior to any intervention. That is, an assessment tool is administered to all groups at the onset. Each sample group then experiences a different intervention. One group may be designed as a control group (receives no intervention).

The same or a similar measure is applied to the groups after the intervention. Group mean scores from all of the groups on both measures are compared using an ANOVA to look for significant differences. These comparisons include pretest/posttest differences for both groups, pretests between both groups and posttests between both groups. Post hoc tests are used to determine which group mean score comparisons are significant.

Group 1	Pretest $\Rightarrow$	Intervention 1 $\Rightarrow$	Posttest
Group 2	Pretest $\Rightarrow$	Intervention 2 $\Rightarrow$	Posttest
Group 3	Pretest $\Rightarrow$	Intervention 3 $\Rightarrow$	Posttest

Example: You wonder if music in classroom improves learning. You and your colleague both give your students the same pretest on a math unit. Both of you teach the same unit but in your class you have classical music playing during instruction. You both give your students the same posttest. You use an ANOVA and post hoc analysis to see if the students were different to begin with (pretest comparison), learned anything from the unit (pre/post comparisons for both groups), and whether the groups were significantly different after the unit (comparison of posttests).

Two or More Groups, Intervention and Control Variables (Factorial ANOVA)

Factorial ANOVA is used when you want to measure the effect of two or more independent variables (one which is usually an intervention) on a dependent variable. This study design could be looking at the interaction of two variables with a single group or it could look for the interaction of a second independent variable with multiple groups. A measure of the impact of an intervention is selected. The scores are separated based on each state of each of the independent variables. Group mean scores from all of the subgroups are compared using an ANOVA to look for statistically significant differences. Post hoc tests are used to determine which group mean score comparisons are significant. Mean scores for all sub-groups are plotted to look for interactions of the two independent variables.

	State 1 of Variable 2	State 2 of Variable 2
State 1 of Variable 1	Score	Score
State 2 of Variable 1	Score	Score
State 3 of Variable 1	Score	Score

Example: You want to know if a new homework policy (intervention—independent variable) has an impact on parents helping their children with homework (dependent variable) and you suspect the impact will be different by age of the student (second independent variable). Before you implement the new policy you send a survey home with every child in the district with questions related to helping with homework. Some time after you implement the policy you send the survey again. You use an ANOVA to compare the responses from the parents of the elementary, middle and high school students before and after the intervention (six groups). Post hoc tests tell you specifically where statistically significant differences appear. Charting mean scores of the parent survey indicates if the relationship between implementation of the policy and age remains the same at all age levels.

The power of the factorial design is that it not only tells you if significant differences have appeared (and where) but it also describes whether there is an interaction between the two variables. In other words is the relationship between the two variables different if you are examining different combinations of the states of the variables. This is usually represented in a paper as a line chart comparing the group mean differences for each state of each variable (Figure 9-4).

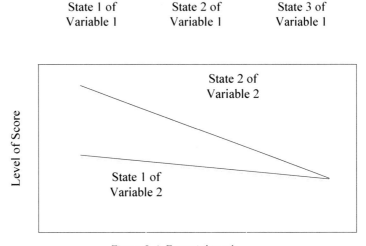

Figure 9-4. Factorial result.

Goodness of Fit (Chi Square)

Chi Square analyses are performed when data collected are in the form of nominal or ordinal variables. Counts of responses to a nominal or ordinal measure (observed frequencies) are compared to a theoretically expected frequency distribution (expected frequencies) of the measure. A Chi Square test is used to determine if the difference between observed and expected frequencies is likely to have occurred by chance.

Example: You want to know if the high school students who drive their cars to school have a preference for the color of their cars. You go into the parking lot and count up the number of cars of each color. You then divide the total number of cars by the number of color categories you used (expected frequency for the distribution of car colors). If there was no preference you would expect the frequency in each category to be the same. Counts in each category (observed frequencies) are compared to the expected frequencies with a Chi Square. If the Chi Square is statistically significant then differences between observed and expected frequencies were unlikely to have occurred by chance and the students then seem to have a color preference. You review the differences between observed and expected frequencies looking for the most likely color category to represent the color preference although the Chi Square analysis cannot tell you directly what that preference is.

Test of Independence (Chi Square)

In this type of Chi Square analysis, sample groups are divided into subgroups on two independent variables. Counts of responses to a nominal or ordinal measure (observed frequencies) are compared to a computed expected frequency distribution of the measure. A Chi Square test is used to determine if the difference between observed and expected frequencies is likely to have occurred by chance.

Example: In your study of high school car color preference you wonder if the preferences may be different based on gender. You identify the driver of each car and the car color. The observed frequencies are plotted into a contingency table (sometimes called a cross tabs) that includes all of the car color categories on one axis and gender on the other. Expected frequencies are computed for each cell in the table. A Chi Square test is used to determine if the difference between observed and expected frequencies is likely to have occurred by chance. If the Chi Square is statistically significant then differences between observed and expected frequencies were unlikely to have occurred by chance. If the Chi Square is statistically significant then the two variables are not independent. Girls have different color preferences than boys. You review the differences between observed and expected frequencies looking for the most likely color category to represent the differences in color preference by gender although the Chi Square analysis cannot tell you directly where the preference difference shows up most strongly.

Below is an example of a Chi Square test of independence table (Figure 9-5). We have included the predicted frequencies because we believe this is valuable information when looking at Chi Square results. Because these simpler forms of Chi Square analysis don't actually point to where significance may be appearing in the analysis many authors only include observed values.

Table 1

Observed and Expected Frequencies[a] for Teacher and Interaction Quality

		Interaction Quality		
		Negative	Neutral	Positive
Teacher 1				
	Observed	211	86	29
	Expected	234.42	59.66	31.93
Teacher 2				
	Observed	347	56	47
	Expected	323.58	82.35	44.07

[a] Chi Square = 24.56; $p < .001$

Figure 9-5. Chi square table.

Aside from getting an overview of the different kinds of quantitative study designs, we also hope through this chapter you are beginning to see that APA tables are as much an art as following rules. Certainly there are specific guidelines that you will always follow but tables vary in order to enhance the presentation of the data. Considerable discussion with your research mentor is appropriate around report table design.

NEXT STEPS

Choosing the right study design to address your research problem is important because the design dictates how you gather and analyze your data. Choosing the wrong design before you start will make your life much more difficult later on. But, there is more to do before you can begin collecting data. You need to review your procedures for collecting data to be sure that you have the best information to understand the problem you are studying. In the next chapter we will investigate survey design and then attach all of this discussion to ideas about validity and reliability.

CHAPTER SELF-CHECK

Having completed this chapter, you should be comfortable discussing the following:
- Pre/post test comparisons
- Gain scores
- Control groups
- Study designs that do not include an intervention
- Study designs that do include an intervention

CHAPTER REVIEW QUESTIONS

1. What kinds of statements can you make about the findings in a correlational study?
2. What kind of study designs can you use to show that an intervention is likely to have caused a result?
3. What are the advantages and limitations of Chi Square analysis?
4. Decide which study design is best for your study and write a paragraph that describes why you believe it to be the correct choice.

REFERENCES

Babbie, E. (1992). *The practice of social science research* (6th ed.). Belmont, CA: Wadsworth Publishing.
Gall, M. D., Gall, J. P., & Borg, W. R. (2003). *Educational research: An introduction* (7th ed.). Boston: Allyn & Bacon.

CHAPTER 10

DATA COLLECTION AND VALIDITY

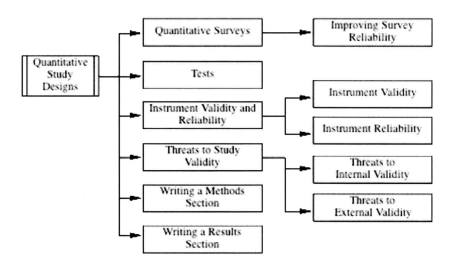

CHAPTER OVERVIEW

Chapter 10 examines how to design quantitative data gathering tools, and reviews issues related to validity and reliability. Writing methods and results sections for a quantitative study are addressed.

INTRODUCTION

Whatever study design you use, the question of whether your intervention caused changes or some other influence was responsible for differences always remains. What follows are some of the most common problems that put the results of any study into question.

QUANTITATIVE SURVEYS

At some point in our lives, we probably all have experienced a really badly designed survey. There are many issues that make designing surveys intended for quantitative analysis very difficult, and unfortunately these issues are often overlooked. The results are studies that are neither valid nor reliable. Later in this chapter we will more fully examine those terms but generally, as we discussed in chapter 4, validity refers to whether the instrument provides you with the information you needed while reliability is a measure of whether those responding to the instrument interpret the tool the same way (i.e., are the findings consistent). With qualitative surveys the point is usually to get people to express themselves around a specific topic. The questions are designed to get people talking (or writing). With surveys designed for quantitative analysis, we are interested in identifying levels of specific characteristics of a group. The purpose is the same for any descriptive statistical activity regardless of how data are gathered. As a rule, direct data gathering is the preferred method of obtaining data. Measuring how tall students are yourself is preferable to having them tell you how tall they are. Or, counting the books that students read during quiet reading time is more likely to be a better measure than having students tell you how many books they have read. Surveys are always **self-report** data and therefore something about which you should be cautious.

This issue of direct data gathering becomes more complicated when you are gathering opinions. So many things can influence how someone responds to an opinion question, that it is actually a good idea to use surveys to elicit this type of information. Using a written instrument not only increases the chances that everyone will interpret the questions in the same way (reliability), but also provides a more "private" way for people to respond. While this is not always the case, using a written survey as opposed to verbal questioning makes it more likely their responses will truly reflect how they feel rather than how they think you want them to respond. The other major reason to use a survey is to standardize responses to questions so the data are easier to statistically analyze with the tools described in the previous chapters.

The biggest problem in quantitative survey design is question construction. Because you are trying to gather data on a specific characteristic, the question has to assure that you will get what you need. Every respondent must interpret the question the same way or your data will be very unreliable. That is not as easy to protect against as it may sound. As an example, respondents are presented with the statement "Teacher inservice is important to a quality school faculty." Then respondents are asked to respond either strongly disagree, disagree, agree, or strongly agree. Here are a few ways in which this question might be interpreted differently by different respondents.

- Younger and more experienced teachers are likely to have had vastly different experiences with inservice. So, what does the term teacher inservice actually mean in this question?
- What is a quality school faculty? Teachers will have very different ideas about what the term quality means here. Using it without explanation increases the chances you will get very inconsistent data.
- The difference between agree and disagree seems fairly obvious but what is the difference between strongly disagree and disagree?

Improving Survey Reliability

What follows are common problems/concerns that affect whether the questions on your survey will generate reliable information about the group you are studying. You hope that your data are reliable enough that applying statistical analysis will make sense.

Bias.   All questions are biased. At least you should start from that point of view. Bias in survey design mostly means that you are leading the respondent to a specific response. Read each question you write and try to imagine if the "correct" answer is implied in the question. If it is, your question is biased toward that answer. It needs to be rewritten to get the respondent's true response.

Language.   A kind of bias is the language used in question writing. If the language is inappropriate for the group who will be completing the survey then your responses will reflect how the group dealt with the way the questions were written more than the issues about which you are surveying.

Complex questions.   Be very careful to avoid asking about two issues in the same question. For example: "Has your school been open to parent participation and taken advantage of the parent teacher organization?" The response could be about parent participation or the PTO or both. It is surprisingly easy to accidentally write questions that address more than one issue simultaneously. We suggest that you avoid the word "and" in question writing as a way to reduce the chances of this happening.

Negatives.   Avoid using negative terms (particularly the word "not") in your questions whenever possible. The respondent must decide if a positive response means agreeing with the opposite. This can get confusing, increasing the likelihood that some respondents will misinterpret the question.

Response categories. When you design response categories for your questions there are two main things to consider: are the categories **mutually exclusive** and are they **comprehensive?** Mutually exclusive means that a respondent will clearly understand which category is the right one for him to choose. If respondents cannot clearly understand the differences between the categories, then the responses will be unreliable (different respondents will interpret the responses differently). Imagine you are asking how often students read at home with the response categories of not very often, sometimes, daily, frequently. Many students might believe that daily was frequently or not know how many minutes rate "not very often" as opposed to "sometimes." There would be confusion about which response category to use, and the findings would be unreliable.

The related problem occurs when respondents cannot find a response category that represents what they think their response should be. In that case, the response categories would not be comprehensive. They would not allow for all possible responses. A question like "What kind of books do you like to read?" with response categories of "sports, travel, mysteries, novels" would suffer from this problem. What if you preferred romance novels? Not providing a comprehensive set of categories will make your data unreliable. The comprehensive problem is why you will see so many survey questions that have "other" as a response category. Although "other" functions as a catchall category for those who do not see themselves in the any of the categories you provided, if "other" shows up often in the responses you get back it is a sign you haven't thought through all of the categories that ought to be available on the form.

Interval response categories. It would improve the power of analysis if survey responses could be compared using the tools we have for comparing group means. That would mean that response categories would have to be interval. Researchers generally do this in two ways: by using indexes and scales. An index counts the number of similar occurrences for a respondent. Questions might be "How many inservices have you attended?" or "How many reading programs have you taught over your career?" The trick in designing an index is that the things counted need to be equivalent for all respondents.

Scales, on the other hand, are used to position a respondent on a continuum. To be interval rather than ordinal data, the steps on the continuum need to be equivalent. To achieve this, specific points on the scale are usually labeled. Questions where respondents are asked to rate their opinion or ability are scale questions. For instance, "Please indicate your ability on a scale of 1 (novice) to 5 (expert)."

Likert scales. Likert scales are a special case of scale questions designed to gather opinions and measure attitudes. It is very difficult to ask for affective responses and to be sure that response categories mean the same thing to all respondents. Likert scales attempt to overcome this problem by converting questions into statements and then asking the degree to which the respondent agrees or disagrees with the statement. Response categories for these types of questions need to be symmetrical and the terms used need to be as unambiguous as possible. By convention the response categories are strongly disagree, disagree, agree and strongly agree. There is some suggestion in the literature that responses are more reliable if the response categories run from negative to positive. A decision you will have to make in designing Likert type questions is whether to include a neutral (center) response category. You will have to decide if, relative to your questions, a neutral response is really a legitimate response and does not mean the respondent does not know how to answer. If you are using this type of scale with younger children, the scale responses can be drawn faces. Primary-age children can be asked to choose the face, like those in Figure 10-1, that matches their feelings.

Figure 10-1. Pictorial scale display.

You should always be cautious using Likert type questions in a survey. They are difficult to design and should only be considered interval data if a series of Likert scale questions around a concept are averaged. One question per concept is very unlikely to produce reliable information in opinion surveys. This brings us to considering theoretical constructs in survey design.

Multiple questions and theoretical constructs. Often surveys are designed to gather information about complex educational constructs. You might be interested in cooperative learning, homework strategies, or learning styles. When designing questions around theoretical constructs like these, you need to be sure that you have done your literature work first. You must develop a solid understanding of the construct to be familiar with the underlying elements involved. You will need to write multiple questions that address each of these elements. No construct can be assessed with a single question. The more complex the issue is, the more difficult it becomes to get a good understanding of a respondent's view of the issue with only a question or two.

Analysis of these types of surveys is done by averaging the responses to all of the questions around each element of the construct. This reduces problems of different interpretations of the questions and increases the reliability of the instrument. Remember you are trying to understand the whole construct you are investigating so breaking the analysis down to individual questions should only be done after you analyzed all of the questions together first.

Pilot testing. We have addressed the topic of pilot testing elsewhere in the text, but it is an important tool worth mentioning again. We cannot tell you the number of times beginning researchers with whom we have been working have designed surveys and sent them out only to discover that the responses they got back were not what they expected. Something in the design of the survey caused a problem. The best way to avoid this is to pilot test every survey you wish to use on a group similar to your study group but that does not include any of the respondents who will be in the final study.

TESTS

Certainly many more instruments are available for data gathering in your study beyond just surveys. Particularly important are instruments designed to measure knowledge or skills. You may have a class in your master's program that focuses specifically on assessment and designing good assessment tools. As a teacher there will be many opportunities to construct assessments throughout your career. In most cases these assessments serve as one element within a broader list of tools we use to understand our students and their progress. When we use these assessments in quantitative research they usually stand alone in determining the impact of an intervention. Therefore, in research circumstances, we need to pay particular attention to the quality of the instruments we use.

Assessment design takes a lot of work. So, when possible, researchers take advantage of the work that others have done to design good assessments. Online access to lists of available tests and instruments has become a bit more difficult over the past few years. If you have trouble finding instruments that fit your needs we suggest you go talk to your reference library for help.

There is nothing wrong with using existing assessments as long as you gain permission where needed and properly cite the authors of the instrument. Changing these instruments to fit your own needs is also permissible; although great care must be taken that the instruments are not changed in ways that make them less capable of doing a quality job of measuring the things in which you are interested. Even relatively simple changes in language may affect the quality and reliability of the instrument. Do so with good reasons in mind and explain the changes you made in the methods section of your research report.

It may seem like chapter end tests and other assessment tools that have been produced by textbook publishers ought to be good quality assessments. This is not always the case. Try your best to find documentation on how the tools were designed and any research that was done to assess reliability and validity of the instruments. Describe what you found when you discuss the instrument in the methods section of your paper. The more you can establish the quality of the instruments you are using, the more confident readers will be in the conclusions of your study. In quantitative studies, regardless of whether you are using surveys, existing assessments or assessments you designed, you need to address the validity and reliability of your data gathering tools.

INSTRUMENT VALIDITY AND RELIABILITY

Reliability refers to the degree to which repeating the strategies you use for gathering data will give you the same results. If instruments cannot gather information in consistent ways, then they are unreliable. When we mentioned reliability earlier in this chapter, each of the examples were situations when questions could be interpreted differently or misinterpreted altogether causing results based on the instrument design rather than differences in the respondents. But, designing instruments that are interpreted similarly by all of the respondents is not enough. The instruments have to be actually measuring what you think they are measuring; that is, instruments must be both valid and reliable. To do this the first step is to establish the validity of the instrument.

Instrument Validity

Establishing instrument validity is rather difficult. Remember we mentioned earlier that newer researchers often avoid instrument construction because of this difficulty. Researchers who develop complex instruments study validity in a variety of ways, but generally these fall into four categories: face validity, content validity, criterion validity, and construct validity.

Face validity. Think of this as the "Mom" test. Would your mother (assuming she is not a psychometrician) think that your instrument makes sense given the topic you are investigating? You might be able to figure out a way to assess students' knowledge of physiology by having them dance the answers to your questions, but many people might think this does not seem like a good way to gather the data around this topic. Your assessment would lack face validity.

Content validity. If you wanted to assess student knowledge of photosynthesis, how would you know that your questions actually represented all of the knowledge that students should have of that topic? Content validity refers to the idea that the questions you pose adequately measure the full domain of the topic being measured. What might you have left out of your questions that is an important component of the topic being assessed? In some ways content validity is similar to face validity except that establishing content validity is usually done by asking a group of experts if they think that the instrument really covers the full breadth of a given topic.

For most of our studies, rather than covering the full breadth of a given topic, we focus on what we actually taught to the students. Does our assessment match our instruction? A panel of experts would look at the testing instrument as well as our detailed lessons plans to see if scope, level, and context all match.

Criterion validity. How good is your instrument at *predicting* an outcome? For example, SAT scores are an excellent predictor of first year attrition of college students. SATs have criterion validity because they do a good job of predicting future student behavior. Criterion validity is usually established statistically by showing the correlation of the instrument with other measures of the construct.

Construct validity. If we wanted to do a study of student motivation to read, the first thing necessary would be to thoroughly understand motivation generally and then specifically how it applies to reading. The questions would then have to be constructed around that subset of motivational factors. We would have to show that the questions we asked were really measuring those constructs and not something else. Establishing this kind of validity is usually done by gathering data around the construct and comparing it to the data generated by the instrument. Often results from the instrument under construction are compared with other instruments that already have established construct validity on related topics.

Think of these as representing increasingly difficult measures of validity. It may be relatively easy to show face validity but being sure that first you understand the construct being addressed and then that your instrument really only measures that construct is no simple task. As you can imagine establishing instrument validity is probably beyond the scope of the work you will be able to do in your early research studies. Even so, paying attention to how others have established the validity of their instruments will help you pick better tools for your work.

Instrument Reliability

Checking the reliability of instruments is easier to do than determining the validity of instruments. Test reliability is important because you want to know that variations in responses are due to differences in attitudes or abilities and not because of variations in how the instrument was interpreted. The idea is to check to see that the instrument performs similarly in a variety of different ways. Most tests of reliability are measurements of the correlation of scores from different forms or

CHAPTER 10

deliveries of the instrument (Gall, Gall & Borg, 2003). When correlations drop below .70 on most measures of reliability the instruments become suspect. Low correlations would indicate that something else is causing variation in the scores other than random error.

There are a number of tests of reliability, and we will mention a few here. **Test/retest** involves delivering the same instrument to the same group with some time lag in between. **Alternate forms** tests are used when two forms of the same instrument are presented to the same group. In **split half** reliability the questions on an instrument are randomly separated into two groups. In all instances, the scores from the two groups of questions are correlated.

Internal consistency measures the degree to which all of the questions in an instrument address the same characteristic. There are two measures of internal consistency, **Cronbach's alpha** (coefficient alpha) and **Kuder-Richardson**.

When question responses contain scale categories, as with a Likert-scale, a Cronbach's alpha assessment is used. This measure requires you to take advantage of a powerful statistical program to determine the instrument's reliability. It is not something that can easily be done with a calculator. When questions can be rated as either correct or incorrect, as with many teacher-made tests, then a Kuder-Richardson test can be used. Imagine what it would be like if you kept doing split-half reliability tests with all of the possible ways that the questions could be divided into two sets and then averaged all of the results. That is essentially what a KR-20 does. There is a simpler and possibly less precise version of this test called a KR-21. Here is the KR-21 formula as it is one that you can compute with just a basic calculator or spreadsheet tools.

$\overline{X}$ =Assessment mean
k   =Number of items in the assessment
σ^2 =Variance (standard deviation squared)

$$\text{reliability} = \frac{k}{k-1}\left(1 - \frac{\overline{X}(k-\overline{X})}{k\sigma^2}\right)$$

Final Words on Instrument Validity and Reliability

It is important that instruments used in a research study be both valid and reliable. Remember that validity tells us if we measured what we set out to measure while reliability deals with the consistency of findings. If an instrument is unreliable, how much weight can you give to its results? If, for example, students do better or worse on a test based on how good the lighting is in the room, could you say with certainty that you were measuring how much students knew about that unit? Obviously, the answer is no. If an instrument is not reliable (i.e., you cannot be sure of the results), then the instrument is also not valid. You can't make a decision based on the test results if you can't be certain of the results! To be valid, an instrument must also be reliable.

What about reliability? Can an instrument be reliable and not valid? Let's say on a test about dinosaurs, you needed five additional points to bring the total point value of the test to 50. You decided to assign five points to students filling in their names. We would expect that the student responses to filling in their name would be quite reliable. They should be able to fill in that blank regardless of when the test was administered. Is asking their name a valid indicator of how much they know about dinosaurs, though? So while this item would be reliable, it would not be valid. Hence, those test scores would not be a good indicator of student knowledge of dinosaurs; the "name question" would be invalid making the overall test invalid. A test cannot be valid if it is unreliable; however, a test can be reliable and not valid. You can have faith in what the students' answered, but it may have nothing to do with the construct/content the test is purported to measure.

In your research paper, instrument validity is "established" by citing the literature published about the instruments you are using. If you do design your own instruments, you must describe in full detail in the methods section of your research report your reasons for asking the questions you did, how you developed the questions, what steps you took to determine the validity of the instrument, and how the instrument was administered. Ultimately, the readers of your work should be able to make their own judgments about the validity of your study from the description you provide.

STUDY VALIDITY

Validity is an important attribute of research studies. In our discussion of instrument validity we asked "does the test actually measure what it is supposed to measure?" For instance, does the test match the instruction that was given? A similar meaning is applied to research validity. Generally, questions of validity ask whether the meaning you have attributed to your study results is justifiable. Problems related to validity appear both when you are designing a study and then again during the process of developing data gathering instruments. The way to minimize most study validity issues in quantitative studies is to randomly select your study samples and to use control groups (recall the discussion of sampling strategies in Chapter 5). Neither of these is possible in many educational studies so it is important to focus on minimizing validity problems directly.

Threats to Study Validity

In order to deal with issues of validity, it is important to get an understanding of what the threats to validity are. Threats to the validity of a study are generally grouped into two categories: threats to **internal validity** and threats to **external validity** (Lissitz & Samuelsen, 2007). Internal validity addresses study design problems. Are there alternative explanations for the results of the study other than the ones you propose? External validity is related to issues of generalizability. Was your study designed in such a way that your results can be applied to groups other than the one from whom you gathered data? Addressing validity threats is done in two places in your paper. First, be sure that sufficient description of the sample, context, instrumentation, and data gathering methods of your study appears in the methods section of your paper. Second, discussion of internal and external validity threats often appears in a section in the conclusions where you discuss problems related to the quality of the data you gathered. If you are aware of what these threats to validity are, you can take steps to minimize them in your study design. Let's look at the main ones.

Threats to internal validity. Threats to internal validity (alternative explanations for study conclusions) fit into a few categories.

History. History effect refers to external influences that cause changes in your subjects similar to those of the intervention but cannot be accounted for by the intervention. Imagine a study investigating the impact of incorporating current environmental issues into a science curriculum. If students learned about issues related to the curriculum from sources other than those provided by the curriculum itself (television or newspaper accounts, for instance) their scores on the curriculum assessment might be positively impacted by those outside resources and not the curriculum.

Maturation. Sometimes those in a study grow naturally over the course of a study. Measuring the impact of physical education instruction on middle school students' physical abilities might suffer from this problem. Students get naturally more coordinated as they mature. It could also relate to mathematics studies; would students' abilities to understand and apply mathematics increase over the course of a semester because of a developmental increase in cognitive abilities? The maturation effect refers to situations in which natural growth influences the measures of your intervention.

Testing. Sometimes study participants learn how to respond to assessments by having taken a similar assessment before. We all do this. We become "test-wise" in certain circumstances. The test turns out to measure our test taking skill rather than changes caused by an intervention. This is a perennial problem in pre/post study designs. The solution to this problem is to be sure that pre and post assessments are of different designs; that is, not identical. Unfortunately, this can cause a related problem—instrumentation.

Instrumentation. If multiple assessments you use around a given issue are dissimilar, respondents may do better or worse because the instrument is a better or worse tool and not because of respondent's actual knowledge. Notice that testing and instrumentation effects are a balancing act. To solve one problem you may cause the other. Sometimes these threats are handled by having sufficient time between pre and post testing so that the student does not "remember" the initial test.

Differential Selection. Since we often use intact groups in our studies, there is always the possibility that our groups are substantially different before the study begins. The way around this problem is to randomly select study participants from the largest possible populations. Since this is not always possible, you will need to compare the pre/post test findings of the two groups using an ANOVA. This will help you assess any differences between the two groups prior to the intervention.

Attrition.   Did those involved in your study at the start remain involved through the study's completion? Imagine that you are studying the impact of a curriculum unit, and by the time the posttest arrives four students have transferred to other schools. They may represent a special subset of the class as a whole and their absence will artificially skew the results of the posttest. A temptation is to not include their pretest scores in the study either, but this causes the same problem. You need to work very hard to be sure that those who are in the sample group in the beginning of the study are still there at the end. When studying students in classes, we have little to no control over this.

Statistical Regression.   This threat to internal validity is a little more complicated but it appears with surprising frequency. If participants in a study are selected because they performed particularly high or low on an assessment, it is very likely that that subgroup will score lower or higher, respectively, on a repeat of the assessment without any other intervention. This is a function of random error which is always a natural part of quantitative studies. As an example, you want to know if one-on-one mentoring will help at-risk students perform better on a standardized assessment. The whole school takes the assessment and you select the lowest ten percent of the students for your intervention. Mostly these students scored lower because they didn't know the answers, *but* some of the lower scores will be attributable to random variation in the group. You won't know the source of that variation but for the students who scored lowest on the test it is likely that they represent the portion of the random variation that makes scores go down. Because this random variation (random error) is random the scores of this sub-group's performance on a repeat of the assessment would be likely to show some increase in scores even if you did nothing else. In other words, these students would tend to score closer to the mean of the total group the second time they complete a measurement tool even if you did nothing with these students. A way around this problem is to give these students who have been selected because they are particularly high or low on some measure, a different assessment to use in a pre/post study design. The scores on the new instrument will now represent the true normal distribution for this group.

Diffusion of Treatments.   If sample groups can communicate with each other during a study, they may teach each other about the impact of the interventions that each group is (or in the case of a control group, is not) getting. Imagine that you are using different instructional strategies in multiple sections of a middle school language arts course. Inevitably the afternoon students will know exactly what has gone on in the morning class. The impact of both teaching strategies may influence both groups because of this natural discussion among students. It may also lead to a related threat to validity—resentful demoralization.

Resentful Demoralization. If groups that are receiving different interventions communicate with each other, it may be that one group will realize that they are not getting something that appears to be desirable. Resentment may occur causing these students to perform differently than they would if they had not known about the other intervention. For example, if you are using web-based inquiry with the afternoon group but not the morning class, the group without the technology might feel they are missing out on a "fun" activity. Some students might feel they are being treated unfairly and become less motivated, thereby scoring lower on the testing measure.

There are other threats to internal validity, although those listed above are the most noted ones. Your job as a researcher is to realize that many things can influence the measures of the impact of things you are doing in your study; you need to put considerable effort into anticipating what they might be to try to avoid them and to be able to discuss what the impact of them might have been on your results.

Threats to External Validity. Threats to external validity refer to problems in translating study results into other study environments. These threats fall into four categories: selection, setting, history and placebo effects.

Selection. If the participants of your study are not representative of the larger group to which you wish to generalize, then you have a problem. Ideally, you should randomly select study participants from the population to which you are generalizing. This is almost never possible in the kind of studies we do. More often than not, we cannot hand pick the students we want to study; we use those students who are enrolled in our classes or school. Consequently, it is very important that you describe your sample in the methods section of your paper so that readers can make their own judgment about whether your study group is similar to those participants in their own or another context.

Setting. Is there something so unique about your study setting that your results might not make sense in other settings? For example, this might be true of the applicability of studies done in parochial schools to public schools, or of studies done in large urban schools to smaller rural schools. Regardless, a full, rich description of the context of your study in the methods section of your paper will help readers make their own judgment in this area.

History. Like history as a threat to internal validity, time also plays a part in determining the external validity of a study. Will studies done at a particular point in some chronological sequence translate to other times in the sequence? For example, if you are studying parent participation in classroom activities, does whether the study was done at the beginning or the end of a school year make a difference? If you are studying teacher conversations in a teacher's lounge, will when you "eavesdrop" make a difference in what you hear (e.g., the start of school, before winter break, during homecoming week)? Or, perhaps more directly, does a study done ten years ago translate well into a current classroom?

Placebo Effects. Sometimes when participants in a study are aware they are being studied, they begin to think about what the researchers are expecting to see and change their behavior accordingly. I suspect you have heard about why medical studies often use placebos to ensure that the changes they see are a function of a drug or other treatment and not a result of a participant simply believing that they are reacting to a treatment. This turns out to be a problem in most studies where the participants are aware they are being observed. The most famous case of this was a study of environmental working conditions in the Hawthorne Plant of the Western Electric Company. No matter what the researchers did to the environment (brighten lights, dim lights), worker productivity increased because the workers knew their productivity was being observed. Consequently you will often hear this threat to validity called the **Hawthorne Effect**.

There is one other common placebo effect. Remember above that we talked about Resentful Demoralization as a threat to internal validity. A version of this may appear as a threat to external validity as well. If a control group sees that they are being compared to a group experiencing something being perceived as better than what the control group has they may try harder to show that what they have is just as good as the innovation. Imagine an example of students receiving an intervention designed to reduce referrals. Students who are not receiving the intervention may decide to show that they do not need the intervention to improve their behavior. Signs of this problem are usually that the control group becomes competitive. In reference to the story of John Henry trying to out perform the steam engine, this is often called the **John Henry Effect**.

Since threats to external validity are primarily judgments made by users of your research, it is very important that you do a good job of helping readers of your research know enough about your study so they can make these judgments about the validity of your research. Writing about the results and conclusions of your study may be the most exciting part of your work, but if you have not put enough time into an adequate description of the design of your study (the methods section), your findings may be ignored.

WRITING A METHODS SECTION FOR A QUANTITATIVE STUDY

Earlier in the this chapter we briefly discussed the importance of ensuring that the methods section of your paper has a sufficient description of what you are doing so the reader of your study report can make her own judgment about whether you have made good methodological choices. Here is a summary of the elements that need to be in the methods section and the order in which they normally appear. While very similar to qualitative studies, there are a few differences. Referring to this section as well as Chapter 6 of this text will be of use when you write this chapter of your research. A sample Methods section to illustrate Methods section writing appears in Figure 10-2.

CHAPTER 10

METHODOLOGY

When we include students in the learning process by providing them with information about how they read, does this influence their thinking about their ability to be a reader, or in other words, their reading self-efficacy? This study explored that question. I worked with a group of 15 newly registered students between grades five to nine from an inner city elementary junior high school in a large urban centre in Alberta, Canada. I am a principal co-ordinator assigned out of central office to work as an advisor to seven inner city schools, including this study school. My role is to work with the administration and school staff on a regular basis to provide the best learning environment possible for the students attending there. One area of focus in my work at these schools is around strategies that will best support the development of student literacy competencies. The school's student demographic is typically represented by a student cohort mix that is made up of approximately 40% self identified Aboriginal students, 25% English Language Learners, with the remaining population being Caucasian. The school is within the top five schools identified on the school district's high needs list where schools are ranked according to social vulnerability and poverty data from federal census and city generated community profiles. Many of the students attending the school struggle with learning, read below their enrolled grade level and are statistically more likely to not complete high school.

As part of the September/October process of engaging the students in preparation for a year of learning, the teachers use an individual reading assessment tool to determine each student's comprehension and decoding levels. Students are assessed by their language arts teacher in a one on one process and then included in a debrief conversation around their reading capabilities. For this individual reading assessment teachers use the Fountas and Pinnell Individual Reading Benchmark Tool (Fountas, Pinnell & Heinemann, 2008).

For the purpose of this study I chose to focus on a group of students who were new to the school in September. I chose this group as I was looking at the pre and post self efficacy of students who had not had prior experience with the Fountas and Pinnell. Because the teachers design instruction based on the specific reading abilities of each student and I measured the resultant instructional engagement, I wanted students who were new to this treatment. My student cohort is represented by students between grades 5 to 9 and includes both regular and special needs coded students. Letters of consent to participate in this study were sent out to parents of the cohort students.

Once the student cohort was identified and parental permission confirmed I then worked with the language arts teachers to have them administer The Reader Self-Perception Scale (RSPS) (Henk & Melnick, 1995) with all of the cohort students. The RSPS is a survey tool used to measure student self-efficacy towards literacy. It has been developed to align with Bandura's (1977) four factors related to self-efficacy: Performance, Observational Comparison, Social Feedback, and

Figure 10-2. Example methods section (reprinted with permission of Nancy Petersen).

Physiological States. The tool has a reliability range of .81 to .84 across these four areas. The tool is comprised of 33 questions, uses a five point student response scale, and includes a scoring sheet to assist in analysis of the survey. (See Appendix A) For ease of reading and responding for the participating students the actual survey portion of the tool was typed up and formatted into a separate document. (See Appendix B.)

The students used class time to complete the RSPS prior to their participation in the Fountas and Pinnell. The first RSPS provided me with the student base line self efficacy towards being a reader. For the support and convenience of the participating language arts teachers, I ensured that each teacher received the RSPS copied, stapled and ready to go, along with a labeled envelope for the completed surveys that were to be left in the school office for me to pick up.

The students then completed the Fountas and Pinnell, as did their classmates. In terms of completing the Fountas and Pinnell, each student worked one on one with their language arts teacher. Part of this process is that the teacher had a debrief dialogue with each student individually. During this dialogue the teacher identified for the student what it means to decode and comprehend in relationship to print material and what the student's specific ability was in each area. The teacher also helped the student understand how to pick print materials that are within their ability level for successful reading experiences. After this process the students were then engaged in their regular language arts learning for the next six to eight weeks, with a new understanding of the reading process and who they were specifically as readers.

In early December the language arts teachers had the cohort of students respond to the RSPS for a second time, having worked on their literacy learning with their new information around the reading process and their own ability within this process for the past several weeks. This second response to the RSPS provided the post data for my study.

The scores on the two RSPS survey administrations were compared using a two tailed paired t-test. The results provided insight as to whether student self efficacy towards being a reader changes after they are involved in a discussion on their strengths and weaknesses and participate in a reading program more closely aligned to their instructional reading abilities.

Figure 10-2. Example methods section (reprinted with permission of Nancy Petersen) (Continued).

Problem Statement

It is a good idea to repeat your problem statement at the beginning of the methods section. Every time you refer to your problem statement it should be identical. Small changes in the language used to describe your problem can have major impacts on how the study would be appropriately designed. Once your problem statement is set in the introduction, it should be repeated verbatim whenever it appears again.

CHAPTER 10

Context of the Study

Describe the environment in which your study is conducted. Focus on those things that are directly related to your study. The way to figure out what context issues might be important to your study (and, therefore should be described in the methods section) is to read the literature. In a study of reading comprehension the literature is likely to make many references to social economic status of readers' families or reading differences based on ethnicity. It would be appropriate to describe the social economic status (SES) of your school (usually done through reporting the percentage of students on free or reduced lunch), and you should report the ethnic backgrounds of your students. In other studies (e.g., relationship of physical activity to on-task behavior) those context descriptions might not be necessary. Our experience is that newer researchers often put lots of information into context descriptions that does not help the reader understand more about the study. We see examples of writers describing the mission statements of the school or the number and distribution of teachers in the school when these things do not connect in meaningful ways to the study. Recall that you do need to provide enough contextual information, though, so the reader can make decisions about the generalizability of your work. So, do not skimp on describing your context, but do focus on meaningful descriptors.

One other word about writing context statements: in general you should not refer to the real name of the school in which you are doing your study and in no circumstances should you refer to the real names of the participants in the study. Use pseudonyms or refer to the school generically (a rural middle school in southwest Washington state). This is part of your need as a researcher to protect the participants in your study from unfortunate consequences that might stem from being in your study. It would seem harmless enough to be talking about students who had done better on an exam but you will never know how that knowledge might be used and you have a fundamental responsibility to protect everyone even remotely connected to your study.

Study Sample

This follows the same guidelines as study context, but in this case you are describing the characteristics of the individuals in your study that are relevant to your study. In some cases you might need only provide very general information (32 5th grade students, 18 of whom were female and 14 male). In some cases it may be important that you provide extensive information about your sample—SES, age, gender, previous academic progress, or other information to provide a comprehensive description appropriate to your study. The characteristics of the sample that you are describing at this point are the ones that the reader needs to know about that are not part of the data collection. If you already knew the characteristics of your sample then you would not ask again as part of data gathering. Why these participants were chosen in your study is also included (e.g., a sample of convenience).

Measures

Here you will describe the data that you will gather from your study participants. This is where you will be specific about how you operationalize the measures of your study. If you are interested in increasing achievement for high school biology students, here is where achievement gets specified. In this case, describing the measures you use will define what you mean by achievement. In one study achievement might be unit test scores; in another, semester grades; or in still another, standardized test scores.

If you are using pre-existing instruments you will also describe the source of these instruments (including citations), why you have selected these, and anything that will help the reader know if they are appropriate to your study and if they are valid and reliable.

Instrument Development

If you have developed your own data gathering instruments, here is the place to describe the process that you used for their development, including citations to other literature. Remember that researcher-constructed instruments are often a bit suspect so you need to justify the decisions you made for developing your instruments. Sometimes this will be very straight-forward. If you are measuring improvements in athletic performance, lap times might be the appropriate measure and would not require much justification. If you are measuring interest in reading, you might decide that frequency of library visits was a good measure but your reader is going to want justification for this choice especially if it seems other more conventional measures might be appropriate.

Our preference is to describe the instruments you have developed as completely as possible in the text of the methods section and not to include the instruments as appendices. If something about the appearance of an instrument that is difficult to describe is important to your study then it would be appropriate to include the full instrument as an appendix. Talk to your research mentor about this.

Procedures

There are two parts to this. If you are administering an intervention in your study (teaching a curriculum unit, or using a special instructional strategy) then you need to describe what the intervention was in great detail. This is the point in the study report where you are operationalizing the intervention you are studying. If your study is about increasing participation in cooperating learning for middle school students, what, exactly, do you mean by cooperative learning? Your reader will know that when you describe how you are using cooperative learning in your study. You should also describe the "pre" condition so the reader has a comprehensive understanding of the change made by the intervention.

Then you need to describe any other procedures that are important to your study. These will usually be descriptions of how data were gathered during the study. These would include things like: When were questionnaires administered, how, by whom? What was the time period between pretest and posttest? Recall, anyone reading your methods section should be able to replicate your study procedures.

Analysis

What will you do with the data after they are collected? Are you comparing group scores with a *t*-test or running chi square tests to identify anomalies in ordinal data? Anything that you will do to the data in order to bring meaning to it will be described here. Describe the statistical procedures you will use to make sense of the data you will collect.

It is easy to get into the results and conclusions of your study and to begin to see things that were not initially obvious to you. You might decide that the smiles on students' faces while they were reading was an important indicator of interest in reading or that achievement in high school biology was also affected by gender. Those may be reasonable observations, but in a quantitative study every measure that you will use must be described in the methods section and every analysis procedure that you will use with the gathered data must also be described. There should be a perfect match between the measures and analysis procedures described in the methods section and the data from those measures and the results of the analysis procedures in the results section.

If you are doing a mixed methods study, you will include all the sections described above. You will include both the qualitative and quantitative data collecting tools and methods of analysis for the two types of data. As a final thought, methods sections are usually written in simple past tense. You are describing what you did, not what you are about to do. Often you will be required to write a proposal for your study. Institutional review board proposals are an example. Since those are written before the study those are written in future tense. You have to remember to change to past tense if you include sections of the proposal in your final report.

WRITING A RESULTS SECTION FOR A QUANTITATIVE STUDY

Unlike a qualitative study, often the results section of a quantitative study is the easiest section to write. Since you have described the measures and analysis procedures that you will use in the methods section, your job in the results section is to describe the data gathered and then what happened when you applied the analysis procedures to those data. Generally this is done in two ways. First describe the data in prose form and then present it again in table form. Although this is the order in which it usually occurs in the section, as a researcher you will do this in the opposite order as a prelude to the actual chapter writing.

Once you have gathered your data and analyzed it, the next step is to build the tables to represent what you have found. Once the tables are built it is much easier to write a paragraph or two that describes what is in the table.

If your study includes a large number of measures and analysis procedures you should look for ways to combine your data into fewer tables. Remember that your reader will look first to the tables to understand what you have found and then go back and read the prose if it looks interesting. If there are too many tables it becomes more difficult to keep track of what you are presenting.

In most quantitative studies the results include descriptive statistics about the groups and then indicators of significant findings when the descriptive data are compared. Simply, more often than not, your tables will have the group size, mean and standard deviation for each group's data. Some appropriate indicator added to the table will show if significant comparisons were found. Since the point is usually to highlight significant findings, it may not even be necessary to report non-significant findings in a table at all. Refer to the examples in using APA style in Chapter 11 for help in presenting your tables.

As a caution in writing results sections in quantitative studies, there will be some temptation to start talking about what the results mean right after you present them. Avoid this temptation. Interpretation of the results belongs in the conclusion section of your paper. See Figure 10-3 for an example of a student's results section. A complete results chapter in a quantitative study is generally only a few pages at most.

Results

A total of 26 students were involved in the traditionally taught math class; 30 students were enrolled in the class being taught with constructivist methodologies. All students in both classes took the pre- and post-tests. Table 1 shows the mean, standard deviation and group size for groups receiving traditional and constructivist math lessons. The ANOVA results indicate a significant difference ($p < .01$). Post hoc analysis showed that there were no significant differences in the two groups' pre-test or post-test results. That is, the groups performed similarly on both tests. There were significant differences when each group's pre-test scores were compared to post-test scores. Both groups showed significant increases in scores regardless of instructional type.

Table 1

Mean Test Scores for Traditional Math Instruction and Constructivist Math Instruction Groups

	n	Pretest	Posttest
Traditional	26		
Mean		51.72	64.07
Std. Dev.		19.57	18.74
Constructivist	30		
Mean		52.80	66.00
Std. Dev.		17.96	16.81

$p < .01$

Figure 10-3. Example results section (reprinted with permission of Carlos Gumataotao.).

NEXT STEPS

Most of the hard work is over at this point and you now get the privilege of thinking about what your work means. The next chapter describes how to approach the task of attributing meaning to your work and thinking about how your work might be carried forward into the future.

CHAPTER SELF-CHECK

Having completed this chapter, you should be comfortable discussing the following:
– considerations in designing quantitative survey instruments
– issues around establishing instrument reliability and validity
– issues around establishing study validity
– organizing and writing Chapters 3 and 4 (Methods and Results) for a quantitative study

CHAPTER REVIEW QUESTIONS

1. What does it mean for a study to be valid? What should you do to increase the probability that your study is valid?
2. What are the differences between internal and external validity?
3. List the major concerns you will have when designing instruments for quantitative studies.
4. What does it mean for an instrument to be reliable?
5. How do the elements of the methods section support the validity of your study?

REFERENCES

Babbie, E. (1992). *The practice of social science research* (6th ed.). Belmont, CA: Wadsworth Publishing.
Gall, M. D., Gall, J. P., & Borg, W. R. (2003). *Educational research: An introduction* (7th ed.). Boston: Allyn & Bacon.
Lissitz, R. W., & Samuelsen, K. (2007). A suggested change in terminology and emphasis regarding validity and education. *Educational Research, 36*(8), 437–448.

CONCLUSIONS, IMPLICATIONS AND WRITING IN APA STYLE

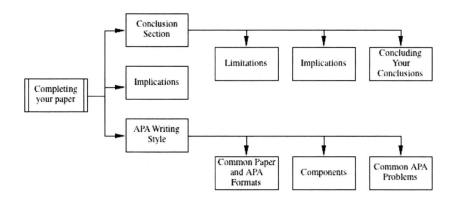

CHAPTER OVERVIEW

Chapter 11 provides the details for wrapping up the paper. It discusses writing a conclusion, discussion, and implications—the "so what" and "what's next" portions of the paper. It also re-addresses the issues of limitations and generalizability. The chapter concludes with a review of writing in APA style.

INTRODUCTION

At the start of this text, we compared educational research to a road trip. Keeping with that analogy, by the time you reach Chapter 5 of your paper, your vacation is done. A friend is asking how your vacation was, and Chapter 5 is your response. You remind her of where you went and you share the highlights. Assuming your friend has also been to that locale, you might compare what you liked and didn't like. You may talk about what you would do again or differently if you went back and where you hope to go on your next trip. Similarly, for your research journey, your conclusions/implications chapter would cover:
- a restatement of your research problem with your conclusion. Succinctly, what did you learn regarding your problem;
- a discussion of what you found and how it compares to what others have found;
- a listing of the limitations of your study (including generalizabilty);
- the importance of your study results—what do these mean for you and others; how will they affect your practice; what additional questions were raised.

207

Think back to the original questions of analysis (Gay, Mills & Airasian, 2005): what is important in the data, why, and what can be learned from it? Those questions guide your conclusion. "If we can really understand the problem, the answer will come out of it, because the answer is not separate from the problem" (Krishnamurti, 1963, p. 120). Let's see how we construct this "journey's end."

CONCLUSION SECTION

Start Chapter 5 with your problem statement. Then summarize the major findings of your research. Include an interpretation of your findings. If you conducted a quantitative study, answer your research question. If you took a qualitative route, recap the main assertions in your study. If you used both methodologies, answer your quantitative questions and summarize the findings from your qualitative analysis. When possible, your quantitative findings should be used to support your qualitative findings. This summary should be tightly coupled with the results section of your paper. When you are writing this section have your results section open in front of you and be sure you are only talking about things you have stated in the results. You will have a chance later in the conclusions section to talk more broadly about your study. For now, the reader of your report should be able to draw connecting lines from the methods section through the results and to the specific conclusions you are stating.

Our work never stands on its own. We are always contributing to the larger knowledge about our topics. Here is the point in your report where you go back to what you found in the literature review and compare it to what you found in your study. How does your work fit into the larger body of work on this topic? How do your findings compare with what other studies have found? As you discuss your results in light of others, cite the studies. For example, you may say,

> "The literature reviewed revealed some common themes which were, in turn, supported by the results of my survey. The literature indicates a need to develop a sense of community within our schools in order to provide stability in a world that is changing so quickly...The results of this study indicate that teachers who share students and space feel supported in their work and have built strong relationships in their learning community..." (Reprinted with permission of Carolyn Carmeron)

> "The data from the students' surveys support Lyle's (1999) findings about what both high and low achieving students believe about group work." (Reprinted with permission of Sheryl Nash)

If your findings are dissimilar to other studies, can you think of any reasons why this discrepancy may have occurred? Were there differences in samples or methodologies that might have led to different results? Include your thoughts on this as well in your comparison. For instance,

> "Generally, males have been found to possess more positive attitudes toward science than females (Kyle et al., 1986; Simpson & Oliver, 1985). This finding did not appear to be the case with this sample. Perhaps, because of the emphasis

that has been placed on the gender gap in science over the past decade, gender biases are being addressed and this problem is being corrected."

"Von Secker (2002) identified varied results for groups of different race, gender, and socioeconomic status. While race was of little import in this study (the population is very homogenous), gender did appear to be a factor." (Reprinted with permission of Tom Kuntz)

Limitations

As discussed in Chapter 5 of this text, it is important that you identify (own up to) the limitations of your study and any problems that may have arisen with your original design. Limitations are factors that might either have biased or otherwise affected the results and/or generalizability of the study. Addressing your limitations is not a weakness; rather it shows that you have given careful thought to your research design. Omitting limitations that may be obvious to a reader, on the other hand, would raise serious issues on the quality of your work.

Include a statement about generalizability. Do you think your findings would hold true for samples or settings other than those in your particular study? Was your sample or context too unique to consider the findings generalizable? See Figure 11-1 for an example. Your statement on generalizability would flow right into a paragraph detailing the limitations of your study.

Also here is where you would more fully address any problems that might have arisen during the study. Perhaps you were studying schoolyard recess behaviors, but because of unusually cold or wet weather, the number of days you planned to carry out your study was decreased, decreasing the amount of data you could collect. Perhaps you planned to study the effects of being in a blended classroom on the students, but your sample was skewed with more of one grade than the other. You would have addressed any changes to your methodology in your results section, but here is where you would address the impact these unplanned changes might have had on the data you actually collected (i.e., a limitation). Recall that common limitations are small sample size, self-report data, and findings not being generalizable. An example of how limitations have been addressed by students is found in Figure 11-2.

The results of this study may not be generalizable for a number of reasons. The fact that the sample included only my students limits the generalizability because of the small, and selected sample. Additionally, since several instructional assistants are a crucial component in working with the students in my classroom, it is impossible to be certain to what extent their comments and actions may have influenced the students throughout the study. Also, during the last two weeks of the study, illness caused the absence of most of the instructional assistants in my room, resulting in the introduction of substitute staff. This, too, makes it impossible to determine the degree to which students may have been influenced by outside sources.

Figure 11-1. Sample addressing generalizability. (Reprinted with permission of Sherilyn Mooney).

There were some limitations that may have affected my findings. For starters, I had a small group of 21 students. That is not a very large sample. Second, I only conducted the intervention for eight weeks, where most of the previous studies on this topic were for much longer. Gathercoal and Nimmo (2002) went more in depth with their study and it took five years, Angell was two years, Lundenberg et al. (1997), was one year. I believe that my case is similar to Festisoff et al. (2008) in that the amount of time and time of year may have affected the results. I conducted the intervention the last eight weeks on school. I believe that the students did truly grow from dependence to the other three stages, but I feel that, with it being the end of the year, it was harder on the whole class. I know for myself, I was less patient and perhaps was stricter and more insistent on what needed to be done; while the students were getting ready for summer, anxious and less responsive to instructions. I believe this could have accounted for the decrease in stage four. I am disappointed that despite the first two stages showing a large decrease, and most students being at Stage 3 (62%), that the number of students in the autonomous stage didn't increase or at least remain the same. With that being said I believe that perhaps had I done a mixed study and included some systematic qualitative observations I would have had more insight into the reasons for the last stage decreasing.

Figure 11-2. Sample of addressing limitations (reprinted with permission of Krista MacGregor).

Think of this limitations section as a chance to describe how the quality of the data you collected could have been improved. Formally this is a review of the threats to the validity of your study, but additionally it is a chance to discuss that you know that your conclusions are based on evidence that might have alternative explanations. As a researcher, you are providing as much help as you can to others who might continue this work by alerting them to potential problems. If you were going to do this study again, is there anything you would do differently to strengthen your design or confirm your findings? What advice do you have for others who may want to replicate or do something similar to your work? Share the "research lessons" you have learned in the experience. No research is perfect, particularly in social science. Reports on research supported by large grants and written by top researchers in the field still have discussions of the limitations of the studies written into them.

Implications

The implications portion of your research study is where you get to talk about the merits of your study. You get to (finally) insert your own opinions—opinions substantiated by your research. It is the personal section of your paper where you share your thoughts about and ideas generated by your project. The implications section addresses primarily two questions: (1) why your study was important and (2) what further studies might be undertaken to move beyond what you found. This section describes how what you studied is part of the larger picture.

Looking at the first question, how will your results impact your teaching or professional practice? What does it mean for you personally and others in general? Have you learned something about your sample or yourself? What can/will you do with this new knowledge; how might you apply what you have learned? How is what you studied part of a larger picture? For example, if you were examining the academic impact of new curriculum, are you now encouraged to teach with the program? If you were examining the impact of a professional development program, what have you learned that will help you in further working with the faculty or when designing future professional development workshops? Did your study cause you to change your pedagogy or the way you interact with students? Why? How?

The second part of an implications section deals with future studies. Did the study raise additional questions that may serve as the basis for further research? What assertions did you make that need to be followed up? For instance, several of our studies suggest that students' attitudes may be affected by the types of teaching used by their instructors. The next logical study would be to go back and determine whether students' attitudes actually were positively affected if an instructor did, indeed, incorporate more active learning strategies in his repertoire. If you did a quantitative study, did you have a finding you think should be delved into further? Is a qualitative follow up needed? Would your findings hold for a different group or a different context? Did your findings or research journey lead you to several other ideas you would like to investigate further? See Figure 11-3 for a sample implications section.

This study has raised more questions for me than resolving them. To now take this research forward to influence my work in the district could potentially change the way my department delivers supports to leadership staff. Having principals identify areas of concern in their own learning may be the place to start, where traditionally the district decides and presents what information is important for leaders to have. I work with a dedicated group of principals on a Special Education committee that would be a starting point for the information gathering on a larger scale. Mentoring them and supporting their growth and development in this area may inform their work with other principal groups. This in turn could create a demand from principals for a more targeted approach to supporting the work they do at the school level.

Figure 11-3. Sample implications section. (reprinted with permission of Deborah Brandell).

Concluding your Conclusion

At the end of this chapter, you must also bring closure to the entire research paper. This is generally a paragraph or two that ties together your question, findings, and the impact of the importance of your work for you personally and/or for education, broadly. For example, if you focused on a new reading program, what might your findings suggest about reading in school in general? Is recess behavior possibly related to classroom behavior? Are students' views of scientists related to ways we might improve students' attitudes or decrease their science anxiety? Review what you wrote in your Chapter 1 about the importance of your question to help you with this summary. Figure 11-4 shows how some students brought their papers to a close.

EXAMPLE 1. (REPRINTED WITH PERMISSION OF SHERYL NASH)

When addressing an educational question, there is never only one answer; and I feel that educators learn the needs of their classrooms quickly and then strive to provide these needs the best they can. Whether a teacher uses whole class, homogeneous, or heterogeneous groups, they should be trusted in determining how to design their classrooms to best meet the needs of their students. The goal of an appropriate education must be to create optimal learning experiences for all. Equality in education does not require that all students have exactly the same experiences. Rather, everyone is promised to have an equal opportunity to learn as much as they can.

EXAMPLE 2. (REPRINTED WITH PERMISSION OF WILLIAM BURNS)

I've learned the teacher's ideal goal seems to be to assist the student towards a formal understanding of mathematics through a constructivist approach. A child's experiences must be closely connected to the language used to describe explorations. There must be a positive environment where participants are encouraged and at ease with oral discussion, a distinct phase of the solution process. This environment can exist in peer discussion if properly facilitated. Teachers should explain new math vocabulary thoroughly and give students copious opportunities to use the vocabulary so as to internalize it. The teacher becomes more or less a sounding board off of which the student bounces clearer and clearer interpretations until the teacher and student understandings are synonymous. The teacher discussion should reflect a strategy of leading students toward discovery, not of revealing answers. In this context, the teacher's role is to question for the purpose of producing quality thinking or extending student thinking. A constructivist approach is effective in helping students to more fully understand mathematics.

Figure 11-4. Samples of closing paragraphs.

APA WRITING STYLE

As stated in the APA Publication Manual (2009), "Good writing is an art and a craft, and instructing in its mastery is beyond the scope of the *Publication Manual* " (p. 31). It is beyond the scope of this book also. What we can tell you are the kinds of things that we have seen over and over again that inhibit good writing; and we can provide a few guidelines to make writing research reports a more straight-forward process. As a reminder, we have included an outline of what is included in each chapter of a typical 5 chapter research paper in Appendix A. Ultimately, how you express your ideas will be a negotiation between you and your research mentor. You may be beginning to see that the manner in which research reports can be written varies enormously, but there are a few rules that can seldom be broken.

The primary rule is to write for clarity. Unfortunately, this may go against ideas that you have developed about good writing in other pursuits. Devices like suspense or inserting the unexpected that are designed for narrative richness probably do not have a place in scientific writing. It is impossible to avoid metaphors in writing, even in scientific writing, but a metaphor is intended to represent something else. In research writing, it is much better to describe the thing directly. Whatever your style, be sure that the language you choose is presenting your ideas as clearly as possible.

Scientific writers use simple past tense for literature reviews and methods sections. Results sections may also be written in this tense but equally you will see results and conclusion sections written in present tense. Remember that if you are required to write a research proposal at the beginning of your study, the methods section is written in future tense as it has not yet been carried out. Do not forget to change sentences copied from your proposal to past tense in your final paper.

Another important rule with research papers is brevity. Try to keep your statements as succinct as possible. Direct, active sentence structure works better than passive voice and sentences with introductory clauses. There is a balancing act with clarity and brevity. It is possible to say too little, making your text less clear. Likewise, it is also possible to say too much, making your meaning murky and risking that the reader will lose track of what you are trying to say.

Inevitably, students may ask two questions: how many references do I need and how long does my paper need to be? Your mentor will answer these questions by telling you that you need as many references as are necessary to support your case, and the paper needs to be as long as is necessary to adequately describe your research project (the responses could be more terse than these). Part of the reason to give these answers is that prescribing a specific length encourages verbose language to fill the assigned space. In reality, the length of a research paper will vary depending on the specific requirements of your project or program and the nature of the study you completed. In general, if your report is 10 pages long then you are probably missing something important in the description of your work. If it is 50 pages long (and not a qualitative or mixed-methods paper) then either you have specific requirements beyond what would normally be included in a published research report or you have included elements that are not necessary to clearly and briefly describe what you have done. Of course, if you are writing a more formal master's thesis or dissertation, the expectation will be for more in-depth writing necessitating a much longer manuscript.

You may be familiar with a number of publication styles depending on your previous experiences in content areas other than education. While specifics vary among the disciplines, every publication style has the same purpose: to make it easy for readers to find information in the publication. You already know something about the idea of finding things easily in APA style articles. Early in your library research work, you may look at nothing but the reference list of an article. While trying to select strategies for gathering data for your study, you may concentrate on methods sections of similar articles. When you are trying to establish a theoretical framework for your study, introductions may seem most important. Even for articles that you read more thoroughly, you may start with the results or conclusions to decide if the article is worth a thorough reading. This non-linear approach to reading research is possible because the style in which the articles are written is predictable. If you are going to contribute to the literature on your topic then you need to follow the same general style rules that others in your discipline are using.

APA style promotes writing about ideas rather than about the people who had the ideas. Here is an example. You might write:

Robert Smith, a long-time, assistant superintendent of curriculum, presents new ideas about teacher inservice in his 2006 book titled *Having an Impact: Teacher Inservice that Matters.*

APA style would focus more on the ideas than the author, suggesting the sentence could be rewritten as:

Smith (2006) suggests avoiding one-shot inservice programs. He advocates periodic tracking of inservice implementation and curriculum needs assessments as components necessary for effective inservice programs.

Because your article is being written in APA style, readers know exactly how to find the shortest path to more information on Smith if they want it. That information is listed in alphabetical order in the back of the article (i.e., the reference list). At the same time, the clarity and brevity rules have been followed by presenting the most important concepts and omitting less important biographical information.

This same approach works whenever you are tempted to talk about yourself in a research report. As noted earlier, acceptance of the use of "I" varies. Writing in first person is sometimes preferred in qualitative research, though some research mentors and publications insist on only third person. For example, "I chose to use a group questioning technique" can be replaced by "Respondents were interviewed in a group setting." In general, it is safe to only include references to yourself or your ideas in the conclusions of the paper or if you need to explain ways in which your presence may have affected data gathering. The reader already knows you are writing the report so references to you are only important if those references clarify the description of the study in some way.

Common Paper and APA Formats

The rules for APA style are published with examples in many places. The best resource is to buy the APA style manual (APA, 2009). Your library will assuredly have copies, and it is likely that others in your university department will own a copy as well. It may be that your library has online resources for using APA. If they do not, numerous libraries around the country do. Check with your research mentor to make sure that the online resource matches your department's requirements, since online resources are often abridged. What follows are some style guidelines for each section of your paper.

Title Page. Typically, a title page consists of the title you have given your research report, followed by your name, university (if your report is part of a degree program) or school/ district (if this is for school/district use), and date. If your paper is part of a university requirement, other information may be requested such as your advisor's name or a statement that the paper is in partial fulfillment of the degree requirements. If you are writing a title page for a paper you wish to have considered for publication, you would include your name, professional affiliation (school or university or district), and contact information (address, phone number, email address).

Running head. Some publications (and mentors) require a running head (header). Running heads are the words that appear on the top of every page of a printed article. If you need to include this it should be only a few words. The running head should be identified on the title page of the paper, be left justified and typed in all capitals at the top of the page.

Pagination. APA suggests that papers are numbered starting with the title page as number one. Page numbers should be formatted to the upper right corner of the page and be preceded by the running head if you use one.

Table of Contents. APA does not list specific style requirements for a table of contents. Generally, a table of contents would not be used if you are writing a journal article length manuscript. Here is another place to talk with your research mentor to see if a table of contents is expected. If you are required to include one, Figure 11-5 shows a typical format.

TABLE OF CONTENTS

Figure 11-5. Sample table of contents.

Note that if you use headers beyond section headings in your paper (see Headers below) they will be indented in the Table of Contents. In more formal papers, you may also be requested to supply a similar content sheet for tables, figures, and appendices included in the paper.

Abstract. An abstract is a summary of the research paper. Because it is short, often having a word limit (typically about 200 words), abstracts are surprisingly difficult to write. A good abstract contains the research question, the basic methodology, the main results and the major conclusions. As you can imagine, it is difficult to cover all these items in a brief overview. If you are writing an abstract for a journal or conference presentation, it is especially important that your abstract "grab" the readers or they will probably not be interested in reading your entire report or attending the conference session. The abstract would be included in the paper immediately following the Table of Contents. Sample abstract are presented in Figure 11-6.

EXAMPLE 1

Student teachers competitively applied for small technology grants to obtain equipment and software to support instruction in their clinical experiences. Self-report summaries of these experiences were examined to identify issues around efficacy of instruction and suggestions for future iterations of uses of technology by these and other teachers. This strategy for moving technology into clinical experiences overcame a number of the inhibitions to infusing technology into teacher preparation identified in the literature.

EXAMPLE 2

The purpose of this study was to examine 5th, 7th, and 10th graders' attitudes toward school and classroom science by means of questionnaires. In particular, the study hoped to determine (a) what students attitudes are; (b) whether a relationship exists between these school and classroom science attitudes; and (c) what relationships grade level, gender, ethnicity, school/community type, expected GPA and science grade have with students' attitudes toward school and classroom science. The results indicated that, although a statistically significant relationship did exist between students attitudes toward school and toward classroom science, the relationship had no practical meaning. Females were slightly more positive about school than males. No gender differences were found with respect to classroom attitudes. Fifth graders held significantly more positive attitudes toward science than upper-grade students. None of the other variables was found to have any practical relationship to either of the attitudes.

EXAMPLE 3

Federal educational technology grant coordinators from seven small liberal arts colleges were interviewed to determine the ways in which technology had been

Figure 11-6. Sample abstracts.

infused in teacher education programs over the life of the grant. Substantive integration of technology had occurred in each of the schools. Traditional change models were unable to explain how change occurred at these institutions. The study suggests a new model of institutional change based on the entrepreneurial efforts and interpersonal connections of local change agents.

Figure 11-6. Sample abstracts. (Continued)

Headers. APA has changed the requirements for the use of headers in its most recent addition of the style manual. Each section of your paper should be separated by a section heading. APA calls these top level headings and they are title case (each major word starts with a capital letter), bold, and centered. The Introduction section heading is omitted because it is assumed the paper starts with the introduction.

Even though each of the chapters (major sections) of your paper includes specific subsections, we encourage you to write fluid transitions from one component to the next. When done successfully, additional headers are not required in the paper. Sometimes, though, your material will be sufficiently complex that you can help the reader by providing an outline of the structure of a chapter of your paper. You would do this by including headers for each of the components of the section. Most of the time you can do this with only one additional level of heading. APA second level headings are the same as first level headings (title case and bold) but they are left justified. If you need an additional subordinate level of heading, you would use a third level heading (indented, bold, only the first letter of the heading is capitalized, ends with a period, and the text follows on the same line).

(Top Level) Centered, Bold, Upper and Lower Case

(Second Level) Flush Left, Bold, Upper and Lower Case

(Third level) Indented, bold, lower case, ending with a period.

(Fourth level) Indented, bold, italic, lower case, ending with a period.

(Fifth level) Indented, italic, lower case, ending with a period.

As a reminder, in a Table of Contents, the section headings would be left justified, with major headers indented and subordinate headers indented again.

Tables and Figures. As described in Chapter 9, tables and figures are often required to present information in a clearer manner than words alone. In quantitative studies it is assumed that data will be summarized in table form. Place a reference to the table or figure at an appropriate point in the text, and insert the table or figure immediately after the referring paragraph. If the insert will not fit completely on that page, continue on with text on that page and place the figure or table at the top of the following page. Continue on with text.

If you are submitting the paper for publication, many publishers require that the tables and figures are included at the end of the manuscript so that their type-setters can determine the appropriate location for the inserts. You would still include the reference to the table or figure at the appropriate point in the text and include a notation in the text approximately where you believe the insert should appear.

Here are key APA guidelines for formatting both tables and figures. Remember to use descriptive, but brief, titles for both. Table numbers are left justified with the word "Table" followed by the table number. On the next line, left justify the table titles which are title case and italic. The body of the table will vary depending on the type of table or figure you are including but the example in Figure 11-7 will give you a general idea of how it should appear.

Table 1

Mean and Standard Deviation of Pretest and Posttest Test Scores for Correctly Reading Words

	Reading Test		
	Pretest ($n = 243$)	Posttest ($n = 243$)	p
Mean	14.72	17.93	$< .001$
Standard deviation	4.13	2.56	

Notes:
1. The table number is not bold.
2. The title is first letter capitals (title case) and italic. Titles do not end in a period.
3. A line runs under the title and another across at the bottom of the table.
4. Sections of the table are separated by lines. In the middle of the section that presents the actual data line separators are not used. There are no vertical separators.
5. Row headers are left justified and data columns are center justified. Data should be decimal point aligned.
6. Actual computed p values are included in the table whenever possible. When it would make the table too complicated, significance levels are indicated by asterisks with the largest p value noted with one asterisk and the second largest with 2 and so on. If you use multiple tables keep the number of asterisks used for specific p values the same among all of the tables.
7. For comparisons of group means, results should be in table form listing means, standard deviations, and sample sizes.
8. Because there are so many forms of data that you may wish to present in table form, try to apply these general design characteristics in ways that make the most sense for your data. Referencing the APA Manual may help.

Figure 11-7. Sample table.

References. The reference list goes at the end of the body of the paper in its own section. It is headed "References." Remember, this is not a bibliography. Do not include sources that were not referred to; that is, cited, specifically in the body of your paper.

References are intended to provide the most efficient path to the original work that is possible. APA reference style is designed to accommodate this. In general, if a publication is available both online and in printed form, you would use the reference to the print document instead of a link to an online version of the publication. For the time being, print references are still more stable than electronic forms. When the reference is only available electronically, of course the electronic reference would be used. As a caution, when you access an article through your library databases that is generally not the *home* of the article. The reference should be to the published source of the material even if that is an electronic source. APA is now suggesting that DOI numbers are included in the reference. This new reference tool overcomes some of the problems around not really knowing the source of materials accessed online.

While we are talking about electronic sources, they only go into the reference section if they are published materials that are accessed electronically. If what you are citing is the contents of a web page, put the url of the web page into the citation in the body of the paper and do not include it in the references.

New users of APA reference style often struggle with the level of detail necessary to type complete references. If you work at understanding the basic components of references, it will help you gather reference information efficiently and reduce the time necessary to correct citations after you have inserted them into your paper. A number of software-based tools have appeared to help you with this, but in our experience none of them does a perfect job of formatting APA references. That means that you need to be familiar enough with the reference style to know when things are not quite right even when you are using commercial tools to assist you.

Appendices. The last physical part of your paper is the appendix. If you have something that you feel should be added to your paper but that would disrupt the flow of the reading if it were included in the body of the report, then it goes in the appendix. Some students (and professors) prefer that items like interview protocols and other data collection instruments be included as appendices rather than placing them directly in the methodology chapter.

The appendix is not a place to include all your raw data! Some of our students feel a need to attach samples of student work or their interview transcripts or a copy of a graded essay assignment. If you have done an appropriate job of analyzing and explaining your data, there is usually not a need to include actual data samples in your research paper. On rare occasions, it might be useful to include raw data as an appendix. For example, if you are analyzing student drawings, you may want to include a sample of a marked picture. Do not feel compelled to find something to put in an appendix section.

As with all parts of the research report, there are guidelines for formatting appendices. Generally, appendices follow the same format as for text or figures in the main body of your paper.

CHAPTER 11

Common APA Problems

Listed below are problems seen with great frequency when students are writing in APA style. Read through these and do your best to avoid them.

References:
- For the title of a journal article, only proper nouns and the first word in the title or subtitle are capitalized.
- Volume numbers are italicized and issue numbers are not. Issue numbers are inside of parentheses and there is no space between the volume number and the issue number.
- In multiple author references, an ampersand is used and not the word and, and a comma is placed before the ampersand separating the last two authors (e.g. Carroll, J., & Morrell, P.).
- Only initials are used for first and middle names.
- All references end in a period.
- The letters "pp" are not placed before the page numbers in a journal reference.
- Web addresses should not be blue and underlined (as MS Word automatically formats them).
- Use single line spacing within references and double line spacing between references. Use hanging indents for each paragraph in the reference list.
- A bibliography is a list of possible resources for a topic. References refer to the citations in a paper. Therefore the reference section of an APA research paper is entitled "References."

Citations:
- Each citation should have an author and date in close proximity. If the citation is done within parentheses, place a comma between the author and date. Multiple citations presented simultaneously are presented in alphabetical order and separated with a semi-colon.
- Carefully match citations and references. The only references appearing on the reference list are those cited in the text. If something is cited in the text, then it must be on the reference list.
- All quotations require a page number at the end of the quotation. Quotations should be used only when an author has used an exceptional turn of phrase that would be difficult for you to paraphrase. Use them judiciously. Your job is to synthesize what you read, not repeat it.
- If a citation appears at the end of a sentence it is inserted before the period.
- There is a temptation to present a series of ideas and then put the citation at the end. When this is happening there is a noticeable pattern of every paragraph ending with a citation. You should try to insert citations when the set of ideas is first introduced.
- When you insert a citation, the same citation should not be inserted again unless there may be some confusion over the person to whom you are referring. Once you cite someone, the reader assumes you are continuing to talk about that work until you give us some clue to the contrary.

Writing Style:
- Avoid using rhetorical questions. Often writers use rhetorical questions as a device to lead to an explanation. This is a bad idea in research papers because the implication is that you will answer the questions that you ask with the research, even if they are rhetorical.
- In APA style the focus is the presentation of ideas. Authors' names are used to give credit and to establish a path to the original sources. In most circumstances, attention should not be given to the author directly—only his or her ideas. So, authors' first names, article or book titles, or any description of authors' positions in life should not be used.
- Do not use et cetera. If there are more components of a list, then list them.
- Try to avoid using parentheses except for citations. If something needs to be in parentheses it is usually because you are trying to add examples or clarification to what you are saying. That information can easily be constructed as a normal part of your paragraph. If it is important to say, say it in a sentence.
- No matter how many authors you read who are doing this, don't use indefinite pronouns. The phrase "one can never know…" should be rewritten in a form such as "the individuals involved in the process can never know…"
- Do not forget page numbers. Page numbering starts on the title page.
- Do not refer to yourself in the third person whenever possible. "This researcher will explore…" Rather refer to the research. "This report is an investigation of …" Remember the part about APA being about the ideas and not the authors. This is in the same vein. However, when writing qualitative research, it is sometimes impossible to avoid using "the researcher" or "I."
- Although it is difficult for us to accomplish much in our language without using metaphors, use them sparingly. Heavy use of metaphors makes the work seem less well informed and trendy, and often have a cultural bias making it difficult for all readers to understand.
- Never use the phrase "research says," or any version thereof, unless it is immediately followed by the citations for the research to which you are referring.

NEXT STEPS

The research is completed. The findings are written. Now what? Celebrate that you have completed a major undertaking! Congratulate yourself. Reflect on your accomplishments and be proud. You have successfully undertaken a journey into educational research. However, do not be content with stopping your journey now. There are many more places to go and people to meet. Take the knowledge and skills you have learned and practiced in this endeavor and start planning your next trip. Chapter 12 will offer some ideas on where you might go from here.

CHAPTER SELF-CHECK

Having completed this chapter, you should be comfortable discussing the following:
- organizing and writing Chapter 5, including the conclusion, limitations, and implications
- organizing and writing a Table of Contents, Appendices, Title Page, Reference Section
- APA and general writing tips

CHAPTER REVIEW QUESTIONS

1. List the major elements of a conclusion section.
2. What is the purpose of APA citation style?
3. Look at some of your recent writing and see if it includes any of the common APA problems.

REFERENCES

American Psychological Association. (2009). *Publication manual of the American Psychological Association* (6th ed.). Washington, DC: Author.

Gay, L. R., Mills, G. E., & Airasian, P. (2005). *Educational research: Competencies for analysis and applications* (8th ed.). Upper Saddle River, NJ: Prentice Hall.

Krishnamurti, J. (1963). *Life ahead: On learning and the search for meaning*. Novato, CA: New World Library.

WHERE TO FROM HERE?

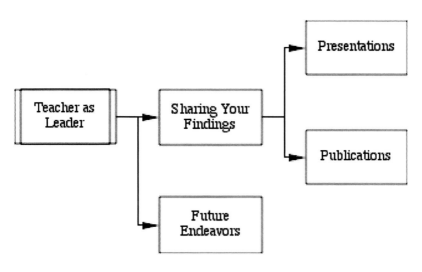

CHAPTER OVERVIEW

Chapter 12 branches away from the research paper and delves into the issues of life-long learning. It is focused on two main areas: immediate and future steps. It talks about what you can do with your current research study and suggests how to decide on future studies. Additionally, the chapter presents ideas for teacher leadership outside the walls of the classroom.

INTRODUCTION

Since we started this text with a trip metaphor, it seems appropriate to return to that to close the text. At the end of your journey, you have pictures and stories to share, ideas of what you want to do and where you want to go for your next trip, and tips you've learned about traveling in general. The research journey is similar. You have findings and processes to share, a whole implication section of ideas of new things to try, and a "suitcase" of new skills in case you want to branch into a new research direction.

TEACHER AS LEADER

Often, people who teach do not really understand the complexity of the discipline of teaching and learning. Think back to your own impressions about teaching before you began your research project. In all likelihood, you have a very different view of teaching now. You may have thought teaching was more of an art than a discipline. What you know about each of your students mixed with your own experiences as a teacher help you to make decisions in and for your classroom and students. We imagine that at this point you realize that your behaviors are more than just the result of luck or experience. Research, by yourself and others, has guided your actions. The courses you took in college were research-based, and much of how you teach and work with your students is shaped in large part by empirical research (both your own and that of others). Education is a content area much the same way that social studies, mathematics and science are. It has its own theories, postulates, guiding principles, body of knowledge and skills. Teaching is not just a set of behaviors, it is a set of guided behaviors, and those behaviors (and their results) are continually being studied. Teaching is an enormously dynamic profession. Teachers, administrators, and communities need to work together to establish an environment of continuous improvement. Given your research experience, you can more easily contribute to the decision-making process from an *informed* point of view. You can help others to be sure that their points of view are informed as well. You can continue to develop the skills to be a teacher leader. Being a leader involves letting others know about the discoveries you have made whenever you complete a research project.

SHARING YOUR FINDINGS

If you are like most of us, you have spent a lot of blood, sweat, and tears in designing and completing your first major research project. Something that was worth so much of your personal investment is worth sharing. Think of who would benefit most from hearing what you did and what you found. Remember, even if what you found was that there was no significant difference that is still probably an important finding.

Presentations

Generally the people most closely related to your study context will be inherently interested in your findings. If you studied students in your class, the other teachers in your building would be interested in what happened. If the scope of your study was school wide or district wide, the entire faculty might like to hear about your research. If you did your project as part of a master's program, your fellow classmates will generally be interested in hearing about your work. It is also possible (and probable) that others in the educational community would be interested in what you studied and what you found. We can all learn from the works of others.

Local Dissemination. Consider who, locally, would be your target audience. Who would benefit most from learning what you researched: your school's faculty/staff, the district's faculty/staff, administration, the school board. Arrange to present your findings to the appropriate group. Talk to your principal or super-intendent and ask for time on the agenda of a faculty meeting, district inservice, board meeting, and the like. Prepare a 10–15 minute Power Point presentation that succinctly highlights your research plan, findings, and implications and allow time for questions and discussion with the audience.

Professional Meetings. You may want to consider presenting your research findings at a local, statewide, regional or national professional education conference, as well. Contact your state department of education or content area groups for a list of conferences. Your first step is to find organizations that seem to have similar interests to yours. If you are interested in meeting with other teachers to talk about classroom issues, look to professional organizations around content areas (e.g., National Science Teachers Association or National Council of Teachers of English). If you are interested in presenting to other researchers, ask your professors where they suggest presenting. Organizations like the American Educational Research Association or the Association for Supervision and Curriculum Development might be right for you. Most national organizations, both content and research oriented, have state affiliates who sponsor smaller, more informal venues, which serve as good places to begin to develop conference speaking skills.

Go to the organization's web site and look for links to materials on conventions or meetings. There you will find dates and locations for the meetings in addition to descriptions of how to submit a proposal. Often you will find links to previous meetings. Search through these to get a sense of the kinds of presentations that are being made at the meeting in which you are interested to be sure you have picked an appropriate venue to share your work. The deadline for proposal submissions is generally several months to a half year before the conference date and the proposal submission requirements vary, so plan ahead. If you have missed the date for proposal submission for the next annual conference, just mark your calendar for the following year so you will have a concrete reminder of when to work on your proposal application.

Most professional meetings post a request for proposal (RFP) six to eight months before the meeting. Read the instructions in the RFP carefully and follow them when you are writing a proposal. Sometimes proposals are rejected without even being read because submitters have not followed instructions. Do not let yourself be in this category. Proposal writing is not difficult but be sure that you have described your project clearly and efficiently. What will proposal reviewers need to know to see that your presentation will be valuable? Your proposal should highlight your findings and their importance, and minimize your literature review, although some organizations (mostly research conferences) want to see evidence that you are working from a clear theoretical construct which will require some reference work.

Before you commit to doing a presentation, be sure that those for whom you are working (e.g., your principal or superintendent) know that you want to attend this meeting. Often your district will have professional development money to assist you in attending. More important, it is considered very bad form to commit to a presentation and then back out after the program for the meeting has been set. Be sure you have the approval of your principal or superintendent before accepting an invitation to present. You may also find that a number of teachers in your building will want to attend, as participants if not presenters. Attending conferences is a type of professional development activity that seems to provide extra benefit when teachers participate as a learning community.

Conference proposals are peer-reviewed, and reviewers' comments are sent to the authors. This is an easy way of getting feedback on your proposal. If you were successful in getting your presentation accepted, use the reviewers' comments to help strengthen your presentation. If you are not successful, do not lose faith. It is likely that you chose the wrong conference for your work or you did not write the proposal in a way that expressed what you did clearly. The feedback you received should help you in either deciding on a different conference venue or in rewriting your proposal for the next conference. Like most things in life, practice makes perfect.

Presentation Tips. Presenting to any group can be intimidating. Whether you are presenting to your colleagues or at a national convention, a few rules should be followed. First, know what your audience expects to hear. Are they after knowing how the students responded to your new curriculum or do they want to know the methods and analytical procedures used in your study? With a little thought you can figure out how to design a presentation that meets the needs of your audience. It is unlikely that anyone will want to sit and listen to you read a paper to them. Whatever you decide to present be sure that you can communicate in a comfortable, authoritative style without reading directly from your prepared materials. It is very much like presenting a lesson to your students.

The second most important rule is to stay within the time allotted for your presentation. This requires planning and practice. If you have not rehearsed your presentation you will most likely underestimate the time needed to say or do what you had planned. The result of this is that either you will have to end your presentation before you have gotten through what you planned or you will take time allocated to others on the program. Neither of these is a good outcome.

Third, try to anticipate what the venue will be like in which you present. How big is the room? What equipment will be there for you to use? What support will be available if problems with the equipment occur? What back up plans do you have (overhead transparencies in case the computer crashes or the bulb on the in-focus project burns out and no one is there to replace it)? After attending national meetings for decades, we are still amazed at the number of presenters who have not planned well for their presentations. This is so much of a problem that some organizations now have instructions for presenters. See, for example, the presentation tips listed under the "meetings and events" menu on the site for the American Educational Research Association (http://www. aera.net). Your goal is to have your audience be excited about the content of your presentation and not be uneasy about the manner in which your presentation was made.

When you do get accepted to present your research, it is natural to feel nervous. We tend to think that because we stand up in front of a room full of students all day and are obviously experienced "presenters" we should be able to easily speak at a conference. Speaking in front of a peer group is very different from speaking in front of your students. It is more like having a formal teaching observation. We tend to be a little nervous and self-conscious at the start, but usually find our groove. Good PowerPoint slides help to augment your talk, give the audience something to look at besides you, and serve as prompts for what you want to orally share. Rehearsing, as noted above, is a good pre-conference strategy to help you become and remain more calm and confident.

So, rehearsing would be the fourth rule. Practice in front of some friends or co-workers or by yourself. Time your talk. Make necessary modifications. If you have trouble with a particular transition, make an extra Power Point slide to help guide you. Continue to rehearse until you feel sure and comfortable with your presentation. We encourage our students to practice a speech; we need to take that same advice.

Publications

There is something extremely satisfying about seeing things you have written in print. Getting your writing accepted for publication will be time consuming but worth while. If your research mentor has guided you into writing in a style that would be acceptable for a journal or other publication, you may be well on your way to being ready to submit a manuscript. If your project report was prepared in the more formal style of a thesis you will more likely have a bit of rewriting to do. Here are a few ideas for increasing the likelihood that your manuscript will be accepted.

Start the same way you would with finding a meeting you would like to attend. Who would most benefit from your research? Who would want to read what you have to say? Is your research so specific that teachers outside the district would not be impacted; does your research have generalizability to a state-wide level; or would any teacher learn from what you have done? Choose an appropriate venue: district newsletter, statewide teacher publication, national journal. There are hundreds of publications oriented toward classroom profes- sionals, hundreds for educational researchers, and still hundreds more that are for more general audiences but publish articles on educational topics. If you do not already have a publication source in mind, with a little effort you will be able to find links to various educational publications online (e.g., http://journalseek.net/ educ.htm).

You will need to do two things as you search for an appropriate publisher. Foremost you need to find publications that represent the groups with which you are most aligned. Are you looking for teacher practitioner journals, a policy journal or maybe a research journal? Do you want to focus on a content area or speak more broadly about educational issues? Make a list of those publications that look like good candidates.

If you are interested in publishing research, the *Cabell's Guides to Publishing* are very useful. There are three of these in areas of education: Educational Curriculum and Methods, Educational Psychology and Administration, and Educational Technology and Library Science. Your college library is likely to have these. They not only list journals in each of the topic areas, but contain a considerable amount of information about each journal including the percentage of submitted articles the journal accepts for publication.

Once you think you have found a publication that might be a good match for your work, you need to review past issues of the publication. Often you can find these online at the web site for the publication; but, just as often, you may have to go to the library to find hard copies of the published materials. Read these carefully looking for levels of complexity and writing style that are similar to your work. If you decide to submit to a publication, it is important that your writing fits the style of the journal; reading previous articles is the best way to figure this out. You can only submit your article to one publisher at a time. In fact you may have to sign an agreement that the manuscript has not been submitted to anyone else. The more ground work you do before you submit your article, the better the chances your publication target is appropriate and your paper will be accepted. Going from submission of an article to publication can be a long process for many publishers, often taking several months just for the paper to be reviewed. If your writing concerns issues that are time-dependent you particularly want to find the right journal the first time through.

Each publisher has a submission guide. Find this on the publication's website or in the journal itself and make a copy. Read this guide carefully. Even though most publishers of education-related articles use APA style, there is considerable variation in the details of what each publication wants. In addition there will be details about page limits, format requirements, and how to submit your article. Most publishers now want you to submit manuscripts only in electronic form. Be sure you have followed the guide for types of documents that can be submitted. If in the end you cannot figure out exactly what a publisher wants from you, call or email them before you submit. The contact information will be on the submission guide.

Getting this all straight the first time you submit something for publication seems like a lot of detail work. It is, but doing it right the first time will increase your chances of having something accepted for publication. As with a conference proposal, if your article is not accepted the first time around, do not give up. Like proposals, the two biggest hurdles to publishing are fit and clarity. And, like a proposal, you will receive reviewer feedback. Use the reviewers' comments to redraft and improve your paper. It is not always easy to condense your research paper to a publishable length; and because we are so close to our own research, what we have done is often not as clear to someone removed from the study and just reading our written words. Frequently, if a submission is rejected, it is typically because your work is a bad match for the publication. Any rejection of writing is disappointing but the more effort you make up front, the better you will get at picking the right journal the first time and submitting manuscripts that are accepted without difficulty. Use rewrites—if needed—as learning opportunities.

WHAT TO DO WITH YOUR DATA

An important consideration once you are done with your study is what do you do with the research data? There are generally guidelines you have to follow according to your Institutional Review Board plan. We recommend our students shred their data after their final written research paper has been accepted by our institution as meeting degree requirements. If, however, the students plan to do any presenting or publishing, data are typically kept in a secure (locked) place for three to five years after the completion of the study. Ethical considerations are the reason for this care in keeping and discarding research data. Data on individual subjects should not be able to be identified by anyone, except, in certain circumstances, by the author of a study.

FUTURE ENDEAVORS

The last chapter of your research paper included a section on implications. What do your findings mean to you? What future studies might be conducted to further validate or extend the original findings? Here is a game plan of what you might want to do next. If you have learned something in your study, see if it holds true with your next class. Check to see if making suggested changes has the hypothesized results. Do what you suggest needs to be done. AND make notes and collect data and write up those findings. If you are following the same line of research, you have almost all of your literature review done already. You just need to adjust your methods and analyze your new findings.

If you do a longitudinal study, you will determine if the results of your initial study hold true for future classes; that is, are generalizable. Think of how much stronger that makes your conclusions and recommendations, and how much more publishable the findings are and more worthy of presenting to larger, more diverse audiences. The first research paper is always the hardest. Do not allow all your experience to go dormant. Continue researching, and writing, and sharing!

We hope through your experiences with designing and conducting your own research, you have become a more reflective practitioner. Do not allow the skills you have been developing as a researcher go unused. Continue to look at your practice and your school and your students. Plan to do some systematic research on your new curriculum or instructional strategy, or school's behavior modification plan. You now know how important it is to read what others have done and discovered. Continue to add to that body of knowledge so others can learn from your experiences. Education as a discipline relies on updated research to be vibrant.

NEXT STEPS

"Enough!" you may be saying. "I'm done with my project. No more!"

Sorry, once a researcher, always a researcher. Use the critical skills you have been developing to analyze new changes suggested (or mandated) by the administration. Will these new curricula, testing methods, or school reconfigurations really have the desired effect? Conduct a study and collect data to see. You know gut feelings will not change anyone's mind. Hard data may.

How can you improve your own classroom teaching? Does making certain changes in assessing or seating or grouping really make a difference? Find out! You do not always need to write a formal proposal, conduct a literature review and plan elaborate methodologies; but you can do simple studies, collect data, and have concrete evidence to help you guide your practice instead of just relying on instinct. And you will be more likely to convince your colleagues to implement or abandon similar practices if you can show them results.

Even if you do not formally conduct a research study ever again, you have learned important skills and a new way of looking at your practice. You will not be content with accepting what you read or what others say blindly. A little voice inside your head will be saying, "But where's the proof? Where are the data to back that up?" And you can use those little voices and skills informally to continue to improve your own professional practice and to effectuate change in your own school setting.

CHAPTER SELF-CHECK

Having completed this chapter, you should be comfortable discussing the following:
- education as a discipline
- disseminating your research findings through presentations and publications: choosing a venue, getting a paper accepted, and tips
- using your research skills in your daily professional life
- deciding on future research topics

CHAPTER REVIEW QUESTIONS

1. Education, itself, is a content area. Do you agree or disagree with this statement? Why?
2. Where might you present your research findings?
3. Where might you publish your research findings?
4. How do you go about choosing a venue for either publication or a presentation?
5. What are some tips for a successful research presentation?
6. Given your research experience, what do you plan to do next?

REFERENCES

Cabell Publishing. (2007). *Cabell's directory of publishing opportunities in educational curriculum and methods* (8th ed.). Beaumont, TX: Author.
Cabell Publishing. (2007). *Cabell's directory of publishing opportunities in educational psychology and administration* (8th ed.). Beaumont, TX: Author.
Cabell Publishing. (2007). *Cabell's directory of publishing opportunities in educational technology and library science* (8th ed.). Beaumont, TX: Author.

APPENDIX A

OUTLINE OF A TRADITIONAL RESEARCH PAPER

Chapter 1: Introduction
- – What do you want to know?
- – What is the logical argument that leads to the need to know this?
    - – This might include some description of the study context.
    - – It probably will include some reference to theoretical constructs.
    - – Why is it important to know this?
- – Operationally define any important terms that may have multiple meanings.
- – What is the research question precisely?

Chapter 2: Literature Review
- – What do others already know about your problem (focusing on the most current empirical research)?
- – On what work is this knowledge based (theoretical construct)?
- – How can you summarize this literature (what is most important for your study)?

Chapter 3: Methods
- – What is the context in which the study will be done?
- – Who is to be studied?
- – How were they selected?
- – What are your role and responsibilities as they relate to the sample?
- – What procedures will be used for data collection?
- – What tools will be used for data collection?
- – How were those tools developed?
- – How will the data be analyzed?

Chapter 4: Results
- – What data were gathered?
- – This section is substantially different for quantitative and qualitative studies
    - – Quantitative—A dispassionate description of the gathered data in text and table forms including how the data appear after the analysis procedures have been applied.
    - – Qualitative—Identification of themes with discussion and supporting examples

Chapter 5: Conclusions
- – What is the answer to your question?
- – What do your results mean?
- – Compare your results to what is known in the literature.
- – How might this study be enhanced (limitations)?
- – What do we still need to know?
- – What implications does this have for education or your classroom?

APPENDIX B

Sample Student Paper (reprinted with permission of Tia Martini)

This appendix presents an inservice teacher's first attempt at educational research. We include it as another example of many of the things that we have talked about in the book. All research reports, even by experienced researchers, could be rewritten to improve the presentation. Our intent is to show a good example realizing that you might choose to do things differently in your study.

Test Anxiety and Self Esteem
Tia Martini

CHAPTER 1 - INTRODUCTION

There are two constants in human existence, we are born and we will eventually die. It is what happens between these two events that make up a life. This life is unique and distinctive to each human. Some are meek and some are bold, others are highly intelligent whereas others struggle developmentally. As children and adolescents a vast majority of their life is spent in the educational environment of school. During this period in their lives, these children and teens are discovering what they think and believe as well as what kind of person they will become. Unfortunately, it is not enough to say that these are the only goals we have for our students as educators and a society. Certain content- specific standards and knowledge have been deemed important and thus placed in what is referred to as the curriculum. Once formalized, it is not enough to merely say; yes I have covered the curriculum, but rather, some form of accountability must come in to play.

Parents, guardians, students and community officials want to know to what extent our students are meeting the goals and standards of the curriculum. As a result, not only do educators assess content area in their classrooms to generate report card marks, but are asked to use standardized tests to serve as a check to school officials and society. In Alberta there is a significant amount of standardized testing occurring. All students are tested in the four core content areas of Language Arts, Science, Math and Social Studies at grades three, six and nine in Provincial Achievement Tests. These same students are later required to write diploma exams in the same content areas in order to graduate from high school. The diploma exams account for half of a student's course mark. It is with these marks that students then apply to post secondary and technical institutions or enter the world of work. Every school in the province has their students' performance on these standardized tests compared in the public forum of newspapers. High stakes testing such as this seems to be a straightforward way to gauge the extent and depth to which the students are achieving. Tests such as these also create a large volume of stress for the students. This trend of high accountability testing does not seem to be fading. If anything, more and more accountability testing seems to be on the horizon.

Recently, my Language Arts classes wrote their mid-term exams. As I watched my students take the test I noticed some of my students immediately got down to the task at hand and began writing. They seemed confident in their ability to complete the test. As I circulated through the test area, I noticed other students staring blankly at their test papers. It seemed to take them a long time to begin their tests. Perhaps they were in preparation to begin, but they also appeared wound up. It appeared that if I would have questioned them, I'm sure they would have jumped out of their seat. Near the end of the exam, some of the students looked panicked and anxious as if there would never be enough time for them to complete the test. After the exam, I thought to myself, what were those students thinking? Were they just nervous because they were writing a mid-point exam and the nervousness manifested itself as a difficulty in organizing their thoughts? Or was this a case of mental blocking and these students had gone "blank" as a direct result of the significant impact the exam would place on their course mark?

As I marked the exams, a seemingly normal distribution emerged, some failed, some excelled and a fair number achieved an average acceptable standard. Some of the anxious students scored very well and others preformed disappointingly: there seemed to be little connection between the behavior during the exam and the results of the test.

After semester break, I asked my classes what they thought of the exam. As expected, some thought it was hard, others thought it was easy. When I returned the exams to my students, I noticed something I was oblivious to before: students who felt confident about how well they did on the exam seemed shaken when the mark was lower than expected and students anticipating a poor result, seemed exceptionally elated by a mark slightly above what they were anticipating.

I began to reflect on the situation and wonder if there was a relationship between the anxiety my students experienced during the exam and how they thought about themselves. Was there a connection? If a student assumed they could achieve on a test, would they take the test in a manner to achieve their goal? Conversely, if a student's self talk was negative and they told themselves that they would do poorly, would this anxiety towards the test impede their performance? Did their self esteem have any impact on the level of test anxiety that they experience during the exam?

As a teacher, evaluation is a necessary and important component of the educational process. So long as there are government- regulated curriculums, testing will not disappear: if anything, it will increase. More testing will definitely have an impact on students with anxiety by increasing their general level of stress. I question whether or not the achievement potential of these students is somehow impacted by their perceptions of self. The purpose of this study is to examine if there is a relationship between students' self reported levels of self-esteem and their general level of test anxiety.

CHAPTER 2 - REVIEW OF LITERATURE

Testing in Education Today

There appears to be a discrepancy between our desire for our school systems to create well- rounded. independent thinking problem solvers, and the near exclusive usage of standardized academic testing to gauge student achievement (Rothstein, 2004). Not only are low stakes teacher- developed and administered tests on the rise in schools, but so too are high stakes government generated standardized tests (Supon, 2004). Conceivably, it is related to the volume of educational reforms that center on high standards, accountability and methods of measuring achievement statistically as opposed to focusing on the skills required to attain academic success (Fulk, 2003).

For whatever reason, more testing is happening in schools. Bass, Burroughs, Gallion and Hodel (2002) report that in 1950, students emerging from public schools had taken a federal, state and district exam to complete their studies, whereas in 1990 the average senior had taken 19 standardized tests to finish their secondary education. Rubenzer (2002) views tests as success benchmarks; they lead to stress or success. Is it any wonder that the fear of failure from assessments is a common problem among students today? This fear of failure from testing and evaluation may begin as early as preschool due to unreal expectations from teachers or significant others and their negative reactions to poor results from tests (Burke, 1999).

Testing is not all bad. It is an effective method to gauge the level of knowledge students possess and the skills they have developed in a particular curricular area. Problems arise when the testing is used to make comparisons among individuals for the purpose of exclusion (Goonan, 2003). Goonan goes on to assert that students are fine with testing if it is used to help identify an area in need of improvement and are resentful when assessments are used as a screening tool for things like getting into post-secondary education or receiving financial assistance. In general, it communicates the message that test scores indicate an individual's worthiness.

Test Anxiety

Most students experience some level of anxiety during a testing situation. When this anxiety begins to affect academic performance it becomes a problem not only for the student (as low grades) but also for the teacher (as an inaccurate measure of a student's ability or level of achievement). Anxiety in general is a basic human emotion consisting of fear and uncertainty that typically appears when an individual perceives an event as being a threat to the ego (Harris, 2003; Sarason, 1980). This fear and uncertainty can assist in keeping students focused. However, in some cases, it can cause students to become excessively concerned with the embarrassment or negative consequences associated with giving a poor performance on an exam (Goonan, 2003). The nervousness and tension experienced before, during and after an examination can serve as a negative trigger for the test anxious. It becomes a larger issue when these feelings begin to interfere with the ability to perform on examination, thus impairing the potential (academic or otherwise) of the test taker (Bass, Burroughs, Gallion & Hodel 2002; Hembree, 1988).

What is known about test anxiety, also referred to as test stress anxiety or merely test stress, is that it is a stable personality characteristic that prompts an individual to react to the threatening situation of a test or exam with sometimes debilitating cognitive, affective and behavioral responses (Hancock, 2001; Cheek, 2002; Sarason, 1980; Hembree, 1988; Sapp & Farrell, 1994; Burke, 1999; Collins 1999 & McDonald, 2001). These three components each manifest in unique ways.

The cognitive component of test anxiety focuses on the thoughts and emotions of the individual (Sapp & Farrell, 1994). Some individuals find that in a testing situation it is difficult to concentrate on the task before them due to the mentally distracting activity of their thoughts (Burke, 1999, McDonald, 2001). Harris (2003) maintains that these thoughts and emotions generate worry within the individual and are due to a lack of self confidence in their academic abilities. The negative messages the student tells themselves become the only thing of importance and can interfere with the actual taking of a test.

The affective component of test anxiety is a composite of physiological reactions that can range from increased heart rate, nausea, clamminess, sweaty hands and dry mouth (Harris, 2003; Burke, 1999). These autonomic arousals are not only physically strenuous, but are also psychologically exhausting (McDonald, 2001). The stress of the test anxiety can tire students out more than physical activity can (Rubenzer, 2002). This tiring physical strain associated with test anxiety can interfere with a student's ability to focus on completing a test (McDonald, 2001; Rubenzer, 2002).

The behavioral component of test anxiety can be attributed to a variety of actions taken by the test anxious that interfere with the ability to achieve on an exam. It is interesting to note that for those who experience test anxiety, there are behaviors that are commonly exhibited. Harris (2003) maintains that procrastination, inefficient study skills and poor test taking strategies are common to the test anxious. Supon (2004) categories the test anxious into one of three groups: those with weak study skills, those who have the study skills but fear failure and those who perceive themselves as having no study skills. In a study by Birenbaum and Nasser (1994) the researchers made an effort to categorize two different groups of students: those deficient in test-taking skills and those deficient of study skills. They found that despite the formality of the evaluative condition, students with test-anxiety showed significant trouble with retaining memorized facts.

The cognitive, affective and behavioral components to combine create behaviors that respond to the deeply rooted belief that failure is the inevitable outcome of any testing situation (Sapp & Farrell, 1994). The three components overlap and/or interact continuously during the testing situation and cannot be entirely separated because any approach or attempt at an intervention only demonstrates success if all aspects are considered in unison (Sapp & Farrell, 1994).

Collins (1999) identifies that test anxiety derives from four general areas. First, test anxiety is a learned behavior resulting from the expectations of parents, teachers or significant others in the student's life. Next, test anxious students created a strong association that grades and test performance measure their level of self worth. Subsequently, within the test anxious there exists a deep fear of disappointing or alienating friends, family and/or parents because of poor performance or imperfect academic ability. Finally, there exists a perceived lack of control and/or an inability to change one's present life situation. Any single or combined area can cause an individual to experience test anxiety (Collins, 1999).

Test anxiety can impact all students; it does not discriminate on the basis of age, race, ethnicity or grade level (Harris, 2003; Birenbaum & Nasser, 1994). There are no consistent findings to support any gender, socioeconomic or racial differences in the prevalence of test anxiety in students (McDonald, 2001, Hembree, 1988). Test anxiety is individual specific and should not be thought of merely by these demographic generalities. Instead, test stress should be thought of as a personal continuum of impairment, to what extent it exists, rather than if it is present or absent (McDonald, 2001).

What is known about test anxiety is that once it is present, it creates a self-sustaining feedback loop (Goonan, 2003). Fulk (2003) calls this a cycle of failure. Poor performance on exams and tests breed anxiety in students and as the anxiety builds the achievement level on exams continues to drop. As more anxiety becomes evident the performance level continues to plummet (Fulk, 2003). As the cycle grows it can affect the learning, encoding and retrieval of information in the test anxious (McDonald, 2001). McDonald (2001) goes on to state that test anxiety creates an increasingly widespread fear of exams in students and it has a detrimental effect on test performance. It should be noted however that interventions can break the feedback loop while at the same time assist students in developing a positive self esteem (Goonan, 2003).

There is extensive empirical evidence of the negative effects of test anxiety on academic performance. Hembree (1988) in a meta-analysis of 562 studies that related test anxiety and academic achievement found that test anxiety routinely causes poor performance. Chittooran (2001) also agrees that test anxiety is associated with poor academic performance but that it is also has a component related to the presence of a negative or low self esteem. Harris (2003) believes that many students have the cognitive ability to do well on exams, but may not do so because of high levels of test anxiety. If the students do not learn how to manage the test anxiety, they may experience consequences that reach beyond the classroom into the world (Bass et al. 2002). Possible examples of these consequences could include not getting into a desired college due to poor entrance exam scores, not receiving a driver's license due to failure on the general knowledge test or even being passed over for a promotion at work as a result of scoring poorly on career promotion testing.

On the other hand, Hancock (2001) does not accept that the presence of, or predisposition to, test anxiety as a reason for reduced achievement. Instead, it is the level of evaluative threat that has an impact on achievement. Students discern for themselves the value of a test and then act accordingly. The greater the stakes the exam holds, the higher the effort to receive a score better than typical. Woo and Frank (2000) contend that low grade point averages are more a case of insufficient effort rather than a lack of ability. Bass et al. (2002) assert that less successful students feel powerless to control their success. These students feel victimized by tests that validate their low performance.

Defining Self Esteem

It cannot be touched, but it can affect how an individual feels. It cannot be seen, but it is there when individuals look at themselves in the mirror. It cannot hear, but it is loud and clear in the self talk of an individual. What is this ethereal thing? It is an individual's self esteem. Brubaker (2000), in the Encyclopedia of Special

Education, uses the terms self-esteem and self-concept interchangeably and defines self-concept as "an individual's evaluation of his or her own abilities and attributes" (p. 1610). In this discussion, self confidence can also be used interchangeably with the aforementioned terms.

Emler (2001) contends that good self-esteem is a vital personality component because it empowers individuals to believe in themselves, while providing the courage to try new things. The key to a healthy self esteem is for individuals to become aware of personal strengths and accepting the limitations of their abilities. Developing a positive self concept is widely valued internationally as a vital outcome of schooling (Humphrey, Charlton & Newton, 2004). However, schools are mocked if they teach a self esteem curriculum designed to enhance student beliefs that they have control over their environments and that their actions have personal consequences in addition to academics rather than just focusing on those academics (Rothstein, 2004). It is the non-cognitive skills that are a stronger predictor of future earnings rather than test scores. A high self concept is one such non-cognitive trait that predicts labor market success (Rothstein, 2004). To support this point, Rothstein (2004) reports that after being out of school for ten years, graduates with high self esteem earned more than graduates with similar academic scores but lower levels of self esteem.

Nonetheless, it should be noted that high self esteem is not enough to produce superior academic achievement in students (Humphrey et al., 2004). Academic competence is significantly more likely to have an impact on the self esteem; this is especially valid for lower achievers in comparison to their high achieving classmates as it breeds disaffection (Humphrey et al., 2004). As mentioned earlier in this review, test anxiety creates a self sustaining feedback loop. Self esteem can also factor into the loop intensifying its effects while negatively impacting the self esteem of the test anxious. The student who does not do well in school may begin to experience a lack of confidence in their academic abilities (Bass et al., 2002). Couple this lack of confidence with the stress of test anxiety and it is no wonder poor performance on tests occur (Bass et al., 2002). Low self esteem to some extent is self-imposed due to the fact that an individual is misperceiving his/her basic worthiness relative to others. Low self esteem is a direct result of the criticism individuals tell themselves creating feelings of inferiority (Emler, 2001).

Emler (2001) believes that self-esteem is "trivially related to later educational attainments" (p. 28), and that the "level of global self-esteem does not have much impact on what young people want or try to achieve" (p. 28). In a study dealing with mathematics students, Waxman and Huang (1996) found that students possessing a high academic self concept were more motivated in class, more satisfied with their classes and more resilient than their lower academic self concept classmates.

Connecting Self Esteem to Test Anxiety

Successful students are often praised by teachers and peers. This creates an environment that allows students to rebuild positive attitudes towards their school, their ability to perform (on tests and exams) and themselves (Collins, 1999).

Students with higher academic self-esteem viewed grades as more valid indicators of their academic ability than did those with lower self esteem (Woo & Frank, 2000). Sapp and Farrell (1994) believe that high academic self concept is one of the strongest psycho educational predictors of achievement. This is due to the behaviors exhibited by the academically self confident. They exhibit low levels of self defeating thoughts, reduced fear of failure self talk and lower rates of absenteeism and tardiness. Fulk (2003) regards the motivation that causes students to dropout of school as being a result of the negative self perception created by their inability to perform well on tests in school. What is the point of staying in school if you continually feel bad about yourself because you are not being rewarded (with personally acceptable marks) for your effort?

Anderson and Anderson (1992) argue that developing a student's sense of pride in test performance is a strong motivator for students to inherently want to prepare more carefully for an examination and, as a result, students score better on tests. Consequently, if schools increase their focus on personal, social and emotional development, this may facilitate achievement beyond predictions (Humphrey et al., 2004). The confidence built from doing well on tests can then be carried into a student's life when faced with other challenges (Rubenzer, 2002).

It was interesting to find in my search of the literature that there are strategies teachers and schools can make that tie together methods of reducing test anxiety while at the same time supporting the development and maintenance of positive self esteem. Rubenzer (2002) believes students can learn how to think calmly under test pressure by creating reality checklists. The anxiety of test stress is not the focus; it is instead the building of stress smartness. Rubenzer (2002) goes on to offer many strategies directed at assisting students in dealing with test anxiety while at the same time helping to support their self concept. These include:

- Helping students remain optimistic and to focus on the silver lining of a situation.
- Developing students' skills in appreciating the personal satisfaction they can receive from their own work.
- Have teachers become positive supports for stressful situations.
- Assisting students in focusing their thoughts on the big picture (year of schooling), not just isolated events (a quiz or an assignment).
- Supply students with a variety of stress relieving strategies such as controlled breathing and test preparation taking and preparation skills.

All of these strategies approach the problem of test anxiety holistically and deal with many facets of the issue while at the same time supporting and attempting to enhance the self esteem of students. Bell (1997) offers that evaluations where students remain anonymous are less threatening and create less anxiety because the students perceive that purpose for the evaluation is more effective as a tool in identifying problem areas students have in understanding the content areas.

In conclusion, if a student's self concept is developed and nurtured while taking efforts to reduce levels of test anxiety, the ability to do well on tests will increase. If achievement levels on tests can be increased, students will be able to determine where they will go to receive career training and inevitably end up doing what they want to in life.

CHAPTER 3 - METHODOLOGY

The purpose of this study was to examine if a correlation exists between a student's level of self esteem and the level of test stress anxiety reported. The test group for this study was made up of two grade eight classes at a community high school just outside of Edmonton (43 students in total). The students were enrolled in Language Arts classes that were a part of my current teaching assignment. Students were members of a combined junior and senior high school situated in a rural setting. The school had an enrollment of 267 pupils from grades 7–12. Most students were bussed from the surrounding community to the school site. Overall, the population of the school by and large was Caucasian with middle-class socioeconomic familial backgrounds. Agriculture is the primary economic base of the surrounding community.

All the students in the grade eight Language Arts classes were approached for participation in the study. Permission forms from the students' guardians as well as from the students were distributed prior to administration of the testing instruments. Students with returned forms began testing in March 2006. All testing was conducted during class time. Care was taken to select days where most students would be present for testing. Missing and absent students completed the tests upon their return. For their participation in the study students were given a pen. Students who did not, or had parents that did not give their permission to participate in the study, were not penalized for their non-participation. They, too, received a pen and continued on with class course work while the rest of the students completed the instruments.

For the purposes of this study, two different instruments were used to collect data. In an attempt to prevent the sensation of being monitored or judged during testing, respondents were coded for identification if an intervention was called for due to ethical professional responsibility. The instruments were administered in consecutive class periods. Prior to the administration of each instrument, students were informed of the anonymous nature of the study and urged to respond in an honest and truthful nature. Again it was reiterated that the intent of the study was not to target or single out any one student, but rather to look at the group as a whole seeking a pattern or trend.

The first instrument administered was the Culture Free Self-Esteem Inventory (CFSEI-3) developed by James Battle (2002). The CFSEI-3 has three forms for different age groups, primary (6 to 8 years of age), intermediate (9 to 12 years of age) and adolescent (13 to 18 years of age). The adolescent form was used for testing as this is the appropriate related age for these students. The inventory consists of 67 statements worded in question form. All items are related to self-esteem and are answered with a response of either yes or no. The recommended testing time is 10–15 minutes. The CFSEI-3 scores student responses in five subscales: academic, general, parental/home, social and personal self-esteem as well as providing a global self-esteem quotient. The students' responses were transferred to a separate scoring form to assess their levels in each subscale. Each student respondent generated two scores for use in this study. The first score was the academic subscale of the instrument. This subscale has a range of 0 to 10. The second was a global self esteem quotient that took into account all of the five subscales. The quotient has a range of 5 to 95. This instrument was purchased through a company called Mind Resources and can be contacted through their website at www.mindresources.com.

The second instrument called the Test Anxiety Scale (Appendix A) was adopted from a study by Bass et al. (2002). The Test Anxiety Scale divides items into three categories: student self-esteem, anxiety during testing and physical and mental anxiety. The scale comprises 23 items where respondents evaluate their responses on a four point Likert Scale. The Likert Scale responses are: never, almost never, almost always and always. The students' responses were scored according to the key in Appendix A. The higher the student score, the higher their level of test stress anxiety. The maximum score on this instrument is 92.

Individual student results were entered into a Microsoft Excel document to determine if a correlation existed between test anxiety scores and academic self esteem scores as well as test anxiety scores and global self esteem scores. From the resulting values, it was then possible to see if a positive, negative or no correlation exists to between students' self reported levels of self-esteem and their general level of test anxiety.

CHAPTER 4 - RESULTS SECTION

Of the 43 students solicited for participation in the study, 42 returned parental and personal consent forms. Only one student's parents did not wish for their child to participate. This brought the sample number to 42 students.

The Test Anxiety Scale was given on a day when all students were present shortly after the consent forms were collected. It took both classes only 5 minutes for all students to complete the instrument. Luckily, the next day all students were again present. The CFSEI-3 instrument took each class 15 minutes for all students to complete. Students reported that this was due to the increased number of items. When all students were finished the second instrument, the pens were distributed to every student.

The instruments were then hand scored and the means and standard deviation of each scale were determined. These data are reported in Table 1 below.

Table 1. Mean and standard deviation for the test anxiety scale, the academic subscale of the culture free self-esteem inventory, and the global self-esteem subscale of the culture free self-esteem inventory

Instrument	N	Mean	SD
Test Anxiety	42	49.36	13.11
Academic Subscale	42	3.31	2.39
Global Self Esteem Quotient	42	77.93	12.77

From the data in Table 1 it is interesting to note that although the academic subscale scores for the group were relatively low placing them in the 9th percentile, the global self esteem quotient also placed them in the average to below average self esteem range (Battle, 2002). This indicates that the group reported an average level of self esteem.

Next, the student results were then transferred into an Excel document and the correlation analysis tool was used to determine how the ranges of the data moved. If the values move together, a positive correlation is apparent. If the measures move in opposite directions, a negative correlation is discernible. Alternately, if the values in both sets moved in an unrelated way, a correlation near zero or no correlation would exist. The relationship between the data sets is presented in Table 2 and the results are shown below.

Table 2. Correlations among the test anxiety scale, the academic subscale of the culture free self-esteem inventory, and the global self-esteem subscale of the culture free self-esteem inventory

Instruments	Test Anxiety	Academic Subscale
Academic Subscale	-0.29	
Global Self Esteem Quotient	-0.69**	0.39*

$*p < .01$, $**p < .001$

As the data from Table 2 show, there was no significant correlation between test anxiety and academic subscale. This may be due to the subscale being so small with only 10 items on the instrument relating to the academic subscale. However, a significant moderate negative correlation (-0.69) was found between test anxiety and global self esteem. This means that the stronger a student's global self esteem is lower their test anxiety score is likely to be. A significant weak correlation (0.39) also appeared between the academic subscale and the global self esteem quotient which might be expected because the two scales are not independent.

CHAPTER 5 - DISCUSSION / CONCLUSION

In reviewing the statistical analysis of the data, the results showed a negative correlation existing between self esteem and test anxiety. The data suggested that the higher the self reported level of self esteem an individual possesses, the less likely the students were to experience anxiety during a test. This also indicated that an individual's self concept played some role in their level of experienced test anxiety. It seems to make logical sense; if an individual's evaluation of his or her own abilities and attributes is strong then their ability to face challenges, like testing, enables the individual to create an operational framework where they feel more confident in their abilities to perform. This in turn, could be the beginning of a greater academic competence counteracting the problem of disaffection with school.

As discussed in the literature review, once test anxiety has begun to take root in a student, it creates a self-sustaining negative feedback loop (Goonan, 2003). Poor results on tests negatively impact what they tell themselves about their abilities, fostering a negative self concept. The negative self esteem created becomes an insurmountable barrier as the vicious cycle gains momentum. A result of this cycle is the definition of self based on marks and test results. Statements like, "I can't do Math" or "I'm just not as smart as everyone else" are common examples of the negative self talk students tell themselves to justify poor performances on tests.

For a future study, it would be interesting to look at methods and strategies that students could use to help counteract this negative self talk and improve their confidence in test taking. These possible strategies could be preemptive steps to reduce test anxiety and empower students to foster a more positive, active role in controlling their own success, thus breaking the negative feedback loop and creating a healthy positive one in its stead. Tests would no longer cause a system of victimization, but rather become a tool of personal empowerment. In addition, as more confidence is built through reducing test anxiety, the function of the results of testing would change. The results would cease to be a measure of self worth; rather, they would become a tool for self assessment regarding the level of knowledge mastered. The improved self esteem would then aid students in facing the numerous challenges faced in their lives. The challenges would then be dealt with as matters of perspective. Students would then have the confidence to manage their own lives and make changes to their life situations (Collins, 1999).

Testing, in all its forms and varieties, is not going anywhere. In a lot of cases, they are primary assessment tools that teachers use to gauge a student's level of mastery. Test anxiety then is a real problem if teachers are not cognizant of the role it plays in their students' educational experience. In some cases, the stakes for tests can be high and if the role of anxiety is not taken into account, the impact on the self worth of the individual would be incalculable. As a teacher, the more we under-stand how our students think and understand what they experience in the educational process, the better we can prepare to meet their educational needs.

Even though a significant negative correlation was found to exist between test anxiety and global self esteem, it is important to not place too much credence on the correlation. Both test anxiety and self esteem are large multidimensional issues in education. For an issue as complex as test anxiety, many factors play a role in its severity and the impact it has on the self esteem of the student. It would be simplistic to assume that self esteem is the only major influence on the level of test anxiety. Life experiences, personal interactions and intelligences are but a few other components that could possibly affect the level of test anxiety a student experiences. In the future, these aspects of the issue could also be taken into consideration and be examined, like the role of intelligence or outside pressures.

Connected to the above mentioned, there is the possibility of assessment bias due to the sample size being as small as it was and not being representative of a diverse enough group of individuals in fully attend to the topic. The sample group was exceptionally homogeneous in terms of ethnicity, ability and socioeconomic background. As well, despite the fact that students were informed that individual results would not be individually examined, some of the items from the inventories may have been interpreted by the students as good or bad. In turn, they may have responded in a manner which they thought might please their teacher or intensify their feelings towards the subjects on the inventories, skewing the results higher or lower than they actually were.

With these points taken into account, the correlation can still have an impact on teachers and their style of teaching. Not one student in the study scored exceptionally low on the test anxiety instrument. This shows that most students experience anxiety in testing situations to some extent. Teachers should be sensitive to this in preparing their evaluation tools. Perhaps teachers could look at alternate types and methods of assessing the students' knowledge and abilities rather than relying solely on tests. Also, the levels of global self esteem that were reported were not exceptionally high in this study. Perhaps this suggests that you don't have to have an extraordinarily high level of self esteem to feel confident in a testing situation. Perhaps it would be possible for teachers to examine methods that would foster the positive self concept of students and their abilities. It appears that a little bit of confidence can go a long way to quell feelings of anxiety.

With self esteem and test anxiety being the large issues they are, small teacher interventions could go a long way to reducing anxiety while assessing the student's abilities. In the end, if developing a positive self concept is widely valued inter-nationally as a vital outcome of schooling (Humphrey, Charlton & Newton, 2004) how can we not try to make improvements to the system? Teachers are in the foreground of students' lives because of the time they spend with them. Teachers model what it is like to be an adult, and can sometimes be one of the only positive role models in a student's life. It is important to remember that the non-cognitive proficiencies like self esteem can be stronger predictors of future success than test scores. As teachers, do we not want our students to have every opportunity before them?

REFERENCES

Anderson, S., & Anderson, C. (1992, May). Study skills made easy. *School Counselor, 39*(5), 1–4.

Bass, J., Burroughs, M., Gallion, R., & Hodel, J. (2002). *Investigating ways to reduce student anxiety during testing.* Unpublished masters' project. Chicago, IL: Saint Xavier University.

Battle, J. (2002). *Culture-free self-esteem inventories: Examiner's manual* (3rd ed.). Austin, TX: PRO-ED, Inc.

Bell, J. T. (1997). Anonymous quizzes: An effective feedback mechanism. *Chemical Engineering Education, 31*, 56–57.

Birenbaum, M., & Nasser, F. (1994). On the relationship between test anxiety and test performance. *Measurement & Evaluation in Counseling & Development, 27*(1), 1–9.

Brubaker, R. G. (2000). Self-concept. In C. R. Reynolds & E. Fletcher-Janzen (Eds.), *Encyclopedia of special education* (2nd ed., Vol. 3, p. 1610). New York: Wiley.

Burke, E. (1999). Test-anxious learners. *Adults Learning, 10*(6), 23–24.

Cheek, J. R., Bradley, L. J., Reynolds, J., & Coy, D. (2002). An intervention for helping elementary students reduce test anxiety. *Professional School Counseling, 6*(2), 162–164.

Chittooran, M. M., & Miles, D. R. (2001, April). *Test-taking skills for multiple-choice formats: Implications for school psychologists.* Symposium conducted at the Annual Convention of the National Association of School Psychologists, Washington, D.C.

Collins, L. (1999). Effective strategies for dealing with test anxiety. In *Teacher to Teacher Series*. Kent, OH: The Ohio Literacy Resource Center.

Emler, N. (2001). *Self-esteem: The costs and causes of low self-worth*. York, UK: Joseph Rowntree Foundation.

Fulk, B. M. (2003). Concerns about ninth grade students' poor academic performance: One school's action plan. *American Secondary Education, 31*(2), 8–26.

Goonan, B. (2003). *Overcoming test anxiety: Giving students the ability to show what they know. Measuring up: Assessment issues for teachers, counselors, and administrators*. Greensboro, NC: ERIC Counseling and Student Services Clearinghouse.

Hancock, D. R. (2001). Effects of test anxiety and evaluative threat on students' achievement and motivation. *Journal of Education Research, 94*(5), 284–290.

Harris, H., & Coy, D. (2003). *Helping students cope with test anxiety*. [Electronic version]. ERIC Counseling and Student Services Clearinghouse. ED479355.

Hembree, R. (1988). Correlates, causes, effects, and treatment of test anxiety. *Review of Educational Research, 58*, 47–77.

Humphery, N., Charlton, J. P., & Newton, I. (2004). The developmental roots of disaffection? *Educational Psychology, 24*(5), 579–594.

McDonald, A. S. (2001). The prevalence and effects of test anxiety in school children. *Educational Psychology: An International Journal of Experimental Educational Psychology, 21*(1), 89–101.

Rothstein, R. (2004). Accountability for noncognitive skills. *School Administrator, 61*(11), 30–33.

Rubenzer, R. (2002). *How to best handle stress*. North Carolina, NC: Warren Publishing.

Sapp, M., & Farrell, W. (1994). Cognitive-behavioral interventions: Applications for academically at-risk and special education students. *Preventing School Failure, 38*(2), 19–25.

Supon, V. (2004). Implementing strategies to assist test-anxious students. *Journal of Instructional Psychology, 31*(4), 292–296.

Sarason, I. G. (1980). *Test anxiety: Theory, research, and applications*. Hillsdale, NJ: Lawerence Erlbaum.

Waxman, H. C., & Huang, S. L. (1996). Motivation and learning environment differences in inner- city middle school students. *The Journal of Educational Research, 90*, 93–102.

Woo, T. O., & Frank, N. (2000). Academic performance and perceived validity of grades: An additional case for self-enhancement. *The Journal of School Psychology, 140*(2), 218–226.

APPENDIX A

Scoring for Test Anxiety Scale (Bass, Burroughs, Gallion, & Hodel, 2002)

Directions: Mark an X in the box that best shows your opinion.

	NEVER	ALMOST NEVER	ALMOST ALWAYS	ALWAYS
1. If I fail a test I am afraid I shall be rated as stupid by my friends.	1	2	3	4
2. If I fail a test I am afraid people will consider me worthless.	1	2	3	4
3. If I fail a test I am afraid my teachers will belittle me.	1	2	3	4
4. If I fail a test I am afraid my teachers will believe I am hopelessly dumb.	1	2	3	4
5. I am very worried about what my teacher will think or do if I fail his or her test.	1	2	3	4
6. I am worried that all my friends will get high scores in the test and I will get low ones.	1	2	3	4
7. I am worried that failure in tests will embarrass me socially.	1	2	3	4
8. I am worried that if I fail a test my parents will not like it.	1	2	3	4
9. During a test my thoughts are clear and I neatly answer all questions.	4	3	2	1
10. During a test I feel I'm in good shape and that I'm organized.	4	3	2	1
11. I feel my chances are good to think and perform well on tests.	4	3	2	1
12. I usually function well in tests.	4	3	2	1
13. I feel I just can't make it in tests	1	2	3	4
14. In a test I feel like my head is empty, as I have forgotten all I have learned.	1	2	3	4
15. During a test It's hard for me to organize what's in my head in an orderly fashion.	1	2	3	4
16. I feel it is useless for me to sit for an examination; I shall fail no matter what.	1	2	3	4

17. Before a test it is clear to me that I'll fail no matter how well prepared I am.	1	2	3	4
18. I am very tense before a test, even if I am well prepared.	1	2	3	4
19. While I am taking an important test, I feel that my heart pounds strongly.	1	2	3	4
20. During a test my whole body is very tense.	1	2	3	4
21. I am terribly scared of tests.	1	2	3	4
22. During a test I keep moving uneasily in my chair.	1	2	3	4
23. I arrive at a test with a lot of tension or nervousness.	1	2	3	4

APPENDIX C

USING ONLINE RESOURCES

All of the collections of research materials that you will use online are databases. Interfaces allow us to access those materials. This appendix provides a few general comments about libraries and the online interfaces that they provide, other interfaces available for your use, and some basic search tips.

LIBRARY RESOURCES

Perhaps the easiest library interface to use is reference librarians. Reference librarians are highly skilled and are often able to solve complex researching problems with seeming ease. Reference librarians are not content specialists even though they may have considerable content expertise just from helping people in one area or another enough times. Take advantage of the support these professionals can provide when it is available. Many college libraries support online reference desks as well so that you may not even need to enter your school library to get support.

Because online access to college libraries is potentially a path into the computer system for the entire university, all college libraries have security protocols that you must follow. In most cases entry into the electronic library is relatively simple if you are on the same physical campus with the servers that house the library resources. It is more complicated if you are accessing the resources from off-campus. In some instances, libraries/schools assign identifying numbers and passwords to patrons. In other cases access is set up through something called VPN (Virtual Private Network) that disconnects you from all other internet access while you are working in the library. There are a myriad of other means to access secured sites. Regardless of the strategies your institution uses, you need to anticipate accommodating them. Ask your reference librarian for help the first time you are using these services. Get the protocol for accessing the library when you are away from the campus, as well, as these procedures may be different.

As you use these online databases, pay attention to the tools that are available to facilitate your use of the resources. When libraries pay for access to databases, they are buying that access through a provider. Perhaps the biggest of these in college libraries is EBSCO (short for the Elton B. Stephens Company). These providers also include tools for searching through the databases. Typical features included in these interfaces are a variety of ways to filter search terms, selection of searching within multiple databases simultaneously, and the facility to export documents and citations to your own computer.

Since ERIC (Education Resources Information Center) is a primary tool for educational researchers, looking at the EBSCO interface for ERIC is a good place to begin a discussion of search tips. We will also examine the other major path into ERIC—direct access through the U.S. Department of Education sponsored website.

USING ERIC THROUGH EBSCO

Once you are connected to ERIC through EBSCO a screen appears that allows you to enter search terms (if your school uses the newer interface—EBSCO*host* 2.0— then this description applies to the advanced search screen). There are four basic operations available at this point.

1. Enter one or more search terms. You will generally have better results if each term is placed on a separate line. If you are just starting out with your topic and unsure about possible search terms click on the word *Thesaurus* just above the search term fields. Here you find possible search terms assigned by ERIC for that topic.
2. In the drop down menu to the right of each search term select the fields in the database in which you wish to search for your term. If, for instance, you are searching for a specific author then you would enter the author's name in the search field and select *AU Author* from the drop down menu. If you do not select a search field, all fields will be searched.
3. To the left of the search field for the second and subsequent search terms is a drop down menu that allows you to select a Boolean operator. Although there are many of these you can use, the menu provides access to the main three. If you select *and* (the default) the search engine will look for occurrences where both terms are present—for example, looking for biology *and* technology in the same references. If you select *or* the search engine will look for fields that have either search term in them—that is, looking for biology *or* technology simultaneously. If you select *not* then the search engine will not select any field that has that term present—looking for biology but *not* if technology is present in the same reference.
4. Depending on the subscription your college has with EBSCO, it is possible to search multiple databases simultaneously. Right below the search terms you will see a drop down menu (labeled IN) that allows you to select all of the databases you want to use. As a reminder, there is considerable research being done on educational topics particularly in the fields of psychology and sociology. If you want a description of the database to figure out if it is appropriate to your search go to the tab above the search fields and select *Choose Databases*. From this list check the databases in which you are interested and then scroll all the way to the top or bottom of the list and select *Continue*.

You may wish to limit your search in general ways. A number of limiters are provided in the section below the search terms. The one that is most likely to be of use to you is the ability to limit the range of dates in which you wish to find documents. Don't forget to clear these fields if you start another search.

When the results appear, look first to the line at the top of the results that says *All Results*. If the number of hits is really large then the search will not be of much use to you. It may include articles that are not germane to your specific topic. Additionally, since the results window only includes 10 references at a time, it could take you hours to go through large lists. We recommend either going back to the first search screen and entering better search terms or looking to the left of the results window to see if any of the suggestions EBSCO makes for limiting the search make sense. Try to get to a results list of a few hundred.

Similarly, if your results list has too few hits, you also need to rethink your search terms. It is easy to be too specific in your search terms. Even though ERIC uses fairly standard terms to identify entries in the database, remember those terms are chosen by authors. Be imaginative. Use the Thesaurus and look through the few hits that you have gotten for other possible search terms. Regardless, the process of finding the literature appropriate to your topic is iterative. Your searches will become more effective after you have learned more about your topic and gone back after finding some initially useful references.

Once your list is of a reasonable length it is time to find relevant works. As you read through the title list provided, pay attention to other information like author, date of publication and type of publication. Use any hints you can to find the material of most interest. To find out more detail you need to click on the title to view the abstract, keyword list and other bibliographic information. The process of going back and forth between the main results page and the individual article pages can become very time consuming so identifying articles without going to the article page if you don't need to can be a good thing.

Overall, there are two types of ERIC references. If the document is published elsewhere (in a journal or book for instance) then ERIC does not have the rights to provide the document directly to you. You can identify these references because the ERIC number of the document begins with an EJ. Since you are probably viewing the search results list through a connection from your library you will probably see a link below the reference that asks you to search in your library databases for the journal that has the original article. This assumes that your library has an electronic subscription to that journal. Clicking on this link should take you into your library database and with any luck directly to the full text of the article. If this does not work then look to the end of this discussion about other means of access to materials you need.

The other type of ERIC document is a document that is directly accessible through the database. These are papers presented at conferences and other publications that are usually submitted directly to ERIC by the author. Typically the number that references these documents begins ED. Underneath the title of the reference to these documents you will see a PDF symbol which indicates that the document can be downloaded to your computer. If you click on the title, the expanded page for the document the PDF link will be at the top of the page.

To save yourself time, it is wise to move items of interest to a folder. As you go through your results list, read the abstracts, and add articles you want to save to examine further to your folder. If you are on the results page you will see a folder icon to the right of the title that is labeled *Add*. If you are on the expanded page for the reference click on *Add to folder* at the top of the page. When you are done, select the folder icon at the top of the page (either the results page or the expanded document page) and all of the articles in which you are interested will be together. Download what you need from the list.

One other procedure that you will want to do is to download the full reference to the documents you have found. When you are in the folder where you have identified the documents of interest, click on *select all* at the top of the list. If you are not using bibliographic software select *Save* and a dialog box will open asking whether you want a brief citation, brief citation with abstract, or a detailed citation with abstract. Below that selection you can choose the citation format. Select APA, but be forewarned that the reference you get will need style editing. If you are saving lots of citations individually, once they are on your computer be sure to combine them into a single document so you can find them easily later. If you are using bibliographic software, select *Export* and EBSCO will ask you what software you are using so that the resulting document will be correctly formatted.

USING ERIC VIA DIRECT ACCESS

ERIC is sponsored by the US Department of Education and is accessible directly through their web site (www.eric.ed.gov). Perhaps the biggest drawback to using this access to ERIC as opposed to EBSCO is that you cannot search multiple databases simultaneously. There are many advantages to using this access to ERIC. You can control the number of references shown on each page (right above the search results). Being able to scroll though 50 references quickly that include abstracts will save you a great deal of time. The abstracts appear as part of the results list so you do not need to go to the expanded reference to read them. The keyword list for the document also appears in the results list view making it easier to identify more keywords that might assist in your search.

Once on the site, select *Advanced Search* and scroll through the publication types. Note particularly ERIC Digests. Enter a search term into the search field on the home page of ERIC. If you want more control over the search select *Advanced Search* first. Click on *Search*. When the results appear, note that your search term is highlighted in the reference. Selecting items of interest is similar to the EBSCO interface. Click on the *Add* icon to what this site calls your clipboard. Access full-text documents by clicking on PDF icon. *Export citations* allows you to move citations into standard bibliographic software or to save the citation as a text document.

On the results page of a search you will also see links to *Find a Library* and to *Publisher's Web Site.* These work inconsistently but remember that often for documents unavailable though ERIC you can get the full text from an archive at the publisher's site.

GOOGLE SCHOLAR

In addition to ERIC, you might want to try Google Scholar (http://www.scholar.google.com). Google Scholar is a set of search tools that uses the WorldCat database as its primary source. Essentially, Google Scholar links to refereed work where a broader Google search looks at much more diverse references. Be aware that Google keeps working on this and the interface changes periodically without any notice. What we mention here is as of the publication of this book.

Use search terms in the same way you would search any bibliographic database. When results appear note the following:

1. Clicking on the document title will take you to the most complete version of the document that is legally available. Often this is the complete document but you may also run into abstract only versions.
2. Clicking on the *All versions* at the bottom of the reference brings up all other occurrences of the document that Google can find. Often these are earlier drafts or versions that may have been posted outside of the legal database. Our experience is that more often than not even if the main link doesn't give you the whole document, one of these will.
3. The *Cited by ...* link not only counts the number of times this document is cited in the database but also links you to each of the documents in which the original is cited. Finding articles with a large number of citations and then going to the links that cite the original is an efficient way of building a reference list in a very short period of time.
4. The *Related Articles* link uses Google's algorithm to search for related articles. Our experience is that this produces better results than if we try to find related articles using our own search terms.

Advanced Scholar Search. At the right end of the search term window click on *Advanced Scholar Search*. This will look much like other advanced search windows you have seen. Limiting the date range of your searches may be useful. We recommend that you do not limit searches by topic because educational research is published in so many fields.

Scholar Preferences. At the right end of the search term window click on *Scholar Preferences*. Preferences are stored in a cookie on your computer so that you don't have to go back and select them every time you use Google Scholar. If you are working on a different computer, though, your pre-selected preferences won't appear. Whenever you make a change in Scholar Preferences be sure to go to the bottom or top of the screen and select Save Preferences in order to make your selections permanent

1. In the *Library Links* bar, type in *the name of your college* and click on *Find Library*. If your library appears listed below the *Library Links* bar make sure that both WorldCat and your university are checked. Now when you search, every time an article is available through your library's journal subscriptions that link will appear after the reference shown in the search window. Click on *[your library name]* and it will automatically take you into the appropriate database and ask if it has found the reference you are after. If you are working off campus, probably you will be presented with the security login window before going to the database.
2. Lower on the Scholar Preferences page you can select the number of hits you want to appear in the results window. We prefer more rather than fewer. You may have already discovered that you can do this from preferences within the

normal Google search engine; but no matter where you set it, that is the number of hits that appear in all Google search tools.

3. If you are using a Bibliography Manager, select the manager you are using from the dropdown list at the bottom of the Scholar Preferences window. A link will now appear at the end of each hit in the results window that will allow the reference automatically to be downloaded into the application of choice.

A FEW MORE SEARCH STRATEGIES

Here are a few other strategies to try.

1. If you find a journal of interest, search ERIC for all of the articles in that journal. Even though the articles will not be available though ERIC it will tell you if there references of interest to you more quickly than by other means. Then go to the publisher's web site and see if the articles of interest are archived in a downloadable form. Or, EBSCO or Google Scholar and limit the search to the journal in which you are interested but don't put in any search terms. All of the articles from that journal will appear in the search results.

2. If you find an author of interest try to find the author's web site. Authors often post copies of their publications online. Even if the article you want is not there you may find related material.

3. Doing traditional internet searches brings up so much information they tend to be useless to your research; we don't recommend this as a productive strategy. On rare occasions, however, some related topic of interest has appeared from these efforts that we probably would not have discovered from traditional approaches. It may be worth a few minutes to see what happens especially if you have discovered productive search terms using the usual methods.

4. Find conferences that are related to your topic and see if someone has presented research on your topic. If you can not find a specific conference that seems close to your interests, then go to the American Educational Research Association (AERA) website (www.aera.net). AERA is the largest and most well known international professional organization focused on educational research. Look through the conference program for papers of interest. Some conferences publish proceedings that make the conference papers available and these are citable as research publications. Others publish abstracts or just titles and author contact information. If the papers are not directly available, email the authors. Educational research is a community and most of us are more than glad to share what we know.

As a final thought, remember that none of us knows all of the ways in which research may be gathered around your topic. Often the best strategy you can use is to ask questions of anyone who may have insight into your work: your research mentor, other students, published authors, research librarians, other professors, your cooperating teachers or other professional colleagues.

APPENDIX D

Z -TABLE

z Table (Negative)

z	0.00	0.01	0.02	0.03	0.04	0.05	0.06	0.07	0.08	0.09
-2.60	0.00	0.00	0.00	0.00	0.00	0.00	0.00	0.00	0.00	0.00
-2.50	0.01	0.01	0.01	0.01	0.01	0.01	0.01	0.01	0.00	0.00
-2.40	0.01	0.01	0.01	0.01	0.01	0.01	0.01	0.01	0.01	0.01
-2.30	0.01	0.01	0.01	0.01	0.01	0.01	0.01	0.01	0.01	0.01
-2.20	0.01	0.01	0.01	0.01	0.01	0.01	0.01	0.01	0.01	0.01
-2.10	0.02	0.02	0.02	0.02	0.02	0.02	0.02	0.02	0.01	0.01
-2.00	0.02	0.02	0.02	0.02	0.02	0.02	0.02	0.02	0.02	0.02
-1.90	0.03	0.03	0.03	0.03	0.03	0.03	0.03	0.02	0.02	0.02
-1.80	0.04	0.04	0.03	0.03	0.03	0.03	0.03	0.03	0.03	0.03
-1.70	0.04	0.04	0.04	0.04	0.04	0.04	0.04	0.04	0.04	0.04
-1.60	0.05	0.05	0.05	0.05	0.05	0.05	0.05	0.05	0.05	0.05
-1.50	0.07	0.07	0.06	0.06	0.06	0.06	0.06	0.06	0.06	0.06
-1.40	0.08	0.08	0.08	0.08	0.07	0.07	0.07	0.07	0.07	0.07
-1.30	0.10	0.10	0.09	0.09	0.09	0.09	0.09	0.09	0.08	0.08
-1.20	0.12	0.11	0.11	0.11	0.11	0.11	0.10	0.10	0.10	0.10
-1.10	0.14	0.13	0.13	0.13	0.13	0.13	0.12	0.12	0.12	0.12
-1.00	0.16	0.16	0.15	0.15	0.15	0.15	0.14	0.14	0.14	0.14
-0.90	0.18	0.18	0.18	0.18	0.17	0.17	0.17	0.17	0.16	0.16
-0.80	0.21	0.21	0.21	0.20	0.20	0.20	0.19	0.19	0.19	0.19
-0.70	0.24	0.24	0.24	0.23	0.23	0.23	0.22	0.22	0.22	0.21
-0.60	0.27	0.27	0.27	0.26	0.26	0.26	0.25	0.25	0.25	0.25
-0.50	0.31	0.31	0.30	0.30	0.29	0.29	0.29	0.28	0.28	0.28
-0.40	0.34	0.34	0.34	0.33	0.33	0.33	0.32	0.32	0.32	0.31
-0.30	0.38	0.38	0.37	0.37	0.37	0.36	0.36	0.36	0.35	0.35
-0.20	0.42	0.42	0.41	0.41	0.41	0.40	0.40	0.39	0.39	0.39
-0.10	0.46	0.46	0.45	0.45	0.44	0.44	0.44	0.43	0.43	0.42
0.00	0.50	0.50	0.49	0.49	0.48	0.48	0.48	0.47	0.47	0.46

APPENDIX D

z Table (Positive)

	0.00	0.01	0.02	0.03	0.04	0.05	0.06	0.07	0.08	0.09
0.00	0.50	0.50	0.51	0.51	0.52	0.52	0.52	0.53	0.53	0.54
0.10	0.54	0.54	0.55	0.55	0.56	0.56	0.56	0.57	0.57	0.58
0.20	0.58	0.58	0.59	0.59	0.59	0.60	0.60	0.61	0.61	0.61
0.30	0.62	0.62	0.63	0.63	0.63	0.64	0.64	0.64	0.65	0.65
0.40	0.66	0.66	0.66	0.67	0.67	0.67	0.68	0.68	0.68	0.69
0.50	0.69	0.70	0.70	0.70	0.71	0.71	0.71	0.72	0.72	0.72
0.60	0.73	0.73	0.73	0.74	0.74	0.74	0.75	0.75	0.75	0.75
0.70	0.76	0.76	0.76	0.77	0.77	0.77	0.78	0.78	0.78	0.79
0.80	0.79	0.79	0.79	0.80	0.80	0.80	0.81	0.81	0.81	0.81
0.90	0.82	0.82	0.82	0.82	0.83	0.83	0.83	0.83	0.84	0.84
1.00	0.84	0.84	0.85	0.85	0.85	0.85	0.86	0.86	0.86	0.86
1.10	0.86	0.87	0.87	0.87	0.87	0.87	0.88	0.88	0.88	0.88
1.20	0.88	0.89	0.89	0.89	0.89	0.89	0.90	0.90	0.90	0.90
1.30	0.90	0.90	0.91	0.91	0.91	0.91	0.91	0.91	0.92	0.92
1.40	0.92	0.92	0.92	0.92	0.93	0.93	0.93	0.93	0.93	0.93
1.50	0.93	0.93	0.94	0.94	0.94	0.94	0.94	0.94	0.94	0.94
1.60	0.95	0.95	0.95	0.95	0.95	0.95	0.95	0.95	0.95	0.95
1.70	0.96	0.96	0.96	0.96	0.96	0.96	0.96	0.96	0.96	0.96
1.80	0.96	0.96	0.97	0.97	0.97	0.97	0.97	0.97	0.97	0.97
1.90	0.97	0.97	0.97	0.97	0.97	0.97	0.98	0.98	0.98	0.98
2.00	0.98	0.98	0.98	0.98	0.98	0.98	0.98	0.98	0.98	0.98
2.10	0.98	0.98	0.98	0.98	0.98	0.98	0.98	0.99	0.99	0.99
2.20	0.99	0.99	0.99	0.99	0.99	0.99	0.99	0.99	0.99	0.99
2.30	0.99	0.99	0.99	0.99	0.99	0.99	0.99	0.99	0.99	0.99
2.40	0.99	0.99	0.99	0.99	0.99	0.99	0.99	0.99	0.99	0.99
2.50	0.99	0.99	0.99	0.99	0.99	0.99	0.99	0.99	1.00	1.00
2.60	1.00	1.00	1.00	1.00	1.00	1.00	1.00	1.00	1.00	1.00
z	0.00	0.01	0.02	0.03	0.04	0.05	0.06	0.07	0.08	0.09

APPENDIX E

Critical Values for Significant Correlations

Number of Matched Pairs in the Correlation	Levels At Which Computed Correlations are Significant (Two-Tailed Test)			
	0.1	**0.05**	0.01	0.001
4	0.900	**0.950**	0.990	0.999
5	0.805	**0.878**	0.959	0.991
6	0.729	**0.811**	0.917	0.974
7	0.669	**0.754**	0.875	0.951
8	0.621	**0.707**	0.834	0.925
9	0.582	**0.666**	0.798	0.898
10	0.549	**0.632**	0.765	0.872
11	0.521	**0.602**	0.735	0.847
12	0.497	**0.576**	0.708	0.823
13	0.476	**0.553**	0.684	0.801
14	0.458	**0.532**	0.661	0.780
15	0.441	**0.514**	0.641	0.760
16	0.426	**0.497**	0.623	0.742
17	0.412	**0.482**	0.606	0.725
18	0.400	**0.468**	0.590	0.708
19	0.389	**0.456**	0.575	0.693
20	0.378	**0.444**	0.561	0.679
21	0.369	**0.433**	0.549	0.665
22	0.360	**0.423**	0.537	0.652
23	0.352	**0.413**	0.526	0.640
24	0.344	**0.404**	0.515	0.629
25	0.337	**0.396**	0.505	0.618
26	0.330	**0.388**	0.496	0.607
27	0.323	**0.381**	0.487	0.597
28	0.317	**0.374**	0.479	0.588
29	0.311	**0.367**	0.471	0.579
30	0.306	**0.361**	0.463	0.570
35	0.283	**0.334**	0.430	0.532
40	0.264	**0.312**	0.403	0.501
45	0.248	**0.294**	0.380	0.474
50	0.235	**0.279**	0.361	0.451
60	0.214	**0.254**	0.330	0.414
70	0.198	**0.235**	0.306	0.385
80	0.185	**0.220**	0.286	0.361
90	0.174	**0.207**	0.270	0.341
100	0.165	**0.197**	0.256	0.324
200	0.117	**0.139**	0.182	0.231
300	0.095	**0.113**	0.149	0.189
400	0.082	**0.098**	0.129	0.164
500	0.074	**0.088**	0.115	0.147
1000	0.052	**0.062**	0.081	0.104

APPENDIX F

USING EXCEL FOR STATISTICAL ANALYSES

Numerous statistical software packages are available that provide an extensive array of statistical tools. For the dedicated quantitative researcher, having one of these available is a must. The power of these packages comes at a hefty price, though, and much of what is included in these packages is seldom used.

Excel, which is included in the Office suite from Microsoft, is available on most college campuses if you do not already own it yourself. Excel is a powerful tool and will help you accomplish most, if not all, of the statistical tasks related to your research study.

BASICS

We are assuming that you know how to open and save Excel documents, enter data into cells and perform perfunctory style adjustments to documents' appearance. We are approaching this from the point of view of understanding basic functions in Excel to accomplish specific statistical tasks. This is not meant to provide you with a broad understanding of how Excel works or what it can do. There are many excellent texts on this topic if you are interested in finding out more.

EXCEL VERSIONS

As of this writing there are four different versions of Excel with which you might come in contact. They are the Windows versions from Microsoft Office 2003 and Office 2007 and the Mac versions from Office 2004 and Office 2008. The older Windows and Mac versions are very similar and except for talking about different keyboard commands, there are few distinctions that need to be addressed. The newer Windows and Mac versions are very different from each other and from the earlier versions. This has the potential to make things complicated, and we will try to keep the instructions for different versions as clearly separated as possible.

As a recommendation as of the printing of this text, if you are interested in using Excel to accomplish a number of statistical tasks with the least amount of time invested to learn the program (i.e., you are trying to complete your research project as efficiently as possible) use the older Windows or Mac versions of Excel.

ADD-INS

Statistical Add-Ins are small "macros" written in visual basic language. They are intended to reduce the amount of effort you need to accomplish specific tasks. If you installed the minimum installation of Office on your computer you may not have Add-Ins available to use in Excel. If this happens go back to the original Office install disk and follow the instructions to make sure the Add-Ins are available. In most cases following the few instructions that follow is all you will need.

For Older Windows and Mac Versions Setup

1. Select *Tools* and see if *Data Analysis* is listed on the drop down menu.
2. If not, select *Tools* then *Add-Ins*.
3. Then select *Analysis ToolPak* and select *OK*.
4. *Data Analysis* should now appear on the *Tools* menu.

For Windows 2007 Setup

1. Select the *Data* tab and see if *Data Analysis* is listed under Analysis on the right end of the tab.
2. If not click on the Microsoft Office button (top left).
3. Select *Excel Options* at the bottom of the window.
4. Then select *Add-Ins* on the left hand navigation bar.
5. Select Analysis ToolPak and click on *OK* to install.
6. *Data Analysis* should now appear on the *Data* tab.

Office 2008 Mac Version

As of the writing of this text, the Macintosh 2008 version of Office does not support visual basic. Therefore it cannot run the Analysis ToolPak Add-In. Microsoft has recently promised to put visual basic back into Excel, but that will not occur until the next regular upgrade of Microsoft Office for the Macintosh. Best estimates are that that will be late in 2010.

EZ Analyze

EZ Analyze (http://www.ezanalyze.com/) is a free Add-In that was developed to be a bit more capable than the Data Analysis package in Excel. It runs in both Windows and Mac (2004) environments. After you download the software use the installation instructions provided by the author. They essentially follow the same procedures for installing other Add-Ins. You can make your own judgment as to whether this is a better package for you but we will only refer to it in a couple of places where it does analysis that Analysis ToolPak does not.

GENERAL USE OF EXCEL

There are a few skills that you will use over and over again in Excel that you need to practice.

Sorting

In most cases the data you have gathered will be entered in one row for each person from whom you have gathered data. The columns will represent each of the variables in your study. Often you will want to sort the data. For instance you might want to separate the boys and girls in your study and analyze them separately.

It is very easy to re-sort data in Excel in ways that make it impossible to go back to the original form of the data. So, ALWAYS make a copy of the original data in a separate file before you do any analysis.

In most cases you will want to sort data in ways that keep all of the row data (data from one individual) together. By clicking on a row number you will highlight the whole row and when sorted all of the data from that row will stay together. By clicking on a row number and then dragging down you will be able to highlight all of the rows you want to sort. If you are not clicking on row numbers to highlight data you want to sort (you are clicking on the cells themselves) ask yourself why you are doing that. It is probably not what you wanted to do.

Once you have the rows selected you want to sort, go to the *Data* menu and select *Sort*. (In Windows 2007 go to the *Data* tab and select *Sort*). If you want to sort by a single variable select the column by which you want to sort. Excel allows you up to 3 levels of nested sorts. For instance if you wanted to sort by gender first and then sort the students by age within gender you would select the appropriate columns in the same Sort dialog box.

Formulas

Formulas are tools for accessing data from one or more cells, manipulating it in some way, and returning a result. Obvious kinds of things that you might want to do are to add up a column of numbers or count the number of times a specific response appears for a question. Formulas can help you do this.

Excel knows that a cell has a formula in it because formulas all start with an equal sign (=). In the beginning writing formulas is quite easy and often Excel will do it for you. If you get interested, it is possible to do some rather complex calculations using formulas. The more complex these become, the more practice and guidance you will need. For this book we are going to keep it relatively simple. One of the advantages to using the Add-Ins mentioned above is that they reduce the need for you to write formulas at all. Regardless it is worth talking about these as they apply to basic statistical analysis.

When writing formulas it is very important to get cell references correct. The easiest way to do this is to click on a cell or range of cells to which you wish to refer instead of typing in the cell reference into the formula. For instance if you wanted to add a column of numbers you would pick the cell where you wanted the result to appear, then type =SUM(). What goes inside the parentheses would be the cell references to cells you want to add together. Be sure the cursor is in between the parentheses and then move the pointer until you can click and drag over the cells you want to add together. Excel will automatically put the correct cell references into the formula. Hit enter and the result will appear in the cell that has the formula.

Note the formula still appears in the formula bar above the spreadsheet even though you can no longer see it in the spreadsheet. Sometimes you will want Excel to only recognize the result of a formula and not the formula itself. For instance you might want to copy the results and paste them somewhere else. To do this you would highlight whatever results you wanted to move and select copy. Highlight the cell(s) where you want the results to be pasted and select Paste Special from the Edit menu. The resulting dialog box gives you choices as to how you want what you have copied to be pasted back into the spreadsheet. Select Values, hit OK and only the results will be pasted and the formulas will disappear.

Auto-Fill Cells

Frequently when you are working in Excel you will need to put similar information into lots of adjacent cells. Here are a few hints for doing that. All of the following can also be done from menu selections or from keyboard commands. Find the strategies that work best for you.

When you want the identical information to go in a whole series of cells put the item in the first cell and hit enter. Click once on that cell. Then position the pointer on the lower right of the cell (you will see a little square which is the target) and click and drag over the rest of the cells you want to have that information.

If you want a series of numbers to be placed in adjacent cells then put the lowest number of your series in the first cell and hit enter. Click once on that cell. Then position the pointer of the lower right corner of the cell again but this time hold down control key (Windows) or option key (Mac) and drag over the rest of the cells you want to have in the series.

If you need more refinement in this process put the initial value in the first cell and hit enter. Click once on the cell. Position the pointer as before but right-click (Windows) or control-click (Mac) and drag over the remaining cells. A dialogue box will appear allowing you to adjust the series steps or to make other changes in the way data are copied from one cell to another.

Auto-Fill for formulas is a special case. Excel adjusts the cell references as the formula is copied to new cells. For instance, if the formula for the addition of numbers in a column is =SUM(A4:A7) when you click on the cell with the formula and auto fill to the right Excel will rewrite the formula to be: =SUM(B4:B7). It assumes you are trying to move the formula under the next column and want to add up the numbers in that column. Usually this is exactly what you are trying to do.

Sometimes you will want to use Auto-Fill with a formula but you will not want all or part of the cell references to change. You can lock cell references by putting a dollar sign ($) before one or more of the elements of the reference. Remember that the first element of a cell reference is the column indicator and the second is the row indicator. Here are possibilities based on the above example:

=SUM($A$4:$A$7) auto-filled to the right becomes =SUM($A$4:$A$7). No change.

Since the second element of the cell reference is the row indicator and the rows do not change as you move to the right =SUM($A4:$A7) auto-filled to the right becomes =SUM($A4:$A7). Again no change.

If you accidentally missed one of the dollar signs=SUM($A$4:A$7) auto-filled to the right becomes =SUM($A$4:B$7). The result would be the numbers in both column A and B in rows 4 to 7 all added together. Probably not what you intended.

You will often use Auto-Fill of formulas to produce averages or sums for lots of variables without needing to insert the formula for each column. It takes a little practice to know when you need to lock cell references and when it doesn't make any difference. Just be cautious when you are learning and keep an eye out for numbers that do not look right.

USING THE ANALYSIS TOOLPAK

The Analysis ToolPak allows you to use most of the basic statistical tools we have described in the text. In a following section we will list the formulas that you would use if you do not have the Analysis ToolPak which is the case with the Mac Office 2008 version of Excel. In some cases you may find using the formulas faster than using the Analysis ToolPak but for the most part these Add-Ins are simple to use and will give you what you need with the least effort.

General Use that Applies to Most Analyses

Here is a basic list of steps to follow for most analyses:

After data have been entered into a spreadsheet, select *Tools* then *Data Analysis*. Select the required analysis. Be sure the cursor is in the input range bar. In the spreadsheet click and drag over the cells to be analyzed and the cell references will be added to the range.

In the bottom portion of the Data Analysis window you may select where you want the results to go. You may want to move the results to a new worksheet (the default) and then copy and paste if you need to move the numbers somewhere else.

Often the columns in the new worksheet are not wide enough and the labels for the results are cut off. Make the column wider to see all of the labels. The actual results are computed to 8 decimal places. You may wish to reformat the column to 2 decimal places.

Descriptive Statistics

For descriptive statistics the general instructions apply. Select Descriptive Statistics when you open Data Analysis. Do not forget to select *Summary Statistics* in the Output selections.

Correlations

The results for a correlation are always presented in a table. The table compares each variable with each other variable including itself. So, column 1 is compared to column 1 (a perfect match, so a correlation of 1) then column 1 is compared to column 2, etc.

Usually you will only be comparing 2 variables but multiple variables can be compared simultaneously producing a correlation table. To do this the columns for the variables being compared must be next to each other in the spreadsheet.

Excel assumes a correlation of two continuous variables (Pearson's).

t-Tests

Remember to select the correct *t*-test. Use paired if it is exactly the same respondents over two sets of scores (per/post tests are an example of this). Use equal variance if there is reason to believe that the compared groups are similar (two fifth grade classes in a school). Use unequal variance if the compared groups are dissimilar (comparing rural high schools to inner-city) or if the group sizes are substantially different. Be conservative.

When you get the results for a *t*-test be sure to make the first column wider so you can see the difference between a one-tailed test and a two-tailed.

Sometimes Excel computes *p* values that are very small. When that happens the result is presented in scientific notation (7.87647E-13). APA says to report values this small as $p < .001$

ANOVA

Single Factor means comparisons of a variety of groups on a single variable (or a variety of states of a variable on a single group). Data need to be in adjacent columns—one column for the variable scores of each group.

Once significance is observed Excel does not provide the tools for figuring out which group differences are significant. EZ Analyze does provide post hoc analysis. You can make a good guess at the post hocs by running multiple *t*-tests between group pairs. To be sure find someone who has a more powerful statistical application and have him or her do the post hoc tests (or use EZ Analyze yourself!).

Two Factor or more (factorial) ANOVAs allow the comparison of multiple groups on multiple factors simultaneously. These are more complex and are best done in a true statistical program.

WRITING STATISTICAL FORMULAS

Most likely there are only a few statistical formulas you will use with any frequency. If *Analysis Tools* meets your needs you may end up writing none of these. It is good practice to understand these tools' use and try them a few times. You may find that you like some of them better than *Analysis Tools*. Start by picking a cell where you want the result of the formula to appear. Then type in the formula that you need, remembering to start with an equal sign (=). When you get the formula complete hit *Return* or *Enter*.

Formula Format	*Description*
=SUM(range of cells)	Totals values in a range of cells
=AVERAGE(range of cells)	Gives the mean of the values in a range of cells
=STDEV(range of cells)	Computes the standard deviation of values in a range of cells

=MODE(range of cells)	Finds the value that appears most frequently in a range of cells
=MEDIAN(range of cells)	Finds the value in the middle of a range of cells
=COUNT(range of cells)	Counts the number of cells that have a number in them within a range of cells
=COUNTIF(range of cells, item to be counted)	Counts the number of occurrences of a specific value in a range of cells
=TTEST(range of cells for variable 1, range of cells for variable 2, number of tails, type of test)	Gives the probability of a significant difference between two ranges of interval values
=CORREL(range of cells for variable 1, range of cells for variable 2)	Computes a correlation coefficient between two interval variables
=CHITEST(range of cells with actual values, range of cells with predicted values)	Gives the probability of significant differences between actual and predicted values for nominal and ordinal variables.

GRAPHING

Excel includes a fairly powerful set of graphing tools. As a warning, the Mac 2008 version of the graphing tools is not as intuitive as other versions. Regardless, you will have some temptation to display your data in graph form. Although there are times when this is appropriate there are not many of them. Under most circumstances APA suggests tables of numbers instead of graphs. Pie charts are rarely seen in research papers.

GLOSSARY

action research—Type of research (qualitative, quantitative or mixed) undertaken by individuals for their own, personal purpose, generally to improve one's teaching or address a specific, local concern.

alpha level—Significant level in research, set to determine the probability at which you would reject the null hypothesis; generally set at .05 or .01.

alternate forms—A way to establish reliability of an instrument when two forms of the same instrument are presented to the same group.

Analysis of Variance (ANOVA)—Type of statistical analysis used whenever more than two group means are being compared at the same time.

bibliography—A listing which includes all relevant materials read whether they are actually cited in the paper or not.

case study—Type of qualitative model involving a detailed account of an individual or group.

causal-comparative research—Quantitative research model for examining the effect of a variable that you cannot control or manipulate; also known as ex post facto research.

Chi Square—Statistical analysis used when comparing groups when data are in the form of nominal or ordinal variables; it determines if the distribution of observed frequencies differs from the theoretical expected frequencies.

coding categories—A type of qualitative data analysis in which the researcher(s) reads the data, decides on categories in which to organize the data, and then codes the data using those categories.

collaborative action research—A type of action research in which a group of stakeholders collectively formulates the research question; also known as participatory action research.

comprehensive—Describes survey response categories wherein respondents can find a response category that represents what they think their response should be.

construct validity—Describes how well an assessment tool measures the construct it is purported to measure.

constant comparative method—A type of ongoing qualitative data analysis of comparing new data and hypotheses with prior data and hypotheses, refining the hypotheses as new data is continually collected

content analysis—Qualitative method used for analyzing documents.

content validity—Describes how well an assessment tool measures the content that was taught.

contingency table—Used to record and analyze the relationship between two variables. Also known as cross tabs, it is used with Chi Square analyses.

control group—A group that is as identical as possible to the experimental group (the group receiving some kind of intervention or treatment) but does not receive any treatment.

correlation—Quantitative analysis used to describe the relationship between two characteristics of a group.

correlation matrix—Symmetrical table which shows the correlation coefficients for variables.

correlational study—Quantitative model for determining relationships between variables.

criterion validity—A measure of how good an instrument is at predicting an outcome.

critical action research—A category of research wherein the research is conducted by a group rather than an individual; synonymous with collaborative action research.

Cronbach's alpha—A measure of internal consistency (reliability) of an instrument which uses scale categories; also known as coefficient alpha and Cronbach's coefficient alpha.

dependent variable – Factor you are measuring in a study

descriptive quantitative study – Quantitative model used when gathering information to clarify characteristics of a group.

descriptive statistics—Summarizes the characteristics of a group.

discourse analysis—Qualitative method used for analyzing interview data.

Education Resources Information Center (ERIC)—Common database of educational research accessible by anyone via the Internet.

effect size—Standardized computation of the amount of a difference between groups.

empirical research—Research based on observation and experimentation.

equal variance—Type of statistical analysis used if the two groups being compared are similar.

estimating parameters—In quantitative research, using sample data to estimate population statistics.

ethnography—Type of qualitative model used to examine the "culture" of a group.

experimental design—Type of quantitative research used when testing a particular variable.

explanatory design—Type of mixed methods study wherein the quantitative data collection precedes the qualitative data collection.

exploratory design—Type of mixed methods study wherein the qualitative data collection precedes the quantitative data collection.

ex post facto research—Causal-comparative research; quantitative research model for examining the effect of a variable that you cannot control or manipulate on the independent variable.

external validity—The degree to which the study findings are generalizable.

face validity—The degree to which an instrument appears to measure what the tool is purported to measure.

field notes—Anecdotal records taken during an observation which include a description of the setting as well as the action.

frequency distribution—A list of the values of a variable in a sample; usually ordered by quantity and showing the number of times each value appears.

focus group—Type of interview format where several interviewees are purposefully interviewed simultaneously.

generalizability—Describes whether your results will hold true for subjects and settings beyond those in your study.

grounded theory—A type of qualitative model used when generating a theory to understand a problem/situation.

halo effect—Results when the researcher's initial opinion or impressions of a subject impacts interpretation of observations.

Hawthorne Effect—Results when the participants' knowledge that they are being studied changes their behaviors and thereby affects the findings of a study.

histogram—Bar chart made from a frequency distribution.

historical research—A type of research model used to understand events that have already occurred.

independent variable – identifies which comparative group someone is in; it is the grouping variable.

inferential statistics—The use of statistics to make an inference about the population from which the sample is drawn.

informed consent—Written statement signed by research subjects stating they are willing participants in the research project after being briefed about the purpose of the study, any risks and their rights.

institutional review board (IRB)—A group that reviews research proposals to consider the risks involved to the subjects participating in the research study in order to protect the rights and welfare of study participants; studies are categorized as needing full review, expedited review, or exempt from review depending on the degree to which the study will involve and impact the subjects.

internal consistency—Measures the degree to which all of the questions in an instrument address the same characteristic.

internal validity—The degree to which the findings are based on the actual study design; that is, are there alternative explanations for study conclusions other than the variables being tested.

interval variable—Measures responses on a scale with intervals of equivalent size.

John Henry Effect—Results when participants in the control group outperform themselves or perform in a manner that is not typical because they know they are in competition with a treatment group.

Kuder-Richardson—A measure of internal consistency (reliability) of an instrument with question responses that can be coded as correct or incorrect.

Likert-type scale—A measurement tool which lists statements and response categories generally ranging from strongly agree to strongly disagree.

limitations—Conditions that make the outcomes of the study less than perfect; that is, factors that might either have biased or otherwise affected the results and/or generalizability of the study.

literature cited—A precise list of references that includes all of the materials which are actually cited in the paper.

mean—The arithmetic average.

measures of central tendency—Numbers representing where most of the members of the group appear; these are mean, mode and median.

measures of variability—Form of descriptive statistics that represents how far the responses are spread apart in a distribution; includes range and standard deviation.

median—The number where half of the group measures lower and the other half measures higher; the middle number in an ordered list.

member checking—Occurs when the subjects read the interpretation of what occurred (during an observation or interview) to corroborate the findings.

meta-analysis—A study of a number of studies; that is, the data presented in published studies are used as the data sources.

mixed-method—A type of research design that uses both qualitative and quantitative methodologies.

mode—The number that appears most often in a frequency distribution.

mutually exclusive—Refers to survey response categories wherein there are clear, distinct differences among the categories.

nominal variables—Responses that can only be sorted into categories that have no logical order.

normal curve—A standard or bell-shaped curve representing a frequency distribution acting in an expected, symmetrical manner.

null hypothesis—Hypothesis stated in a form that says it is not true; e.g. stating an intervention will have no effect

observer effect—Results when the mere presence of a researcher affects the behavior of those being observed.

one-tailed test—Used when the direction of change is stated in the hypothesis so that the significance is at one end of the distribution.

ordinal variables—Responses that can be sorted into categories in a logical order, but the categories are not necessarily equivalent.

outliers—Data that do not fit the general pattern.

paired t-test—A type of statistical analysis used if the two groups being compared are composed of exactly the same individuals.

participant/observer—Qualitative research design in which the researcher is a part of the study context; the degree of involvement varies along a continuum from complete observer to full participant.

participatory action research—A type of action research in which a group of stakeholders collectively formulates the research question; also known as collaborative research.

Pearson's r—Measure of the degree of a relationship between two variables in a correlation; used with interval variables.

percentile rank—The percentage of students who scored lower on the test than a specific student.

personal journal—A researcher's reflective notes, descriptions of events, personal thoughts; can serve as a qualitative data source.

phenomenology—A type of qualitative model used when looking at something through the eyes of those being observed.

pilot study—A trial run of a study on a small scale.

policy journals—Publications intended to review important issues in education.

political action research – A category of research wherein the question is focused on an issue of widespread rather than local importance.

post hoc tests—Statistical analysis run after an ANOVA to determine which of the comparisons are significantly different.

practical action research—Research whose purpose is to improve teaching and learning or provide necessary information to help in decision making.

practical significance—Describes how useful a statistically significant finding is in real life.

practitioner journals—Publications that help teachers solve specific problems in their own classrooms or schools.

pre/post design—Study design in which data are gathered from the group (a pre-test) before the intervention occurs (a curriculum unit, perhaps) and then more data are gathered from the group after the intervention (a post-test).

probability—The likelihood that something occurred by chance.

proposal—The first three chapters of a research report.

purposeful sample—Specific individuals are hand selected by the researcher to study because of the likelihood that they may have relevant information for the study.

qualitative—School of research that is descriptive in nature.

quantitative—School of research that deals with quantities and statistics; generally measures characteristics of groups.

range—Represents the difference between the highest and lowest responses in a data set.

ratio variables—A special case of interval variables wherein the scale always starts at zero.

regression line—A line drawn through a scatter plot that best represents the relationship between the points; also known as a best fit line.

reliability—The level of internal consistency, stability; in qualitative studies, refers to whether what is observed by the researcher matches what actually occurred in the field.

request for proposals (RFP)—Invitation to submit a proposal for granting, conference and other purposes.

research journals—Publications that contain peer-reviewed current research.

running head—The words that appear on the top of every page of a printed article.

sample of convenience—Participants are chosen for a study because they are close at hand and readily available

sampling distribution of the mean—Distribution of the values of sample means over all possible samples of the same size from the same population.

GLOSSARY

scatter plot—A graph of values of a data set using Cartesian coordinates, generally drawn for correlational studies.

self-report data—Information provided directly by a participant; e.g., surveys or interviews.

semi-structured interview—Interview format wherein guidelines are prepared and followed as closely as possible, but deviations from the script (e.g., follow up questions) are permitted.

significant difference—A difference in mean scores unlikely to have occurred by chance.

snowball sampling—Sampling technique of identifying some individuals for a sample and asking them to identify others who can participate.

sociogram—A type of graphical representation that increases understandings of relationships in a classroom or within a group.

Spearman's rho—The measure of the degree of a relationship between two variables in a correlation; used when one variable is ordinal.

split half—A way to determine reliability of an instrument that involves the questions on the instrument being randomly separated into two groups and then correlating the scores from the two groups of questions.

standard deviation—The average distance the responses are from the mean score.

standard error—The estimated standard deviation in a series of measurements; the standard deviation of a sampling distribution of the mean.

statistically significant—The term applied to group mean differences unlikely to have occurred by chance a set percent of the time (generally $p < .05$).

structured interview—Interview format wherein questions are preplanned and followed like a script.

survey research—Quantitative model that relies on answers to questions.

test of independence—A type of Chi Square analysis to determine if two variables are independent (not related) to each other.

test/retest—A way to establish reliability of an instrument that involves delivering the same instrument to the same group with some time lag in between.

title case—Each word in the heading begins with an uppercase letter, except for prepositions, conjunctions, and articles.

triangulated design—A type of mixed methods design wherein qualitative and quantitative data are collected simultaneously or concurrently.

triangulation—In qualitative research using multiple data sources to help ensure that the data collected are accurate and a true representation of what is being studied.

two-tailed test—Used when the direction of change is not anticipated at the onset of the study so that the significance is at either end of the distribution.

Type I error—A false positive, occurs when the null hypothesis is rejected but should not have been; that is, there really are no differences between groups.

Type II error—A false negative, occurs when the null hypothesis is not rejected when it should have been; that is, there really are differences between groups.

unequal variance—A type of statistical analysis used if the two groups being compared are different from the start.

unstructured interview—Interview format wherein there are no formal pre-planned questions; it is conversational, with no artificial directionality cues.

validity—Determines whether a tool actually measures what it is purported to measure or whether a study can be generalized to other settings.

variable—Specific characteristic of interest in a study.

z score—The distance an observation is above or below the mean in units of standard deviations.

CPSIA information can be obtained at www.ICGtesting.com
Printed in the USA
BVOW05s1140121015

422056BV00003B/7/P